# A Product of RSM Federal

If you have any questions about the content in this manual, please contact us:
RSM Federal | contact@rsmfederal.com | (888) 384-3451 Ext. 3

# Copyright & User Agreement

# Updates, Errors, Corrections or Omissions?

We take great pride in the breadth and detail of this manual. We don't make this statement lightly… it is the most comprehensive educational resource for government sales on the market. However, like any document, we may have missed something or the data in a specific section may require updating.

This manual is updated at least once every year.

If you find an error, believe an update should be made, or there is a topic you feel should be included, please contact us and let us know.

RSM Federal
contact@rsmfederal.com

# Trademarks – Service Marks

**Trademark Notice:** The following trademarks and service marks are owned and licensed by RSM Capital Group LLC dba **RSM Federal** and **Federal Access®**. Realignment Solution Methodology™ (RSM) is trademarked and copyrighted by RSM Capital Group. RSM Methodology has been registered with intellectual patents. All other referenced marks are those of their respective owners. In the absence of a trademark or service mark, all process, methodology, and content are owned by RSM Federal. The following page includes current trademarks and service marks as of this edition. Any questions concerning the use of these trademarks, process, methodology, content, techniques, strategies or manual should be referred to RSM Federal at the following address: 13 Amber Wave Ct, O'Fallon, Missouri 63366, Phone: (888) 384-3451, Extension 1 contact@rsmfederal.com and www.rsmfederal.com

| | |
|---|---|
| Federal Access® | Registered Trademark |
| Realignment Solution Methodology™ (RSM) | Trademark |
| RSM Phased Realignment Model™ | Trademark |
| Competency (Value) Mapping™ | Trademark |
| Advanced Process Simplified Tracking™ (APST) | Trademark |
| Multi-Disciplined Staffing Approach™ (MDSA) | Trademark |
| Bulls-Eye Decision Support System™ (BDSS) | Trademark |

| Trademarks and Service Marks | | |
|---|---|---|
| **Copyright / TM** | **d.b.a.** | **d.b.a.** |
| RSM capital group | RSM FEDERAL The Art and Science of Government Sales | FA FEDERALACCESS Powered by RSM Federal |
| **Resources** | **Podcast** | |
| FA FEDERALACCESS ONLINE TEMPLATES | GAMECHANGERS | |

*Table 1 - Trademarks and Service Marks*

# The Author

**Joshua P. Frank**
Managing Partner, RSM Federal

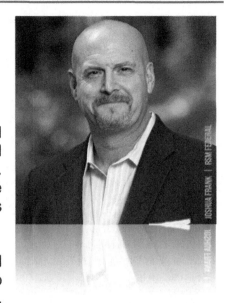

Award-winning business coach, professional speaker, and bestselling author, Mr. Frank is a nationally recognized authority on government sales and business acceleration. With more than 30 years in the government market, he specializes in bridging business strategy with federal sales strategies.

He is a recognized expert in the development and implementation of tactics and strategies required to differentiate, position for, and win government contracts. His seminars are consistently the top rated sessions at national conferences and events. Mr. Frank's coaching has helped companies win more than $13.5 billion in government contracts and $30 billion in indefinite delivery contracts. His tactics and strategies facilitate improved positioning, competitive advantage, and sales cycle acceleration to winning new contracts and increasing revenue. With thousands of testimonials, Mr. Frank's approach is consistently rated as being real-world, highly educational, and thought provoking.

Managing Partner at RSM Federal, Mr. Frank is author of multiple bestsellers including *An Insider's Guide To Winning Government Contracts – Real World Strategies, Lessons, and Recommendations* and *Game Changers for Government Contractors*. Mr. Frank also owns Veteran Warehouse Supply (VWS), a commodity-based business which provides healthcare and hospitality textiles to the Department of Defense and Department of Veterans Affairs.

Mr. Frank has been honored with SBA's award for Veteran Business of the Year; Industry Small Business Advocate of the Year by the Society of American Military Engineers (SAME); and in 2021, Mr. Frank was inducted into the Government Sales Hall of Fame with the inaugural Lifetime Achievement Award.

An avid outdoor enthusiast, Girl Scout and Boy Scout leader, Mr. Frank lives in St. Louis, Missouri with his wife, daughter, and son. A former military intelligence officer, holds degrees in English, a Masters in Management Information Systems (MIS), and a Master's in Business Administration (MBA).

Contact Mr. Frank:  LinkedIn:   https://www.linkedin.com/in/joshuapfrank/
　　　　　　　　　 Email:     contact@rsmfederal.com

# Table of Contents

# List of Figures

# List of Tables

# Introduction

**RSM FEDERAL**
The Art and Science of Government Sales™

# The RSM Federal Ecosystem

**Throughout this Manual I will be referring to *other* resources.**

For example, there is another resource in the GovCon Ecosystem called *An Insider's Guide To Winning Government Contracts* that I also wrote. You'll find it on Amazon. If you don't have this book yet, I highly recommend you stop what you're doing and order your copy today. This Manual is a Deskside Reference, not meant to be read cover to cover. The objective of this Manual is to provide you with a comprehensive understanding of government sales and force you to think about the business processes your company must utilize to successfully and consistently win government contracts. When you have a question about marketing, sales, proposals, any topic, simply pick up the Manual and review those sections. The book *An Insider's Guide to Winning Government Contracts* provides the mental aspect; how you should approach the market! And then you have the Federal Access Coaching and Training Platform with the templates and step-by-step strategies you need to execute the concepts in this Manual and the Insider's Guide.

In addition to An Insider's Guide, I have also co-authored (under RSM Federal Publishing), several other books. They include the books Game Changers and Becoming a GovCon Expert. You'll find all of them on Amazon under my author page.

We also cover all of these GovCon topics in the Podcast Game Changers for Government Contractors on iTunes, Soundcloud, or wherever you listen to podcasts.

You have this Manual. You may have one of our books. You listen to the podcast Game Changers when you're driving to work. All of these resources will help you accelerate into the government market. But all of these resources work in parallel with our flagship the Federal Access Coaching and Training Platform. Federal Access provides all the templates, tactics, videos, and step-by-step strategies that you're learning about in this manual, that you read in our books, that you listen to on the podcasts.

Now, what if you don't learn this way? What if you need a coach to simplify the process? Then you work with an RSM Federal Certified Coach.

When you combine all of these resources, you have the most comprehensive coaching and training ecosystem in federal space. It's why our clients and Federal Access members have won billions of dollars. Welcome to RSM Federal.

Figure 1 - Federal Access CTA

# You Want Templates?

## *Marketing • Sales • Proposals*

**As you open this manual, you will notice the Federal Access icon** on various pages and within various graphics and tables. This manual is the foundation for every product, program, and service provided by RSM Federal. This manual is one of hundreds of resources in the Federal Access Platform. With more than $13.2 billion in government contracts the last several years, the tactics and strategies in Federal Access are one of the most proven, comprehensive and cost effective business resources on the market for small, mid-size, and large businesses. 95% of companies that are Federal Access members - *win contracts*. These tactics, templates, and strategies earned RSM Federal the SBA Veteran Business of the Year award, the Industry Small Business Advocate of the Year award by the Society of American Military Engineers, and the inaugural Lifetime Achievement Award from the Government Sales Hall of Fame.

A complete business resource with hundreds of templates and resources, Federal Access has everything you need to succeed in government sales. Federal Access is **NOT** a bid-matching tool. There are plenty of online systems for finding opportunities. Federal Access helps you win opportunities **before** and **after** you've identified them.

Federal Access will accelerate your success in the market. Federal Access provides all of the tools that you'll see referenced in this Manual. If you purchased this manual through one of our affiliates or partners – after reviewing the manual, and when you're ready to take the next step, we invite you to join Federal Access.

## https://federal-access.com/manual

# Introduction to Realignment Solution Methodology (RSM)

This manual is the foundation of how we educate our clients on the government market. Since 2001, we have collected, evaluated, tested, and documented the most successful business processes, tactics, and strategies successfully utilized to engage and win government contracts. These tactics and strategies have directly resulted in billions of dollars in government contracts for our Clients and Federal Access Members.

We help companies position, tailor, and market the strengths and solutions of their company in order to differentiate the value of their capabilities and win government contracts. In 2006, these tactics and strategies were consolidated and streamlined to provide a foundation for *Realignment Solution Methodology*™ (RSM) and two years later RSM Federal opened for business. All of RSM Federal's products, programs, and services are designed around proven tactics, processes, and strategies which align and synchronize the customer and your internal business units, most notably sales, marketing, proposal, and management.

These tactics and strategies are performed in parallel while creating a competitive advantage within the prospect's decision cycle. Our experience is based on the best practices of larger defense contractors as well as thousands of successful smaller businesses, both private and public sectors.

This Manual is designed to accelerate the maturity of your business by **three** to **five** years when combined with the templates and step-by-step strategies provided in the **Federal Access Platform**.

# Our Mission

There are thousands of government startup guides for entrepreneurs and small business owners which target business development and sales. Most consultants claim to have expertise in positioning a company's solutions. However, there are very few consulting or coaching firms that successfully target and synchronize all business activities and verticals *critical to achieving recurring annual revenue growth.*

Many companies are unable to afford the expertise of larger consulting firms and there are few qualified coaching firms that can provide the expertise these companies need at a cost which they can afford.

*RSM Federal's mission is simple* – provide companies with the tools and resources

they need to increase revenue and grow their companies. This manual is a stand-alone resource. Your next step is joining the more than 1,000 other companies who take advantage of Federal Access. If you are not a member of Federal Access, that's your next step.

# How To Use This Manual

This manual is a *deskside reference* and is **not meant to be read cover to cover**. However, our clients and Federal Access members rarely follow our advice and we often receive feedback about their late-night readings. Whether you are a business developer, a marketer, a proposal manager, or senior management, this manual is split into modules that allows you to quickly locate specific competencies or activities you wish to improve. Each tactic and strategy is designed to help you win government contracts.

This manual provides strategies on not only how to improve your sales, but how your actions impact other employees as well as your prospects, existing clients, and teaming partners. **You do not have to follow every step of every process.** Every company has a unique set of solutions and corporate strategy, as well as employee maturity and capability. Every company will utilize this manual *in a different way*.

If you have the digital version of this manual, we recommend you purchase a printed version because you will take a ton of notes as you tailor strategies for your company. Keep this on your desk and refer to it when needed. *You will want to take notes.* If you have any questions or have challenges in implementing a specific tactic or strategy, please contact us at contact@rsmfederal.com

# Measuring The Value Of This Manual

Since 2001, I have measured the success of our tactics and strategies based on the following metrics:

→ Increased revenue and decreased costs
→ Increased focus and stronger capture management
→ Improved prospect engagement and customer relationships
→ Streamlined business development process and sales strategy
→ Improved partnerships and Programmatic Teaming Strategy™ (PTS)

# Return on Investment

The table below are metrics on the value of key activities. The speed at which you implement these strategies define how quickly you will increase revenue and Return on Investment (ROI). The table below provides general ROI percentages to help you understand how the tactics in this manual will impact and drive revenue. ROI percentages are listed as individual activities *in a vacuum*. Each company will focus on different activities at different times. This is a solid baseline for any size business.

| ROI Points and Metrics | | |
|---|---|---|
| **Activity** | **Module** | **ROI Percentages** |
| Competency-Mapping | Branding, Differentiation, Shaping, and Positioning | 25 |
| Market Sales Strategy | Business Development and Sales | 25 |
| CRM System | Business Development and Sales | 10 |
| Pipeline and Dashboard | Business Development and Sales (metrics) | 5 |
| Programmatic Teaming | Teaming and Partners | 25 |
| Other Tactics & Strategies | All Modules | 5 to 25 |

*Table 2 - Return On Investment*

# Reevaluate How You Approach Sales!

In general, successful business development and sales is a result of that overused but accurate phrase, "Thinking outside the box." You are asked to move outside the box but internal and external politics, policy, and culture create roadblocks to keep you inside.

Keys to Success:
→ More Professional
→ More Attentive
→ More Detailed
→ More Focused Than Your Competition

This manual will help you position and realign your competencies to facilitate a competitive advantage, accelerate opportunities, and increase revenue.

# The Government Contractor's Blueprint

## Aligning Your Corporate Acquisition Phases

A wide range of professionals in both the commercial and government markets supported the edit and review of this manual. Due to the amount of information and level of detail, a graphical representation was developed to help the reviewers cross-walk key concepts and activities. **This Blueprint is the foundation for Federal Access 4.0**.

*You should review these acquisition phases.* If you are a business developer, in marketing, a proposal writer, or the owner, it will give you a high level overview of what activities you must perform; what is covered in this manual; and every phase in this blueprint has templates, training, and step-by-step strategies at your fingertips when you are a member of Federal Access.

This model is used extensively when RSM Federal coaches provide coaching services to our clients; such as rebuilding business development processes, integrating proposal development with sales and marketing; or facilitating a company-wide shift and realignment to adjust operational focus.

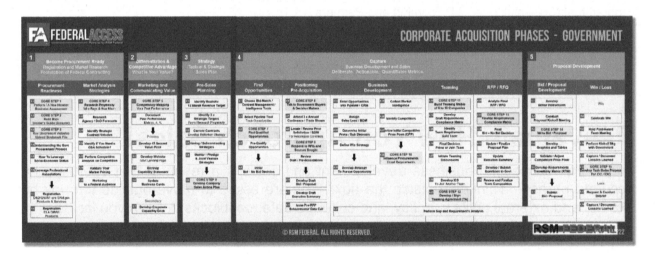

*Figure 2 - RSM Federal GovCon Blueprint*

Download a legible version of the blueprint at
**https://rsmfederal.com/blueprint**

# Legend

| Manual Legend | |
|---|---|
|  | **Federal Access Knowledge-Base**<br>Every major tactic, strategy, and resource listed in this manual is available in Federal Access. When you see this icon, the strategies or templates discussed are available online. When you are ready to start downloading templates and step-by-step strategies, visit www.rsmfederal.com or www.federal-access.com |
|  | **Podcast Game Changers for Government Contractors**<br>When you see this icon, there is a Game Changer's episode where our team has interviewed a small business expert on the topic being discussed. You can take a break from the manual and listen to a podcast to improve your understanding. |
|  | Caution. Common error, decision, or process that is often overlooked and may cost your company time, money, or revenue. |
|  | Technique or strategy implemented by corporate management or leadership. |

*Table 3 - Legend*

# Chapter 1
# Introduction to Government Sales

# Where Do I Find Opportunities?

As expected, this is the number one question that companies have when they first enter the government market. However, finding opportunities is the easy part. Positioning to win those opportunities is the hard part. It's the whole reason we built the RSM Federal ecosystem and training resources.

As you read this chapter (and other chapters in this Manual), you'll find hundreds of location and recommendations for prospecting and how to position and communicate your differentiation and value.

If you sell product, you should initiate your focus on SAM.gov as well as DLA's Internet Bid Board System (DIBBS). If you sell predominantly services, you'll focus on SAM.gov. If you have a GSA Multiple Award Schedule (MAS) (a contract vehicle), you'll be focused on the eBuy system as well. There are several other systems but these are the key ones.

The System for Award Management (SAM) is the gateway for most procurements over $25,000.

# The Author's GovCon Bookmark File

As I train sales teams, I provide a copy of a bookmark file that includes government and industry websites for everything from pricing, to opportunities, to agency websites, agency forecasts, marketing, and how to sell to the various agencies and commands. You can upload my personal bookmark file to your computer's Internet browser. It's available for download in Federal Access.

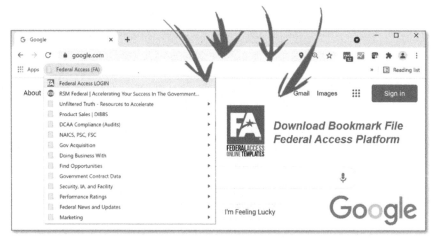

*Figure 3 - GovCon Internet Bookmark File*

# Stay Current On The Federal Market

It is impossible to keep this manual current based on all the changes that take place in government procurement and federal acquisition.

When major updates to content in this manual are identified, we report and discuss them via RSM Federal's LinkedIn page and via our website.

Connect on LinkedIn
https://www.linkedin.com/company/rsm-federal/

Visit RSM Federal
https://rsmfederal.com

# Public Sector (Government) = Commitment

Deciding you want to win government contracts is not a decision to be made lightly. Selling to the government is a long game.

- **Lengthy Planning Process**
  - Requires detailed strategic plan and education (purpose of manual)

- **Standard Sales Cycle of 6 – 24 Months**
  - Commodity / Product sales cycle shorter than Service's
  - Product Sales     6 to 12 months
  - Services           6 to 24 months
  - The tactics and strategies in this manual accelerate these cycles

- **No commercial business? Need 2 years operating expenses**
  - Must have adequate cash-flow

- **Corporate Investment**
  - Dedicated resources, time, and money
  - Commitment by senior management
  - May have to hire non-billable resources to position company
  - Hire functionally
  - Strategy is critical – sales cycle can be long and arduous but the activities are fairly simple

# Competitive Characteristics of Small Biz

If you are a small business, it is important that you understand, at a high-level, what advantages and competitive characteristics you have.

- **Industry Agnostic.** Whether you sell garden hoses, cleaning supplies, software, security products, or janitorial services, the government utilizes small businesses because smaller companies can do things that often elude larger companies.

- **Small Business is expected to provide the government with:**
  - Agility
  - Flexibility
  - Innovation
  - Creativity
  - Responsiveness

> "Competitive characteristics that often elude large companies" Use these to market and differentiate the value of your solutions

- **Make sure to communicate these characteristics:**
  - Via email
  - During discussions
  - In every proposal

Source: Online DoD Personnel and Procurement Statistics, Office Secretary of Defense
Source: Budget, DoD Comptroller

# The Federal Budget

Fiscal Year Starts October 1st
Mandatory Programs include Medicare, Medicaid, and Social Security

| Outlays | 2020 | 2021 | 2022 | 2023 |
|---|---|---|---|---|
| DoD | $713,000,000,000 | $753,000,000,000 | $769,000,000,000 | $782,000,000,000 |
| Federal Agencies | $724,000,000,000 | $733,000,000,000 | $748,000,000,000 | $758,000,000,000 |
| **Total Appropriations** | **$1,437,000,000,000** | **$1,486,000,000,000** | **$1,517,000,000,000** | **$1,541,000,000,000** |
| **Mandatory Programs** | **$2,977,000,000,000** | **$3,010,000,000,000** | **$3,212,000,000,000** | **$3,334,000,000,000** |
| **Total Outlays** | **$4,414,000,000,000** | **$4,496,000,000,000** | **$4,728,000,000,000** | **$4,875,000,000,000** |

*Table 4 - Federal Budget*

# Small Business Set-Aside Percentages

**23% Statutory Small Business Goals**
Based on the Federal Budget, we can identify how much spend is set-aside for small business. *The table below only outlines appropriated funds.* However, many of the mandatory programs require contracts with industry as well.

| | 2020 | 2021 | 2022 | 2023 |
|---|---|---|---|---|
| DoD **(23%)** | $163,990,000,000 | $173,190,000,000 | $176,870,000,000 | 179,860,000,000 |
| Federal **(23%)** | $166,520,000,000 | $168,590,000,000 | $172,040,000,000 | $174,340,000,000 |
| **Total Statutory Goal** | **$330,510,000,000** | **$341,780,000,000** | **$348,910,000,000** | **$354,200,000,000** |

*Table 5 - Small Business Statutory Goals (Appropriated)*

# How Much Goes To Small Business?

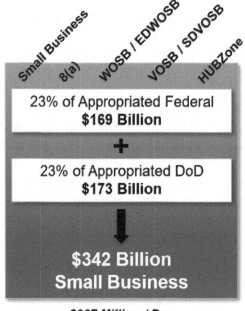

- **2021 Federal Budget**
  - $4.5 Trillion
    - ✓ $1.5 Trillion Appropriated Programs
    - ✓ $3.0 Trillion Mandatory Programs

- **2021 DoD Budget**
  - $753 Billion

*Figure 4 - Small Business Set-Asides*

Source: Online DoD Personnel and Procurement Statistics, Office Secretary of Defense
Source: 2021 Budget, DoD Comptroller

# Department of Defense Small Business Annual Spend

These numbers show that there is plenty of funding as long as your company understands the market and utilizes the right tactics and strategies.

- **Based on DoD Total Obligation Authority of FY2021, DoD spent:**
  - $2.0 Billion per day
  - $81 Million per hour
  - $1.4 Million per minute
  - $22,609 every second

- **Average DoD Total Obligation Authority of FY2021 to FY2023:**
  - $2.1 Billion per day
  - $87.6 Million per hour
  - $1.5 Million per minute
  - $24,353 every second

23% of Appropriated DoD Funding
Small Business Set-Asides
$173 Billion

# Under Secretary of Defense (AT&L)

These tenets are more than a decade old but remain viable and a current focus for not only DoD but the entire government.

- **Strategic Thrusts**
  - Define effective and affordable tools for the Joint Warfighter
  - Responsibly spend every single tax dollar
  - Take care of our people
  - DoD transformational priorities

- **Priorities**
  - Reduce cycle time
  - Increase competition
  - Communicate

- **Directives**
  - Emphasis on Small Business utilization
  - Seek to compete multiple award / IDIQ contracts among small businesses
  - Leverage small business innovation

AT&L – Acquisition, Technology, and Logistics
Source: Office of Under Secretary of Defense for AT&L

# Shifts in Regulations

We often look at regulations changes in a vacuum. Seeing how the government changes regulations, year over year, helps us better understand the direction and impact to business, small and large.

To keep abreast of changes in regulation and acquisition strategies, bookmark www.rsmfederal.com and keep connected with us on LinkedIn by following us at https://www.linkedin.com/company/rsm-federal/

## Fiscal Year (FY) 2021

- **HUBZone Updates**

  - SBA designates over 400 new counties as Qualified HUBZones

- **8(a) Minority and Social Disadvantaged**

  - Program extension, due to COVID, for one year

- **Business Size Calculations**

  - In 2021, companies may choose their revenue average for the last three years or last five years. In January 2022, it formally moves to five years. This will allow some companies that graduated out of small business status to move back into small business status.

- **Minimum Wage**

  - Starting in 2022, all federal contractors are required to pay their employees and contractors a minimum of $15 per hour.

## FY 2020

- **Year of COVID**

- **DUNS Number will remain though spring 2022; to be replaced by new SAM Identifier.**

- **Cybersecurity Maturity Model Certification (CMMC)**

  - Requirement for all DoD contractors to certify their systems for Controlled Unclassified Information (CUI).
- **HUBZone Updates**

  - Change from three year recertification to annual recertification
  - Company may remain HUBZone for up to 10 years, if you purchase the building, regardless of the area being a designated HUBZone
- **Woman Owned Small Business (WOSB) Updates**

  - Updated certification methods with SBA as new certification authority. While third party certification is still authorized, the SBA requires that those third party certifiers provide certification at no cost.

- **8(a) Minority and Social Disadvantaged**
  - Income and Net Worth Eligibility Standards Increased
  - Retirement accounts no longer count towards net worth
  - 8(a) Joint Ventures no longer required to be approved by SBA prior to award of a competitive contract. However, joint ventures for sole-source awards still require SBA approval of the JV prior to submitting proposal.

- **Veterans and Service Disabled Veteran Owned Small Business (VOSB / SDVOSB)**
  - VA CVE verification appeals must be filed with the SBA versus the VA

- **Tiered Evaluations**
  - Many agencies, especially the Department of Veterans Affairs (VA) moves toward tiered evaluation where they start with SDVOSB, then Small Business, and then large business.

- **Mentor – Protégé**
  - 8(a) Business Development Mentor-Protege Program consolidated into SBA's All-Small Mentor-Protege Program.
  - SBA final rule allows mentors to own 40% (equity stake) of protégé and perform top to 60% of a contract with the protégé executing 40%.

- **Joint Ventures**
  - Three-in-Two Rule – SBA eliminates the three contract limit under a Joint Venture but retains the two year rule.

# FY 2018
- **Strategic Sourcing and Category Management**
- **To the detriment of smaller businesses, multiple large initiatives pushing for increased strategic sourcing**
  - BEFORE you decide to sell to the government, FIRST verify if the products or services you sell are already under a strategic sourcing initiative
  - Strategic sourcing is discussed more online via RSM Federal's LinkedIn page

- **Micro Purchase Thresholds**
  - Department of Defense increased from $3,500 to $5,000 per 2017 NDAA
  - Federal Agencies increased to $10,000 per 2017 NDAA

- **Simplified Acquisition Threshold**
  - Procurements using FAR Part 13, Simplified Acquisition Procedures, have increased from $150,000 to $250,000
- **Acquisition Strategies Continue...**
  - Consolidation and Bundling of smaller contracts (Strategic Sourcing)

- Large increase in Indefinite Delivery / Indefinite Quantity (IDIQ) contracts
- Complement Contracts for Small Business
- Performance Based
- 5 Year Base with one 5 Year Option (10 Years)

- **RFPs and Proposals**

  - 2 Week Bids (Only two weeks to develop proposal)
  - Quality Assurance / Quality Control becoming more important
  - DoD 8570.01-M Information Assurance (IA) Workforce Improvement Program

- **Risk**

  - Government trend of contractors paying for "Scope-Creep"

- **Architectural and Technological Direction**

  - Service Oriented Architecture (SOA)
  - Net Centric Enterprise Services (NCES)
  - Cloud Computing

# FY 2016

- Small Business Administration (SBA) published final rule allowing sole source awards to Women-Owned Small Businesses (WOSBs), a provision that was enacted as part of the FY2015 National Defense Authorization Act (NDAA).

  - However, WOSB still requires rule of two for competition.
  - Therefore, 8a is still one of the only true sole source vehicles

# FY 2015

- Government starts cancelling GSA Schedule contracts for non-performance

# FY 2014

- Socio-economic size standards are increased for most NAICS codes

# FY 2012

- Although number of government contracts decreased, small business set-asides remain above 22%.

- Small businesses expected to retain large percentage of government spend

# FY 2009

- President Obama orders overhaul of "broken" contracting system
- Government contracts have doubled to $500 Billion since 2001
- Shrink outsourcing of government operations
- Minimize number of non-competitive contracts
- Preference to fixed-price contracts
- Increased accountability and oversight

# Handling Recessions & Budget Constrained Environments

Depending on which political party is in power and the normal ups and downs the government experiences in funding; when combined with shifts in enterprise strategic sourcing → recessions and constrained budgets impact government sales:

- Cancel redundant software and hardware contracts

- Consolidate smaller contracts for less acquisition overhead

- Increase reliance on process versus technology

- Software as a Service (SAAS)

- Virtualization

- Utilize collaborative technology

- Move from thick to thin clients and eliminate perpetual software licenses

- Minimize travel (Conference, Trade Shows, etc.)

- Loyalty to current system integrators (small and large)

- Increase reliance on metrics

- Postpone new contracts and increase FTEs on current contracts

# Corporate Culture & Attitude

In general, a corporate culture is market and industry agnostic. You either have a positive outlook and your employees have the right attitude, or it doesn't matter what you sell.

- **Culture and Attitude – You can sell in any market!**

- **You Must:**
  - Believe that your products and services provide value
  - Ability to communicate and differentiate the value of your solutions
  - Always be honest
  - Focus on prospect and customer needs – not yours
  - Solve problems – don't push a product or service – push value
  - Do not initiate the sale until you understand the prospect's requirements
  - Present your solutions without pressure
  - Understand the customer's language (acronyms)

  - Eliminate sales language

- **The Customer Is Looking For:**

  - Trust
  - Ethical dealings
  - Belief that your solution will solve their problem

---

# Relentless Persistence

In general, the government market requires more "touches" than the commercial market. Set expectations that the business development process is longer, not necessarily harder.

- **Government is a competitive market**

- **Your attitude is key**
  - Prospects pick-up on hesitancy, fear, and lack of confidence
  - In a budget-constrained environment, your prospects will sense your desperation

- **When everything else fails, superior relationships close contracts**
  - Persistence is just as important as the strategies in this manual

- **The Touch Rule**
  - Commercial = 7 to 10 "touches" to make the sale
  - Government = 7 to 20 "touches" before you're properly positioned for the sale

- **Network, Network, Network – and Network**
  - Keep in touch with ALL your contacts (including teaming partners)
  - The 25% Rule. Every quarter, touch 25% of your network.

- **Ignore the pessimists – their attitudes are contagious**

# Typical Small Business Focus

This is one of the more important graphics and concepts. It's natural for companies new to government sales, especially smaller businesses, to spend too much time behind their computers. Successfully winning government contracts requires that your business development strategy **focus on pre-acquisition strategies**.

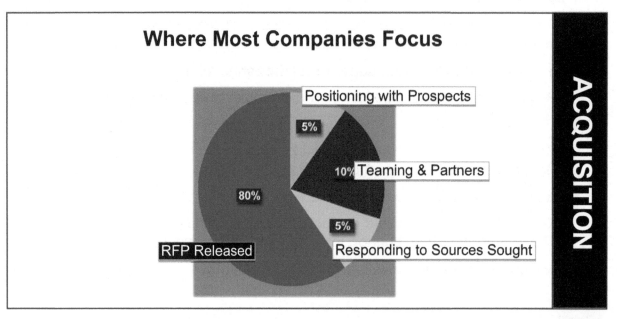

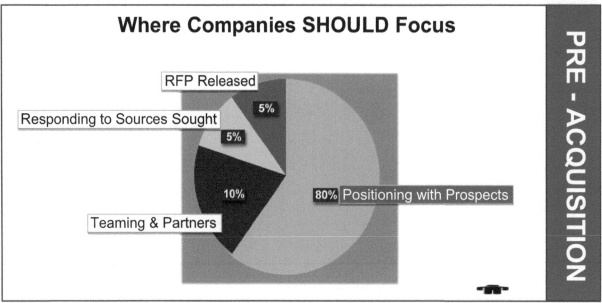

*Figure 5 - Typical Small Business Focus*

# The Business Development Triad

When you sell to the government, you have to understand how you will grow your company through Channels, Partners, and Contract Vehicles. It's not complicated. Channels are more for product-based / commodity-based companies. Who are your resellers and distributors *who already sell* to the government? Or, maybe you're a channel for another company's products, you're the reseller.

Partners are just that – teaming partners. When two or more companies join forces, they can be more competitive. Contract vehicles are just what they sound like. These are vehicles you obtain in order to open doors. Every military command or federal agency you engage has their favored vehicles. It's how they like to buy from industry.

As you progress, you will increase all three. To be successful, you need to increase all three.

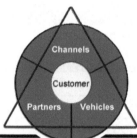

| Strategy Cornerstones | |
|---|---|
| **Channels** | Extends distribution of your products and services to a larger geographical region or market than you can distribute on your own (e.g. distributor or reseller) |
| **Partners** | Creating some form of alliance, partnership, or teaming arrangement. May be legal and contractual or a loose and verbal agreement. Exclusive partnerships must be mutually beneficial or will tend to disintegrate. (A Partner can also be a Channel) |
| **Vehicles** | Method used to simplify the buyer's job; significantly reducing procurement lead time and lowers acquisition costs associated with managing complex bid procedures. A long term contract vehicle such as the Federal Supply Schedule (GSA Schedule) or Government Wide Acquisition Vehicle (GWAC) is perhaps the single best mechanism for conducting business with the federal government |

*Table 6 - Strategy Cornerstones*

# Stages of GovCon Business Growth

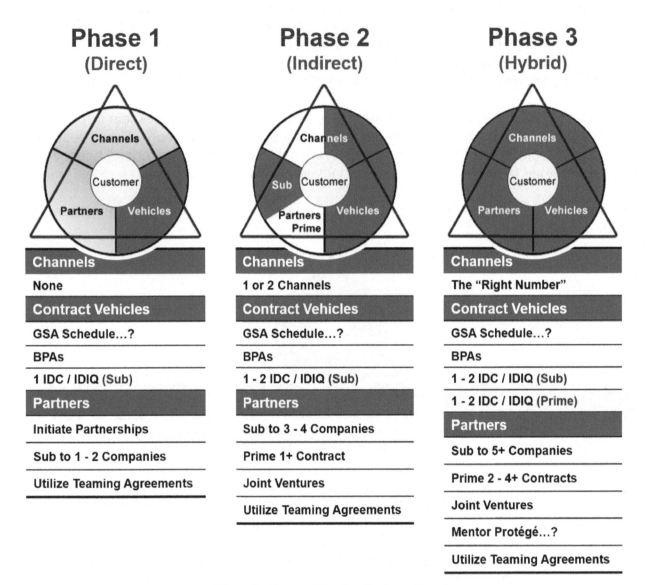

*Figure 6 - Stages of GovCon Business Growth*

**Note. Not every company needs a GSA Schedule**

# Business Growth Requires "One Voice"

Prospects are more comfortable when they receive standardized documentation. You build trust when the customer hears the same position on an issue. Your customers and prospects trust you when everyone they speak with in the organization has the same message.

- **Customers, prospects, and teammates are looking for "One Voice"**
  - Business Cards are standardized
  - Documentation "look and feel" are standardized
  - Website branding matches marketing collateral
  - What is the future direction for your products, services, or company?

- **Inconsistency across the company will:**
  - Make the prospect question what you tell them
  - Make the prospect question your ability to solve their problems
  - Create a perception that your company lacks business maturity

- **Why is it so important that Marketing and Sales have "One Voice?"**
  - What happens when territories are realigned?
  - What happens when you hire new employees?

# Small Business Programs

| Small Business Set-Aside Programs ||
| Program | Ownership |
| --- | --- |
| Small Business (SB) | • SBA NAICS Size Standards |
| Emerging Small Business | • 50% numerical size standard of NAICS code assigned |
| Woman Owned Small Business (WOSB) | • 51% owned ≥ 1 Woman |
| 8(a) Certified Small Disadvantaged Business (SDB) | • Owned by ≥ 51% socially or economically disadvantaged African-American, Hispanic, Asian Pacific, Native American and Subcontinent Asian Americans<br>• Personal net worth of ≤ $750K<br>• Adjusted gross income of ≤ $350K;<br>• and ≤ $6 million or less in assets |
| Historically Underutilized Business Zone (HUBZone) | • Be a small business<br>• 51% owned and controlled by U.S. citizens, a Community Development Corporation, an agricultural cooperative, an Alaska Native corporation, a Native Hawaiian organization, or an Indian tribe<br>• Principal office located in HUBZone<br>• ≥ 35% of employees live in HUBZone |
| Veteran-Owned Small Business (VOSB) | • 51% owned ≥ 1 veteran |
| Service-Disabled Veteran Owned Small Business (SDVOSB) | • 51% owned ≥ 1 service-disabled veteran |

*Table 7 - Small Business Set-Aside Programs*

\* If your company falls within one of the above socio-economic statuses, you should consider getting certified by the SBA. You can then access "set-aside" contracts which have less competition. This provides you with an advantage over other companies.

 **Important Note.** Remember, certifications do not win contracts! Your ability to communicate the value of your company, supplies, and services is what wins contracts. Do not over-rely on certifications. However, they are important "Balancing Differentiators."

# Federal Statutory Goals For Small Business

- Mandated by FAR* Part 19 "Small Business Programs"
- Agencies follow the FAR to varying degrees
  - Not all meet their percentage obligations
  - Some agencies utilize one set-aside more than others
- Small business classification is dependent on your NAICS Codes
- DoD does not have a specific HUBZone goal
  - However, DoD has instructed subordinate commands to work towards 3%
  - It is not a statutory requirement
- DoD does not have a specific goal for Black Universities
  - Until 2010, DoD instructed subordinate commands to work towards 3%
  - It is not a statutory requirement
  - *No longer utilized as of 2010* but still tracked in SAM.gov's Data Bank and USASpending.gov
  - Usage replaced by grants and 8a programs
- End of the Fiscal Year? (July – September)
  - If a specific agency has not met statutory goals, HUBZone is the least used
  - Focus will be on 8(a), WOSB, VOSB, and SDVOSB based on current percentages

| Federal Agency Small Business Statutory Goals | | |
|---|---|---|
| **Percentage** | **Set-Aside** | **Certification Authority** |
| 23% | Small Business (SB) | NAICS Thresholds |
| 5% | Small Disadvantaged Business (SDB) 8(a) | Through SBA |
| 5% | Woman-Owned Small Business (WOSB); and Economically Disadvantaged Woman Owned Small Business (EDWOSB) | Through SBA |
| 0% | Veteran-Owned Small Business (VOSB) | Through VA<br>Transfers to SBA in January 2023 |
| 3% | Service-Disabled Veteran-Owned Small Business (SDVOSB) | Through VA<br>Transfers to SBA in January 2023 |
| 3% | Historically Underutilized Business Zone (HUBZone) | Through SBA |

*Table 8 - Small Business Percentages*

| DoD Prime Contracting Goals | |
|---|---|
| **FY** | **Set Aside** |
| 21.95% | Small Business (SB) |
| 5% | Small Disadvantaged Business (SDB) 8(a) |
| 5% | Woman-Owned Small Business (WOSB) |
| 3% | Service-Disabled Veteran Small Business (SDVOSB) |
| 3% | Historically Underutilized Business Zone (HUBZone) |
| **DoD Subcontracting Goals** | |
| 32.25% | Small Business (SB) |
| 5% | Small Disadvantaged Business (SDB) 8(a) |
| 5% | Woman-Owned Small Business (WOSB) |
| 3% | Service-Disabled Veteran Small Business (SDVOSB) |
| 3% | Historically Underutilized Business Zone (HUBZone) |

*Table 9 - DoD Prime and Subcontracting Goals*

# Order of Precedence – Small Business Programs

- Different for every Agency, for example:
  - Health & Human Services (HHS) → 8(a) HUBZone, SDB 8(a), HUBZone Sole Source, HUBZone Set-Asides, SB
  - Veterans Affairs (VA) → SDVOSB, VOSB, SDB 8(a), WOSB, HUBZone
- Precedence for remaining SB Programs *at agency discretion*
- *Assumes contracting offices are following the guidelines*

| SB Programs – Order of Precedence |
| --- |
| 8(a) HUBZone Small Business Concerns |
| 8(a) Program Participants |
| HUBZone |
| Woman Owned Small business (WOSB); and Economically Disadvantaged Woman Owned Small Business (EDWOSB) |
| Service Disabled Veteran Owned (SDVOSB) |
| Veteran Owned (VOSB) |
| Small Business (SB) |
| Full and Open Competition |

*Table 10 - Small Business Programs - Order of Precedence*

Note. The table above is the general order of precedence for the federal government and military services. Remember, each Agency and Command will adjust the order of precedence for their respective organizations.

# How Do I Certify?

- **8(a) Business Development Program**
  - Certification program managed by the Small Business Administration (SBA)
  - Be a small business
  - Nine (9) year program. Note - Companies that were active in the 8a Program between March 13, 2020, and September 9, 2020 (During COVID) were able to extend program participation an extra year (for 10 years total)
  - Owner(s) must be both "socially" and "economically" disadvantaged
  - ≥ 51% owned and controlled by U.S. citizens
  - Initial net worth less than $750,000
  - Adjusted gross income of ≤ $350,000 (Last 3 year average)
  - Total assets worth ≤ $6 million
  - IRA retirement accounts excluded
  - Do you qualify and want to certify? https://certify.sba.gov/am-i-eligible and https://certify.sba.gov/

- **HUBZone Program**
  - Certification program managed by the Small Business Administration (SBA)
  - Be a small business
  - ≥ 51% owned and controlled by U.S. citizens, a Community Development Corporation, an agricultural cooperative, an Alaska Native corporation, a Native Hawaiian organization, or an Indian tribe
  - Primary office must be in a HUBZone - https://maps.certify.sba.gov/hubzone/map
  - 35% of all employees must live in a HUBZone
  - Do you qualify and want to certify? https://certify.sba.gov/am-i-eligible and https://certify.sba.gov/

- **Woman Owned Small Business (WOSB) Program**
  - Certification program managed by the Small Business Administration (SBA)
  - Be a small business
  - ≥ 51% owned and controlled by women who are U.S. citizens
  - Have women manage day-to-day operations and also make long-term decisions
  - Economically Disadvantaged Woman Owned Small Business **(EDWOSB)**
    - ➤ Falls under the WOSB Program

> ➢ Meet all requirements under WOSB Program

> ➢ Initial net worth less than $750,000

> ➢ Adjusted gross income of ≤ $350,000 (Last 3 year average)

> ➢ Total assets worth ≤ $6 million

- Do you qualify and want to certify? https://certify.sba.gov/am-i-eligible and https://certify.sba.gov/

- **Veteran Owned Small Business (VOSB) Program**

  - Certification program managed by the Department of Veterans Affairs under the VETS First Verification Program. However, there is a congressionally mandated transfer, of certification authority, from the VA to the Small Business Administration. After January 1, 2023, Veteran certification will be handled by the SBA.

  - Requires DoD Form DD-214 (Served in Military)

  - Do you qualify and want to certify? https://www.va.gov/osdbu/verification/

- **Service Disabled Veteran Owned Small Business (SDVOSB) Program**

  - Requires disability determination by Veterans Affairs (VA)

  - Certification program managed by the Department of Veterans Affairs under the VETS First Verification Program. However, there is a congressionally mandated transfer, of certification authority, from the VA to the Small Business Administration. After January 1, 2023, Veteran certification will be handled by the SBA.

  - Requires DoD Form DD-214 (Served in Military)

  - Do you qualify and want to certify? https://www.va.gov/osdbu/verification/

# 2020 – Agency Score Cards For Small Business

Every year the core federal agencies and Department of Defense are scored on their success or failure in meeting their small business set-aside goals. To be clear, the federal government is just as "political" as corporate America. As a result, I should point out that there are many different ways to massage contract data to show a positive outcome. That said, whether the respective agencies and military commands actually meet their goals is immaterial. Even if they miss their goals, we're still talking billions of dollars going to small business.

These score cards come from SAM.gov's Data Bank. You can pull this data on your own but putting it into an easy to understand table or graph is not as simple. RSM Federal has been consolidating this data for more than a decade. These cards will be updated in this manual during the annual update.

## Measuring An Agency's Propensity For Small Business

## 2020 Set-Asides

| Agency | SB | 8(a) | VOSB | SDVOSB | WOSB | HUBZone |
|---|---|---|---|---|---|---|
| SBA Goal | 23% | 5% | 0% | 3% | 5% | 3% |
| DHS | 36.04% | 5.69% | 6.76% | 5.76% | 6.79% | 4.07% |
| DOC | 43.65% | 5.80% | 5.76% | 4.10% | 11.99% | 13.05% |
| DOD | 24.51% | 3.43% | 4.37% | 3.22% | 4.05% | 2.20% |
| DOI | 60.13% | 9.96% | 7.92% | 5.62% | 14.10% | 7.33% |
| DOJ | 32.73% | 5.06% | 7.64% | 6.17% | 5.95% | 2.20% |
| DOL | 40.21% | 6.35% | 7.76% | 6.63% | 12.80% | 5.94% |
| DOT | 34.05% | 6.79% | 5.97% | 3.76% | 8.29% | 3.41% |
| Education | 14.90% | 1.58% | 3.01% | 1.07% | 5.91% | 0.53% |
| Energy | 4.96% | 0.67% | 0.82% | 0.56% | 0.90% | 0.19% |
| EPA | 39.50% | 9.04% | 3.14% | 2.95% | 5.48% | 2.04% |
| GSA | 49.47% | 7.56% | 10.78% | 8.90% | 10.47% | 4.39% |
| HHS | 23.10% | 3.52% | 2.31% | 1.70% | 5.02% | 1.31% |
| HUD | 1.57% | 5.03% | -4.28% | -5.04% | 4.92% | 6.96% |
| NASA | 17.48% | 3.83% | 1.97% | 1.65% | 4.30% | 0.65% |
| NRC | 53.57% | 14.91% | 9.40% | 7.60% | 12.03% | 7.34% |
| NSF | 53.57% | 14.91% | 9.40% | 7.60% | 12.03% | 7.34% |
| OPM | 82.75% | 15.52% | 9.20% | 7.94% | 46.40% | 8.49% |
| SBA | 80.18% | 4.18% | 11.37% | 9.99% | 63.09% | 7.61% |
| SSA | 31.86% | 1.47% | 4.17% | 3.61% | 5.99% | 1.02% |
| State | 28.44% | 10.81% | 6.58% | 4.27% | 4.46% | 6.06% |
| Treasury | 46.26% | 3.90% | 4.00% | 3.12% | 9.06% | 2.41% |
| USAID | 14.91% | 1.97% | 1.05% | 0.48% | 5.69% | 0.66% |
| USDA | 47.21% | 4.73% | 4.21% | 2.45% | 10.00% | 6.74% |
| VA | 26.57% | 0.02% | 20.41% | 20.25% | 2.42% | 1.98% |

| Legend | Met or Exceeded SBA Goals (Regardless of Agency Goals) |
|---|---|
| | Failed to achieve SBA Goals |

| 2020 | SB | 8(a) | VOSB | SDVOSB | WOSB | HUBZone |
|---|---|---|---|---|---|---|
| # Agencies | 19 | 13 | 19 | 16 | 18 | 13 |
| Percentage | 79% | 54% | 79% | 67% | 75% | 54% |

*Table 11 - Small Business Scorecards*

- **FY 2019 Results**
  - Small Business ⬆ 83%
  - 8(a) 63%
  - WOSB 75%
  - HUBZone ⬆ 75%
  - SDVOSB 71%

- **FY 2020 Results**
  - Small Business ⬇ 79%
  - 8(a) ⬇ 54%
  - WOSB 75%
  - HUBZone ⬇ 54%
  - SDVOSB ⬇ 67%

## 2020 Set-Asides

| Small Business | | 8(a) SDB | | VOSB | | SDVOSB | | WOSB | | HUBZone | |
|---|---|---|---|---|---|---|---|---|---|---|---|
| OPM | 82.75% | OPM | 15.52% | VA | 20.41% | VA | 20.25% | SBA | 63.09% | DOC | 13.05% |
| SBA | 80.18% | NRC | 14.91% | SBA | 11.37% | SBA | 9.99% | OPM | 46.40% | OPM | 8.49% |
| DOI | 60.13% | NSF | 14.91% | GSA | 10.78% | GSA | 8.90% | DOI | 14.10% | SBA | 7.61% |
| NRC | 53.57% | State | 10.81% | NRC | 9.40% | OPM | 7.94% | DOL | 12.80% | NRC | 7.34% |
| NSF | 53.57% | DOI | 9.96% | NSF | 9.40% | NRC | 7.60% | NRC | 12.03% | NSF | 7.34% |
| GSA | 49.47% | EPA | 9.04% | OPM | 9.20% | NSF | 7.60% | NSF | 12.03% | DOI | 7.33% |
| USDA | 47.21% | GSA | 7.56% | DOI | 7.92% | DOL | 6.63% | DOC | 11.99% | HUD | 6.96% |
| Treasury | 46.26% | DOT | 6.79% | DOL | 7.76% | DOJ | 6.17% | GSA | 10.47% | USDA | 6.74% |
| DOC | 43.65% | DOL | 6.35% | DOJ | 7.64% | DHS | 5.76% | USDA | 10.00% | State | 6.06% |
| DOL | 40.21% | DOC | 5.80% | DHS | 6.76% | DOI | 5.62% | Treasury | 9.06% | DOL | 5.94% |
| EPA | 39.50% | DHS | 5.69% | State | 6.58% | State | 4.27% | DOT | 8.29% | GSA | 4.39% |
| DHS | 36.04% | DOJ | 5.06% | DOT | 5.97% | DOC | 4.10% | DHS | 6.79% | DHS | 4.07% |
| DOT | 34.05% | HUD | 5.03% | DOC | 5.76% | DOT | 3.76% | SSA | 5.99% | DOT | 3.41% |
| DOJ | 32.73% | USDA | 4.73% | DOD | 4.37% | SSA | 3.61% | DOJ | 5.95% | Treasury | 2.41% |
| SSA | 31.86% | SBA | 4.18% | USDA | 4.21% | DOD | 3.22% | Education | 5.91% | DOD | 2.20% |
| State | 28.44% | Treasury | 3.90% | SSA | 4.17% | Treasury | 3.12% | USAID | 5.69% | DOJ | 2.20% |
| VA | 26.57% | NASA | 3.83% | Treasury | 4.00% | EPA | 2.95% | EPA | 5.48% | EPA | 2.04% |
| DOD | 24.51% | HHS | 3.52% | EPA | 3.14% | USDA | 2.45% | HHS | 5.02% | VA | 1.98% |
| HHS | 23.10% | DOD | 3.43% | Education | 3.01% | HUD | 1.70% | HUD | 4.92% | HHS | 1.31% |
| NASA | 17.48% | USAID | 1.97% | HHS | 2.31% | NASA | 1.65% | State | 4.46% | SSA | 1.02% |
| USAID | 14.91% | Education | 1.58% | NASA | 1.97% | Education | 1.07% | NASA | 4.30% | USAID | 0.66% |
| Education | 14.90% | SSA | 1.47% | USAID | 1.05% | Energy | 0.56% | DOD | 4.05% | NASA | 0.65% |
| Energy | 4.96% | Energy | 0.67% | Energy | 0.82% | USAID | 0.48% | VA | 2.42% | Education | 0.53% |
| HUD | 1.57% | VA | 0.02% | HUD | -4.28% | HUD | -5.04% | Energy | 0.90% | Energy | 0.19% |

*Table 12 - Small Business Scorecards by Set-Aside*

## 2007 - 2020 Small Business Set-Aside Reporting

| Agency | 2007 | 2008 | 2009 | 2010 | 2011 | 2012 | 2013 | 2014 | 2015 | 2016 | 2017 | 2018 | 2019 | 2020 |
|---|---|---|---|---|---|---|---|---|---|---|---|---|---|---|
| **SMALL BUSINESS GOALS - 23%** | | | | | | | | | | | | | **RSM FEDERAL** | |
| DHS | 32.38% | 32.12% | 32.38% | 32.38% | 29.07% | 30.65% | 36.91% | 34.98% | 29.79% | 36.95% | 35.25% | 34.47% | 35.08% | 36.04% |
| DOC | 36.58% | 43.14% | 36.58% | 36.31% | 39.42% | 36.89% | 41.35% | 40.93% | 43.24% | 41.43% | 42.22% | 45.88% | 42.85% | 43.65% |
| DOD | 21.13% | 18.57% | 21.13% | 20.94% | 19.80% | 20.41% | 24.80% | 23.47% | 24.64% | 22.90% | 22.50% | 23.85% | 24.13% | 24.51% |
| DOI | 56.24% | 54.85% | 56.24% | 49.69% | 53.60% | 55.76% | 54.70% | 55.19% | 55.20% | 59.66% | 56.83% | 58.02% | 57.03% | 60.13% |
| DOJ | 24.54% | 30.14% | 24.54% | 29.20% | 26.19% | 29.82% | 25.04% | 32.35% | 29.79% | 31.71% | 29.82% | 34.04% | 31.40% | 32.73% |
| DOL | 36.69% | 32.61% | 36.69% | 34.97% | 34.68% | 34.96% | 38.65% | 35.02% | 34.85% | 36.04% | 39.12% | 38.94% | 40.34% | 40.21% |
| DOT | 38.91% | 38.75% | 38.91% | 35.35% | 40.62% | 44.09% | 41.43% | 45.79% | 50.93% | 51.77% | 48.57% | 33.43% | 37.49% | 34.05% |
| Education | 16.40% | 16.51% | 16.40% | 15.95% | 18.18% | 19.83% | 27.47% | 28.78% | 28.43% | 23.35% | 26.84% | 34.90% | 30.96% | 14.90% |
| Energy | 6.32% | 5.82% | 6.32% | 7.60% | 5.33% | 5.15% | 3.76% | 5.25% | 5.40% | 5.38% | 5.27% | 5.13% | 5.85% | 4.96% |
| EPA | 47.32% | 44.36% | 47.32% | 43.27% | 42.26% | 44.02% | 44.03% | 40.25% | 39.75% | 40.09% | 40.35% | 43.33% | 43.90% | 39.50% |
| GSA | 27.04% | 39.38% | 27.04% | 28.67% | 38.83% | 39.98% | 41.69% | 39.20% | 44.15% | 39.22% | 42.42% | 38.80% | 42.13% | 49.47% |
| HHS | 17.05% | 22.79% | 17.05% | 22.01% | 23.94% | 22.39% | 23.90% | 21.60% | 23.30% | 23.02% | 22.32% | 22.13% | 25.13% | 23.10% |
| HUD | 49.69% | 61.39% | 49.69% | 27.96% | 36.06% | 40.34% | 14.95% | 40.29% | 38.20% | 46.34% | 48.97% | 40.73% | 28.10% | 1.57% |
| NASA | 15.08% | 15.85% | 15.08% | 15.46% | 17.82% | 19.00% | 15.90% | 18.33% | 17.32% | 16.67% | 16.50% | 16.69% | 17.30% | 17.48% |
| NRC | 33.06% | 36.30% | 33.06% | 28.70% | 33.76% | 32.98% | 35.16% | 35.50% | 31.13% | 37.12% | 36.68% | 40.99% | 57.67% | 53.57% |
| NSF | 16.88% | 18.18% | 16.88% | 15.10% | 17.65% | 15.38% | 19.15% | 17.81% | 21.67% | 18.63% | 18.78% | 11.18% | 16.03% | 53.57% |
| OPM | 13.98% | 13.48% | 13.98% | 18.70% | 18.16% | 20.25% | 20.54% | 23.45% | 33.84% | 31.40% | 33.97% | 30.92% | 30.63% | 82.75% |
| SBA | 64.65% | 73.29% | 64.65% | 66.99% | 67.07% | 70.92% | 79.07% | 77.48% | 78.18% | 73.70% | 79.53% | 77.99% | 81.02% | 80.18% |
| SSA | 32.47% | 33.48% | 32.47% | 32.19% | 35.02% | 30.76% | 37.45% | 38.73% | 39.75% | 36.66% | 31.32% | 32.57% | 35.89% | 31.86% |
| State | 33.94% | 32.81% | 33.94% | 34.62% | 34.26% | 39.03% | 30.39% | 43.48% | 43.94% | 28.56% | 22.85% | 27.58% | 31.65% | 28.44% |
| Treasury | 26.71% | 28.45% | 26.71% | 30.17% | 34.51% | 38.55% | 39.99% | 36.70% | 34.68% | 36.16% | 35.55% | 42.31% | 42.65% | 46.26% |
| USAID | 8.66% | 15.43% | 8.66% | 8.13% | 13.74% | 11.99% | 100.00% | 20.46% | 18.12% | 13.11% | 13.17% | 14.03% | 14.75% | 14.91% |
| USDA | 52.68% | 53.80% | 52.68% | 55.17% | 52.40% | 52.83% | 52.01% | 53.64% | 49.99% | 56.24% | 57.95% | 63.12% | 57.78% | 47.21% |
| VA | 34.94% | 35.15% | 34.94% | 37.35% | 33.66% | 35.01% | 39.75% | 34.48% | 30.79% | 29.87% | 29.37% | 30.56% | 31.12% | 26.57% |

*Table 13 - Small Business Set-Aside Reporting 2007 - 2020*

# 2007 - 2020 8(a) Set-Aside Reporting

| 8(a) GOALS - 5% Agency | 2007 | 2008 | 2009 | 2010 | 2011 | 2012 | 2013 | 2014 | 2015 | 2016 | 2017 | 2018 | 2019 | 2020 |
|---|---|---|---|---|---|---|---|---|---|---|---|---|---|---|
| DHS | 5.96% | 6.10% | 5.96% | 4.80% | 11.50% | 12.83% | 7.82% | 7.07% | 7.21% | 6.35% | 5.50% | 5.56% | 6.57% | 5.69% |
| DOC | 5.73% | 8.11% | 5.73% | 6.25% | 15.36% | 14.68% | 5.88% | 6.60% | 7.34% | 6.53% | 6.23% | 6.28% | 5.45% | 5.80% |
| DOD | 4.37% | 3.12% | 4.37% | 4.12% | 6.90% | 7.30% | 5.04% | 4.38% | 4.40% | 3.95% | 3.45% | 3.41% | 3.13% | 3.43% |
| DOI | 12.62% | 12.08% | 12.62% | 11.74% | 20.77% | 21.92% | 13.16% | 11.70% | 11.53% | 11.12% | 9.95% | 9.88% | 10.74% | 9.96% |
| DOJ | 3.61% | 3.29% | 3.61% | 4.23% | 6.79% | 8.63% | 3.45% | 4.55% | 4.02% | 4.96% | 4.49% | 5.79% | 5.16% | 5.06% |
| DOL | 7.95% | 6.36% | 7.95% | 7.87% | 19.15% | 17.89% | 7.98% | 6.99% | 6.66% | 7.10% | 5.31% | 7.01% | 5.55% | 6.35% |
| DOT | 9.19% | 11.53% | 9.19% | 9.80% | 19.45% | 17.98% | 12.71% | 13.48% | 13.06% | 11.39% | 12.58% | 7.02% | 7.91% | 6.79% |
| Education | 1.81% | 1.42% | 1.81% | 2.14% | 5.53% | 5.19% | 1.51% | 1.92% | 1.94% | 1.58% | 1.52% | 1.65% | 1.65% | 1.58% |
| Energy | 0.87% | 1.07% | 0.87% | 1.36% | 1.94% | 2.28% | 0.61% | 0.97% | 1.15% | 1.21% | 1.01% | 0.78% | 0.75% | 0.67% |
| EPA | 5.90% | 7.09% | 5.90% | 8.91% | 14.82% | 15.70% | 7.38% | 7.30% | 7.51% | 6.64% | 8.06% | 8.77% | 8.00% | 9.04% |
| GSA | 6.43% | 7.28% | 6.43% | 7.97% | 19.02% | 19.16% | 9.90% | 9.10% | 10.71% | 9.73% | 10.19% | 8.63% | 8.03% | 7.56% |
| HHS | 3.66% | 4.20% | 3.66% | 5.02% | 9.16% | 9.16% | 5.07% | 4.79% | 5.65% | 5.54% | 5.30% | 5.38% | 5.51% | 3.52% |
| HUD | 17.75% | 17.15% | 17.75% | 8.84% | 21.89% | 27.96% | 12.42% | 8.26% | 13.58% | 13.88% | 9.62% | 10.71% | 5.87% | 5.03% |
| NASA | 2.95% | 3.56% | 2.95% | 3.18% | 7.09% | 7.65% | 3.74% | 3.96% | 3.73% | 3.88% | 3.79% | 4.03% | 3.95% | 3.83% |
| NRC | 12.36% | 11.95% | 12.36% | 10.28% | 14.11% | 16.39% | 11.76% | 15.34% | 56.24% | 12.83% | 12.28% | 10.48% | 15.10% | 14.91% |
| NSF | 4.39% | 4.42% | 4.39% | 5.04% | 8.47% | 6.13% | 5.38% | 8.49% | 10.88% | 10.04% | 11.47% | 5.42% | 4.93% | 14.91% |
| OPM | 0.54% | 1.38% | 0.54% | 0.78% | 4.39% | 5.02% | 4.90% | 7.96% | 6.24% | 5.97% | 4.78% | 3.58% | 5.65% | 15.52% |
| SBA | 21.41% | 9.75% | 21.41% | 27.63% | 47.39% | 44.93% | 28.73% | 31.61% | 24.65% | 23.61% | 34.20% | 21.98% | 32.79% | 4.18% |
| SSA | 5.25% | 5.32% | 5.25% | 6.70% | 12.07% | 9.12% | 3.74% | 2.90% | 2.93% | 2.96% | 2.51% | 2.28% | 2.01% | 1.47% |
| State | 10.77% | 8.91% | 10.77% | 11.82% | 16.74% | 19.92% | 9.70% | 16.95% | 15.74% | 8.84% | 6.50% | 7.68% | 11.41% | 10.81% |
| Treasury | 6.14% | 5.20% | 6.14% | 7.92% | 13.17% | 14.74% | 9.32% | 7.73% | 8.45% | 7.78% | 6.65% | 4.24% | 4.88% | 3.90% |
| USAID | 0.36% | 0.75% | 0.36% | 1.28% | 7.67% | 7.13% | 0.40% | 3.05% | 2.23% | 1.30% | 1.66% | 3.23% | 2.38% | 1.97% |
| USDA | 7.36% | 5.93% | 7.36% | 8.40% | 13.27% | 12.46% | 7.58% | 6.57% | 5.64% | 7.15% | 5.86% | 6.05% | 6.85% | 4.73% |
| VA | 1.21% | 1.99% | 1.21% | 0.90% | 8.41% | 7.91% | 0.28% | 0.31% | 0.21% | 0.12% | 0.12% | 0.05% | 0.07% | 0.02% |

*Table 14 - 8(a) Set-Aside Reporting 2007 - 2020*

# 2007 - 2020 Woman Owned Small Set-Aside Reporting

| WOSB GOALS - 5% Agency | 2007 | 2008 | 2009 | 2010 | 2011 | 2012 | 2013 | 2014 | 2015 | 2016 | 2017 | 2018 | 2019 | 2020 |
|---|---|---|---|---|---|---|---|---|---|---|---|---|---|---|
| DHS | 7.86% | 6.57% | 7.86% | 7.03% | 5.95% | 6.43% | 8.98% | 7.33% | 7.34% | 7.67% | 7.86% | 7.43% | 7.81% | 6.79% |
| DOC | 7.27% | 9.42% | 7.27% | 8.83% | 9.70% | 9.27% | 12.01% | 12.24% | 13.39% | 11.58% | 11.80% | 12.77% | 11.91% | 11.99% |
| DOD | 3.37% | 2.72% | 3.37% | 3.59% | 3.43% | 3.38% | 4.22% | 3.97% | 4.43% | 4.10% | 4.05% | 4.06% | 4.24% | 4.05% |
| DOI | 10.37% | 10.55% | 10.37% | 11.30% | 11.99% | 12.16% | 10.49% | 11.22% | 12.67% | 12.85% | 13.87% | 13.06% | 13.61% | 14.10% |
| DOJ | 4.27% | 4.96% | 4.27% | 6.04% | 6.28% | 6.59% | 6.82% | 6.71% | 6.01% | 6.12% | 6.62% | 6.64% | 6.37% | 5.95% |
| DOL | 7.06% | 6.57% | 7.06% | 7.17% | 6.95% | 6.62% | 8.73% | 8.84% | 10.00% | 12.02% | 14.80% | 12.62% | 12.62% | 12.80% |
| DOT | 10.94% | 6.57% | 10.94% | 7.85% | 11.14% | 8.77% | 11.34% | 12.12% | 9.10% | 10.64% | 11.40% | 8.47% | 10.32% | 8.29% |
| Education | 5.83% | 5.48% | 5.83% | 5.47% | 5.42% | 5.76% | 9.06% | 9.51% | 9.01% | 5.95% | 7.53% | 9.48% | 9.42% | 5.91% |
| Energy | 0.89% | 0.98% | 0.89% | 1.14% | 0.93% | 1.24% | 0.98% | 1.27% | 1.11% | 1.23% | 1.27% | 1.18% | 1.12% | 0.90% |
| EPA | 4.62% | 4.71% | 4.62% | 4.77% | 5.35% | 6.02% | 5.91% | 5.87% | 6.98% | 5.88% | 6.31% | 5.44% | 4.99% | 5.48% |
| GSA | 5.79% | 7.58% | 5.79% | 5.93% | 9.15% | 9.06% | 9.48% | 8.07% | 9.29% | 9.31% | 8.82% | 8.55% | 10.06% | 10.47% |
| HHS | 4.51% | 5.57% | 4.51% | 5.69% | 6.43% | 6.60% | 7.57% | 6.54% | 7.49% | 7.29% | 6.53% | 6.37% | 7.20% | 5.02% |
| HUD | 16.12% | 17.04% | 16.12% | 10.98% | 13.68% | 14.65% | 15.30% | 14.85% | 12.35% | 20.11% | 17.98% | 15.40% | 12.61% | 4.92% |
| NASA | 2.37% | 2.48% | 2.37% | 2.24% | 2.79% | 2.94% | 2.58% | 3.29% | 336.00% | 4.05% | 4.39% | 4.61% | 4.50% | 4.30% |
| NRC | 4.73% | 7.15% | 4.73% | 5.35% | 5.82% | 7.07% | 12.80% | 10.07% | 8.78% | 10.19% | 9.52% | 13.84% | 14.89% | 12.03% |
| NSF | 4.64% | 6.53% | 4.64% | 4.73% | 5.27% | 5.00% | 5.63% | 5.76% | 6.13% | 2.67% | 3.57% | 2.77% | 3.82% | 12.03% |
| OPM | 5.60% | 2.96% | 5.60% | 8.86% | 7.89% | 7.48% | 7.10% | 8.99% | 9.19% | 9.66% | 15.45% | 21.94% | 14.87% | 46.40% |
| SBA | 19.99% | 21.81% | 19.99% | 25.19% | 19.62% | 13.46% | 20.10% | 23.74% | 23.08% | 21.72% | 20.25% | 28.52% | 24.17% | 63.09% |
| SSA | 3.76% | 3.28% | 3.76% | 4.06% | 6.36% | 10.80% | 14.99% | 10.65% | 12.93% | 13.39% | 7.45% | 6.29% | 9.45% | 5.99% |
| State | 4.08% | 3.50% | 4.08% | 4.70% | 4.99% | 9.65% | 6.50% | 9.69% | 9.76% | 6.23% | 4.47% | 5.59% | 5.33% | 4.46% |
| Treasury | 8.26% | 7.10% | 8.26% | 8.93% | 12.75% | 13.23% | 12.51% | 9.83% | 9.08% | 11.59% | 13.08% | 12.35% | 11.48% | 9.06% |
| USAID | 3.47% | 4.31% | 3.47% | 4.34% | 4.67% | 4.36% | 0.40% | 5.90% | 3.67% | 3.36% | 3.83% | 4.45% | 5.52% | 5.69% |
| USDA | 6.81% | 6.84% | 6.81% | 8.08% | 8.16% | 7.50% | 7.96% | 9.65% | 9.71% | 9.86% | 9.53% | 10.43% | 10.31% | 10.00% |
| VA | 3.40% | 4.00% | 3.40% | 3.54% | 3.86% | 3.30% | 3.29% | 3.42% | 2.95% | 3.03% | 2.71% | 2.55% | 3.04% | 2.42% |

*Table 15 - WOSB Set-Aside Reporting 2007 – 2020*

# 2007 - 2020 Veteran Owned Set-Aside Reporting

| VOSB GOALS - NO FEDERAL MANDATE (table uses 3%) | | | | | | | | | | | | RSM FEDERAL | |
|---|---|---|---|---|---|---|---|---|---|---|---|---|---|
| Agency | 2007 | 2008 | 2009 | 2010 | 2011 | 2012 | 2013 | 2014 | 2015 | 2016 | 2017 | 2018 | 2019 | 2020 |
| DHS | 4.33% | 4.78% | 4.33% | 5.48% | 6.02% | 6.72% | 7.74% | 8.10% | 7.26% | 7.57% | 7.50% | 7.26% | 7.30% | 6.76% |
| DOC | 4.04% | 4.66% | 4.04% | 4.59% | 4.96% | 5.47% | 8.82% | 6.39% | 6.31% | 6.74% | 6.09% | 6.12% | 5.71% | 5.76% |
| DOD | 3.14% | 2.38% | 3.14% | 3.62% | 3.70% | 3.85% | 4.76% | 4.57% | 5.18% | 4.78% | 4.54% | 4.82% | 4.51% | 4.37% |
| DOI | 5.91% | 5.87% | 5.91% | 4.87% | 6.12% | 7.08% | 6.52% | 6.71% | 7.53% | 8.19% | 7.57% | 7.77% | 6.96% | 7.92% |
| DOJ | 2.49% | 3.83% | 2.49% | 3.44% | 3.56% | 4.39% | 3.90% | 5.25% | 5.53% | 5.46% | 6.60% | 6.69% | 6.27% | 7.64% |
| DOL | 4.26% | 6.48% | 4.26% | 3.90% | 3.89% | 5.34% | 5.22% | 5.00% | 5.01% | 5.91% | 6.46% | 6.74% | 8.44% | 7.76% |
| DOT | 5.83% | 5.14% | 5.83% | 5.78% | 7.67% | 8.58% | 9.68% | 8.39% | 8.62% | 7.48% | 7.44% | 6.53% | 6.86% | 5.97% |
| Education | 0.98% | 1.16% | 0.98% | 0.94% | 1.27% | 0.96% | 0.58% | 0.95% | 1.31% | 1.45% | 2.07% | 3.08% | 3.84% | 3.01% |
| Energy | 1.42% | 0.76% | 1.42% | 1.28% | 0.77% | 0.63% | 0.53% | 0.87% | 1.11% | 1.02% | 0.97% | 0.99% | 1.06% | 0.82% |
| EPA | 9.64% | 6.47% | 9.64% | 7.19% | 9.77% | 7.81% | 5.06% | 6.10% | 5.73% | 4.40% | 4.49% | 5.28% | 4.30% | 3.14% |
| GSA | 3.71% | 6.42% | 3.71% | 3.61% | 5.35% | 4.83% | 5.65% | 6.84% | 6.51% | 7.18% | 8.05% | 8.79% | 7.96% | 10.78% |
| HHS | 2.29% | 2.09% | 2.29% | 2.58% | 2.50% | 2.50% | 2.58% | 2.33% | 2.78% | 2.72% | 2.56% | 2.86% | 3.54% | 2.31% |
| HUD | 8.23% | 9.03% | 8.23% | 1.84% | 2.57% | 7.05% | 3.96% | 3.93% | 2.74% | 4.52% | 5.78% | 8.62% | 4.64% | -4.28% |
| NASA | 3.28% | 3.66% | 3.28% | 2.61% | 2.29% | 1.98% | 1.41% | 1.46% | 1.67% | 1.49% | 1.67% | 1.58% | 1.87% | 1.97% |
| NRC | 6.33% | 4.74% | 6.33% | 6.51% | 9.61% | 7.72% | 3.23% | 4.99% | 4.76% | 7.71% | 8.38% | 7.13% | 12.48% | 9.40% |
| NSF | 3.16% | 3.25% | 3.16% | 2.88% | 4.18% | 3.01% | 3.24% | 3.45% | 3.98% | 3.68% | 2.86% | 2.44% | 2.19% | 9.40% |
| OPM | 1.05% | 1.50% | 1.05% | 1.00% | 1.64% | 2.09% | 1.71% | 1.31% | 0.84% | 2.17% | 3.66% | 1.39% | 3.00% | 9.20% |
| SBA | 4.61% | 3.27% | 4.61% | 3.30% | 7.35% | 9.37% | 9.85% | 6.70% | 8.67% | 14.24% | 21.11% | 15.65% | 25.89% | 11.37% |
| SSA | 9.46% | 5.56% | 9.46% | 5.48% | 4.56% | 3.04% | 4.44% | 4.03% | 3.87% | 4.06% | 4.67% | 5.19% | 4.93% | 4.17% |
| State | 6.33% | 8.09% | 6.33% | 6.62% | 6.16% | 6.89% | 6.28% | 7.84% | 8.91% | 7.33% | 4.21% | 4.65% | 4.84% | 6.58% |
| Treasury | 4.64% | 3.97% | 4.64% | 6.84% | 7.71% | 8.41% | 5.50% | 6.32% | 6.19% | 6.60% | 5.60% | 4.91% | 5.64% | 4.00% |
| USAID | 0.23% | 1.86% | 0.23% | 0.61% | 3.00% | 1.62% | 99.60% | 4.21% | 3.73% | 1.45% | 1.07% | 0.57% | 0.59% | 1.05% |
| USDA | 5.17% | 4.94% | 5.17% | 5.61% | 4.65% | 5.10% | 5.18% | 6.15% | 6.44% | 7.15% | 6.77% | 10.55% | 5.85% | 4.21% |
| VA | 19.98% | 14.88% | 19.98% | 23.08% | 20.50% | 22.60% | 24.86% | 20.94% | 18.63% | 19.07% | 20.62% | 22.24% | 22.88% | 20.41% |

*Table 16 - VOSB Set-Aside Reporting 2007 - 2020*

# 2007 - 2020 Service Disabled Veteran Set-Aside Reporting

| SDVOSB GOALS - 3% | | | | | | | | | | | | RSM FEDERAL | |
|---|---|---|---|---|---|---|---|---|---|---|---|---|---|
| Agency | 2007 | 2008 | 2009 | 2010 | 2011 | 2012 | 2013 | 2014 | 2015 | 2016 | 2017 | 2018 | 2019 | 2020 |
| DHS | 1.91% | 1.91% | 1.91% | 3.21% | 3.96% | 5.34% | 5.81% | 6.19% | 5.37% | 5.98% | 5.70% | 5.55% | 5.84% | 5.76% |
| DOC | 1.99% | 1.91% | 1.99% | 2.92% | 2.88% | 3.43% | 7.21% | 4.76% | 4.95% | 4.87% | 4.54% | 4.11% | 3.92% | 4.10% |
| DOD | 1.43% | 0.94% | 1.43% | 1.82% | 2.02% | 2.33% | 3.04% | 3.01% | 3.45% | 3.35% | 3.23% | 3.47% | 3.25% | 3.22% |
| DOI | 2.38% | 2.45% | 2.38% | 2.32% | 2.78% | 3.33% | 3.77% | 3.87% | 4.57% | 5.02% | 4.51% | 4.76% | 4.36% | 5.62% |
| DOJ | 0.80% | 1.04% | 0.80% | 1.10% | 1.48% | 2.62% | 2.99% | 3.51% | 3.63% | 3.68% | 5.10% | 5.08% | 5.11% | 6.17% |
| DOL | 2.66% | 4.34% | 2.66% | 3.08% | 2.98% | 3.93% | 4.06% | 3.09% | 3.21% | 4.72% | 4.79% | 4.52% | 6.70% | 6.63% |
| DOT | 1.71% | 1.78% | 1.71% | 2.33% | 2.46% | 3.15% | 3.53% | 3.24% | 3.59% | 3.11% | 3.04% | 3.59% | 4.14% | 3.76% |
| Education | 0.48% | 0.45% | 0.48% | 0.65% | 0.99% | 0.82% | 0.45% | 0.74% | 0.89% | 1.16% | 1.69% | 2.45% | 2.52% | 1.07% |
| Energy | 1.20% | 0.52% | 1.20% | 0.86% | 0.33% | 0.38% | 0.21% | 0.43% | 0.70% | 0.64% | 0.62% | 0.64% | 0.83% | 0.56% |
| EPA | 7.76% | 3.67% | 7.76% | 5.15% | 7.26% | 6.68% | 4.34% | 5.29% | 4.35% | 3.95% | 3.78% | 4.78% | 3.96% | 2.95% |
| GSA | 1.90% | 4.01% | 1.90% | 2.22% | 2.63% | 3.17% | 3.57% | 4.46% | 4.79% | 5.32% | 6.44% | 5.62% | 4.75% | 8.90% |
| HHS | 0.94% | 0.70% | 0.94% | 1.00% | 0.97% | 1.02% | 1.14% | 1.07% | 1.31% | 1.55% | 1.65% | 1.93% | 2.76% | 1.70% |
| HUD | 1.03% | 1.30% | 1.03% | 1.34% | 1.50% | 6.01% | 0.71% | 3.63% | 2.49% | 4.40% | 5.97% | 7.91% | 4.00% | -5.04% |
| NASA | 1.42% | 1.32% | 1.42% | 1.53% | 1.29% | 1.02% | 0.64% | 0.57% | 0.71% | 0.86% | 1.02% | 1.02% | 1.35% | 1.65% |
| NRC | 2.26% | 0.69% | 2.26% | 2.43% | 2.40% | 3.76% | 2.69% | 4.47% | 3.88% | 6.13% | 7.06% | 6.20% | 9.90% | 7.60% |
| NSF | 0.33% | 0.02% | 0.33% | 0.35% | 0.91% | 2.30% | 3.08% | 3.20% | 3.61% | 3.12% | 2.77% | 2.19% | 2.25% | 7.60% |
| OPM | 0.15% | 0.95% | 0.15% | 0.06% | 0.97% | 0.84% | 0.84% | 0.49% | 0.34% | 1.46% | 2.81% | 1.16% | 2.26% | 7.94% |
| SBA | 3.05% | 0.84% | 3.05% | 1.90% | 6.57% | 6.45% | 7.35% | 4.47% | 7.02% | 11.20% | 18.65% | 13.96% | 24.17% | 9.99% |
| SSA | 2.85% | 2.04% | 2.85% | 3.03% | 2.82% | 1.15% | 2.84% | 2.66% | 2.85% | 3.15% | 3.36% | 4.14% | 4.19% | 3.61% |
| State | 1.87% | 2.01% | 1.87% | 2.59% | 2.71% | 4.05% | 4.08% | 5.19% | 5.83% | 5.40% | 3.69% | 3.88% | 4.13% | 4.27% |
| Treasury | 2.41% | 2.06% | 2.41% | 3.86% | 4.07% | 4.15% | 2.43% | 4.02% | 3.84% | 4.14% | 3.74% | 3.56% | 4.28% | 3.12% |
| USAID | 0.25% | 0.10% | 0.25% | 0.53% | 2.65% | 1.37% | 99.60% | 3.88% | 3.36% | 1.19% | 0.84% | 0.35% | 0.38% | 0.48% |
| USDA | 2.59% | 2.09% | 2.59% | 2.76% | 2.24% | 2.92% | 3.36% | 3.79% | 3.54% | 3.98% | 3.22% | 3.58% | 3.53% | 2.45% |
| VA | 16.96% | 11.78% | 16.96% | 20.05% | 18.22% | 19.24% | 22.09% | 18.70% | 16.80% | 17.75% | 19.49% | 21.29% | 22.52% | 20.25% |

*Table 17 – SDVOSB Set-Aside Reporting 2007 - 2020*

Note. Contrary to what many believe, there is no congressional, Defense, or statutory set-aside requirements for Veteran Owned. Only 3% for Service Disabled.

# 2007 - 2020 HUBZone Set-Aside Reporting

| HUBZONE GOALS - 3% | | | | | | | | | | | | | RSM FEDERAL | |
|---|---|---|---|---|---|---|---|---|---|---|---|---|---|---|
| Agency | 2007 | 2008 | 2009 | 2010 | 2011 | 2012 | 2013 | 2014 | 2015 | 2016 | 2017 | 2018 | 2019 | 2020 |
| DHS | 2.70% | 3.14% | 2.70% | 2.66% | 2.96% | 3.03% | 4.22% | 3.87% | 4.04% | 4.21% | 3.60% | 3.85% | 4.08% | 4.07% |
| DOC | 0.86% | 2.19% | 0.86% | 1.08% | 0.78% | 0.73% | 1.07% | 1.08% | 1.46% | 4.22% | 5.82% | 9.27% | 11.83% | 13.05% |
| DOD | 3.26% | 2.15% | 3.26% | 3.00% | 2.58% | 2.18% | 2.35% | 1.92% | 1.86% | 1.57% | 1.49% | 1.94% | 1.88% | 2.20% |
| DOI | 10.30% | 10.01% | 10.30% | 9.08% | 9.39% | 7.90% | 7.06% | 5.80% | 5.25% | 4.86% | 5.07% | 5.29% | 6.03% | 7.33% |
| DOJ | 0.68% | 1.08% | 0.6805+AE | 0.79% | 0.74% | 1.01% | 0.70% | 1.01% | 0.85% | 1.05% | 1.08% | 2.28% | 1.70% | 2.20% |
| DOL | 1.08% | 3.53% | 1.08% | 3.15% | 3.12% | 0.69% | 1.25% | 1.08% | 2.23% | 2.76% | 3.24% | 3.88% | 5.14% | 5.94% |
| DOT | 7.08% | 7.31% | 7.08% | 6.83% | 6.54% | 7.04% | 4.48% | 6.12% | 10.73% | 10.85% | 3.62% | 1.82% | 2.97% | 3.41% |
| Education | 0.80% | 0.57% | 0.80% | 0.72% | 0.66% | 0.29% | 0.13% | 0.22% | 0.21% | 0.58% | 1.32% | 1.84% | 2.21% | 0.53% |
| Energy | 0.13% | 0.20% | 0.13% | 0.72% | 0.24% | 0.39% | 0.26% | 0.58% | 0.39% | 0.14% | 0.12% | 0.15% | 0.19% | 0.19% |
| EPA | 2.13% | 2.22% | 2.13% | 0.98% | 1.07% | 2.53% | 2.60% | 1.92% | 1.33% | 0.61% | 1.62% | 2.40% | 2.25% | 2.04% |
| GSA | 3.24% | 6.56% | 3.24% | 3.22% | 4.39% | 3.81% | 3.41% | 3.25% | 4.35% | 3.88% | 4.94% | 3.98% | 3.95% | 4.39% |
| HHS | 1.03% | 1.19% | 1.03% | 1.42% | 0.96% | 0.73% | 0.69% | 0.61% | 0.73% | 1.02% | 0.80% | 0.93% | 1.49% | 1.31% |
| HUD | 3.06% | 2.10% | 3.06% | 1.13% | 0.90% | 0.83% | 1.09% | 0.70% | 0.68% | 1.19% | 2.94% | 3.44% | 3.60% | 6.96% |
| NASA | 0.73% | 0.85% | 0.73% | 0.89% | 0.77% | 0.68% | 0.58% | 0.86% | 0.62% | 0.51% | 0.47% | 0.53% | 0.82% | 0.65% |
| NRC | 4.66% | 4.09% | 4.66% | 3.59% | 3.88% | 4.01% | 1.79% | 2.54% | 3.09% | 2.89% | 2.23% | 3.44% | 13.24% | 7.34% |
| NSF | 1.07% | 0.11% | 1.07% | 0.66% | 0.96% | 0.69% | 0.98% | 1.88% | 2.14% | 2.37% | 2.71% | 1.70% | 1.85% | 7.34% |
| OPM | 0.47% | 1.92% | 0.47% | 0.07% | 0.03% | 0.46% | 1.64% | 2.78% | 1.63% | 3.19% | 3.29% | 1.85% | 3.18% | 8.49% |
| SBA | 8.64% | 11.84% | 8.64% | 3.33% | 3.78% | 5.21% | 6.01% | 6.98% | 5.56% | 6.53% | 7.45% | 11.17% | 6.74% | 7.61% |
| SSA | 1.45% | 2.27% | 1.45% | 1.93% | 1.97% | 2.01% | 1.54% | 1.37% | 1.31% | 1.57% | 1.39% | 1.03% | 0.95% | 1.02% |
| State | 2.71% | 2.11% | 2.71% | 2.82% | 2.27% | 2.49% | 1.51% | 1.97% | 3.21% | 2.36% | 2.46% | 4.70% | 5.67% | 6.06% |
| Treasury | 1.83% | 1.51% | 1.83% | 2.24% | 4.11% | 4.65% | 2.45% | 3.33% | 4.08% | 4.49% | 4.78% | 3.46% | 3.49% | 2.41% |
| USAID | 0.71% | 0.26% | 0.71% | 0.29% | 0.58% | 0.70% | 0.00% | 0.21% | 0.16% | 0.19% | 0.18% | 0.42% | 0.62% | 0.66% |
| USDA | 8.22% | 6.60% | 8.22% | 9.90% | 5.56% | 4.39% | 2.96% | 3.57% | 3.01% | 3.94% | 4.03% | 5.68% | 7.02% | 6.74% |
| VA | 2.12% | 2.69% | 2.12% | 2.16% | 2.24% | 1.73% | 1.48% | 1.49% | 1.68% | 1.58% | 2.14% | 2.19% | 2.83% | 1.98% |

*Table 18 - HUBZone Set-Aside Reporting 2007 - 2020*

# Chapter 2
# Small Business Government Updates

**RSM FEDERAL**
The Art and Science of Government Sales™

# Small Business Updates

The majority of this manual was developed for entrepreneurs and small business owners who are fairly new to government sales. This short chapter outlines some very important changes that have taken place the last several years.

- **New Small Business Mentor-Protégé Program**
    - In past, only 8(a), SDVOSB → Now all small business can participate
    - Mentors can be large or small businesses
    - SBA must approve MP relationship
    - Mentor limited to one protégé at a time (Up to three with different NAICS)
    - Unlike 8(a) MP, protégé must only qualify as small – not half the size of small
    - Formal Mentor-Protégé Agreement (MPA):
        - ➢ Focuses on protégé's business plan
        - ➢ Minimum 1 year agreement
        - ➢ Maximum 3 years (but may be extended 3 years) – Maximum 6 years
    - Annual reporting with detailed list of "assistance provided"

    Note. I do not recommend you seek out mentors to participate in the Mentor-Protégé program. Why? Because from a business perspective you "back-into" these relationships. If you don't know how and have not successfully won contracts under standard prime / subcontractor relationships, you will not succeed in finding a quality company to mentor you. Yep, everyone talks about Mentor Protégé but many companies get into these relationships and fail… for many reasons. If you're new to government, focus on prime / subcontracting first.

- **Mentor-Protégé Joint Ventures**
    - Compete for set-aside contracts
    - Exception to affiliation
    - Enables large businesses to qualify as "small" as part of JV

- **Limitations on Subcontracting**
    - Elimination of the 50% rule
    - Excludes percentage of the award amount to *similarly situated contractors*
        - ➢ Effectively allowing you to count work performed by other small businesses as your own
    - Example: WOSB set-aside contract
        - ➢ Your company will prime and account for 40% of revenue / profit
        - ➢ Before, this rule change, you would have to account for 51%
        - ➢ If you subcontract to *another* WOSB that gets 25% revenue / profit →

➢ Now you have 65% of revenue / profit going to WOSB(s)

➢ Therefore – prime accounts for 65% and meets 51% threshold

- **Mixed Type Contracts**

  - Contracting officers must now determine if supplies or services have greatest percentage of contract value – and assign the appropriate NAICS code.

  - Limitations on subcontracting then apply to the principal NAICS code

  - Example: Small Business set-aside contract

    ➢ DoD construction project – both service and supply components

    ➢ Contracting officer projects $2 million services and $500,000 in supplies

    ➢ Greatest percentage contract value is for services (primary NAICS code)

    ➢ Small business prime must account for 50% of $2 million in services ($1 million)

    ➢ Remember, limitations on subcontracting applies

    ➢ The $500,000 in supply components can go to *ANY size business*.

- **Department of Veterans Affairs Act "Rule of Two"**

  - Kingdomware Technologies Protested VA's move away from Veteran Companies

  - GAO sided with Kingdomware but the VA refused to follow GAO guidance

  - Went to the Supreme Court

  - In an 8-0 decision, the Supreme Court upheld that a contract must be awarded to a veteran owned or service disabled veteran owned business if it meets two criteria:

    ➢ Contracting officer reasonably expects that **two or more** VOSB or SDVSOB will submit an offer

    ➢ Award can be made at a **fair and reasonable price**

- **Sub Contracting Plans**

  - Primes that identify a small business by name in a proposal MUST now notify the subcontractor in writing prior to turning in the proposal

  - This eliminates large businesses from using small businesses to win contracts and subsequently not using those small businesses after award

  - Prime's sub-contracting plan will have on-site compliance reviews to validate that the small businesses used to win the contract are being used

- **Calculation of Annual Receipts for Size Status**

- Before June 2016, some companies omitted passive income. New rule states all income, including passive income, is required in calculation of annual receipts.
- Starting in 2020, companies had the option of using 3 or 5 year average
- Starting January 2022, all companies will use the 5 year average of annual receipts

- **Affiliation**
  - Generally, affiliation exists when:
    - ➤ One business controls or has power to control another
    - ➤ Third party controls or has power to control another
    - ➤ Control may arise via ownership, management, or interaction
    - ➤ Minority shareholder has ability prevent quorum or block actions per charter, by-laws, or shareholder's agreement (defined as negative control)
  - Firms owned / controlled by married couples / civil unions
    - ➤ Share or provide loans, resources, equipment, locations, employees
    - ➤ Must show a clear "line of fracture" between the firms
  - Economic Dependence
    - ➤ 70% receipts from another concern over previous three fiscal years
  - Partnering with Large Business
    - ➤ No change to affiliation
    - ➤ Large businesses owns major share of small business or all receipts through large business

# Chapter 3
# Government Contracts & Vehicles

**RSM FEDERAL**
The Art and Science of Government Sales™

# Admin & Registration for Government Sales

## Getting Started In Public Sector

There are nine (9) primary registration requirements that small businesses should complete in order to sell to the government.

Since the government often changes requirements on each, we keep them updated in the Federal Access Coaching and Training Platform.

Rather than duplicate content, you can download government registration steps when you join Federal Access.

https://rsmfederal.com/federal-access

You should NOT pay any company to register you in the System for Award Management (SAM) or pay to renew or maintain your account. Companies that charge you for these services are con-artists and the government has been trying to shut them down for years. What they do is not illegal. However, it is unethical. If you need help registering your company, your local Procurement Technical Assistance Center (PTAC) will help you for free.

*Figure 7 - Government Registration*

If you need to register and have not yet engaged your local PTAC, contact them: http://www.aptac-us.org/

# Getting Started in Public Sector

- **Marketing Partner Identification Number (MPIN)**
  - You will receive your MPIN automatically after registering in SAM
  - Utilized for registering with other required government sites
  - You will need the MPIN to update your SAM registration and to open and review your CPARS ratings (contract evaluations)
- **Online Representations and Certifications Application (ORCA)**
  - Now Built into the System for Award Management (SAM)
- **Commercial and Government Entity Code (CAGE)**
  - SAM will send you a CAGE code automatically when SAM registration is approved
  - A CAGE code identifies a specific company at a specific location
  - Used for pre-award surveys, automated bidder lists, and accounting
  - Critical for product sales via DLA's Internet Bid Board System (DIBBS)

# Getting Started in State and Local

- **Most States have online opportunity and bidding systems**
  - Daily review of multiple opportunity websites takes too much time
  - Utilize a bid-matching system to quickly identify State RFPs/RFQs and opportunities
  - Contact RSM Federal for recommendations
- **Some States require annual registration fee**
  - Most states will allow you to review opportunities without registering
  - Most states require a state tax identification number to register
  - Depending on the city you target, may require additional licenses
- **State and Local Contracts are the least regulated in Public Sector**
- **Relationships are key**
  - Must identify the specific needs of each State agency you target

# Federal Contracts – Overview

- **Basics**
  - Heavily regulated
  - Contract terms are more defined than private sector
  - Disputes handled by the Command or Agency, the Government Accountability Office (GAO), and the Court of Federal Claims

- **To be successful in the federal space:**
  - Must align your products and services with as many contract vehicles as possible
  - The GSA Schedule may or may not be required for your company
  - Each year you want to compete for and gain access to additional contract vehicles

- **The government makes decisions on type of contract**
  - Key decision is based on "Distribution of Risk"

# Government Acquisition Cycle

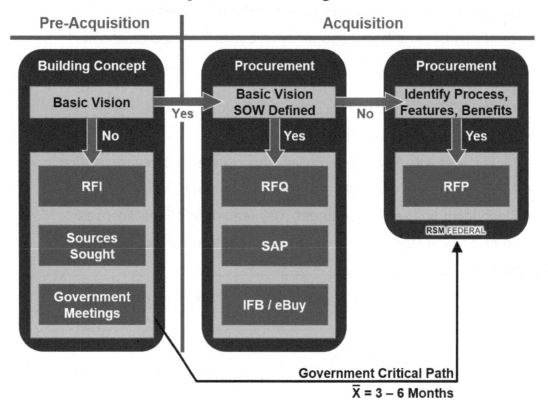

*Figure 8 - Government Acquisition Cycle*

# Government Pre-Acquisition Tools

- **Request For Information (RFI)**
  - Used to gain information or to learn about market capabilities
  - Not an invitation to bid (but critical for positioning and teaming)
- **Sources Sought (SS)**
  - Determine if Small Business Set-Aside is Appropriate
  - FAR Part 10 Market Research
  - Assess market's ability to support government's requirements
  - Determine acquisition strategy

# Government Acquisition Tools

- **Invitation for Bid (IFB)**
  - For acquisitions over $100,000
  - Government gives you numbers for everything they want – you provide price
  - Less paperwork than an RFP or RFQ
- **Request For Proposal (RFP)**
  - Government states a problem and asks vendors to submit a <u>method</u> for solving
  - Customer has an idea of what benefits and features are required
  - Most <u>flexible</u> and most <u>complicated</u>

- **Request for Quote (RFQ)**
  - Scope of work is already defined
  - Provide a dollar value for given set of benefits and features

Connecting Business with Government
A Leading Authority On To How To Win Government Contracts

# Simplified Acquisition Procedures (SAP)

- Simplified Acquisition Procedures (SAP)
- Under FAR 13 for acquisitions up to $250,000
- Provides both government and vendors with flexibility and decreases burden
- Faster and less expensive way to buy and sell
- Only for small businesses
- Still promotes competition per FAR Part 6 but can be sole source with justification
- Contracting Officer must document four (4) items:
    1) Brief description of how they awarded the contract
    2) Number of offers
    3) Tailored explanation for contract award decision
    4) If sole-source, provide justification
- Does NOT have to be posted on System for Award Management (SAM)
- Formal debriefings are not required

## So which agencies and services use SAP?

 This is the one million dollar question. There are no listings for simplified acquisitions. No organization is the same. You have to build relationships and ask the contracting officers! Some military commands and federal agencies use SAP more than others.

Remember, acquisitions under $250,000 are normally posted on SAM.gov but not all. That said, you can query SAM.gov's Data Bank or USASpending.gov to find which agencies or commands buy under the SAP threshold for your products or services (NAICS or PSC codes), how often they buy, and who the buyers are. Takes a bit of elbow grease, but you can identify who has used SAP in the past and then target them in the future.

# Sources Sought & Requests For Information (RFI)

- If you are a small business - very important that you take advantage of these!
- **Used by government to facilitate acquisition strategy**
  - Should they release as full and open, small business, woman owned, etc.?
  - Will RFP be released under NAICS code 541112 or 541119?
- **Excellent opportunity for you to position *before* the RFP is released**
  - What requirements would you like to see in the RFP? (Even if they don't ask)
  - What competition weaknesses would you like to ghost* into the RFP?
- **The Contracting Officer is *not obligated* to share your response with other companies.**
- **Released for new opportunities or refining an existing opportunity**

\* **Ghosting** – Process of influencing requirements which are your strengths and your competition's weaknesses. For a complete overview of how to influence an acquisition, read the Insider's Guide to Winning Government Contracts. Available on Amazon.

# Responding to Sources Sought and RFIs

- **Government Market Research To Obtain:**
  - Capability from vendors with relevant experience
  - Provide description of similar supplies, projects, or services
  - Applicable industry certifications at individual and organizational level
  - Investments in quality / process improvement activities
  - Certification in applicable security and cybersecurity

- **Response Often Includes:**
  - Comments regarding government's contemplated acquisition strategy
  - Comments about currently selected NAICS codes
  - Comments on acquisition strategy for small or large business
- **Common Instructions:**
  - No more than five to ten pages and 5Mb
  - Mark "business sensitive" to ensure government does not "accidentally" share
  - Responses will not be returned and receipt not always confirmed
  - Potential offeror's responsibility to monitor for release of solicitation

# Contract Vehicles – Overview

- Method used to simplify the buyer's job, significantly reducing procurement lead time and lowering acquisition costs associated with managing simple and / or complex bid procedures.

- A long-term contract vehicle like a GSA Schedule or Multiple Award Task Order Contract (MATOC) is perhaps the single best mechanism for conducting business with the federal government. BUT, before you get a Schedule, make sure you really need one!

- Last several years, the government is increasingly releasing contracts with a base period of 5 years with 5 one-year options. The standard contract period for large DoD or Federal Agency contracts is now 10 years. This is why it's important that you strategically identify which agencies and commands you will target so you are aware of key procurements *prior* to acquisition.

# 5 Primary Acquisition Entry Points

| Acquisition / Procurement Entry Points ||
| --- | --- |
| **Vertical** | **Note** |
| **Micro-Purchase**<br>FAR 2.101 | ≤ $10,000 (Federal Agencies and DoD)<br>This is sole source<br>Must accept Government Purchase Card (Visa / MC)<br>**NOT** advertised on SAM.gov |
| **Simplified Acquisition**<br>**(FAR Part 13)**<br>* Allocated for Small Biz | ≥ Micro-Purchase and ≤ $250,000<br>Maximum $7M (or $13M for commercial items) in support of contingency operation<br>Does **NOT** need to be advertised on FBO |
| **Public Bids**<br>Supplies and Services | ≥ $25,000<br>www.sam.gov<br>Online Bid-Matching Services<br>Opportunities formally advertised<br>3 to 10 month cycle (Notification to Award)<br>If you review for first time on SAM, *probably* too late |
| **Public Bids**<br>Supplies | www.dibbs.bsm.dla.mil<br>≥ Micro-Purchase and ≤ $250,000 → And RFPs ≥ $250,000 |
| **GSA Schedule**<br>Multiple Award Schedule<br>(MAS) | Not subject to Full and Open competitive procedures<br>Buyers can restrict notification<br>You must be on their radar |
| **Prime Contractors** | Access subcontracting opportunities<br>Programmatic Teaming Strategy™ (PTS) |

*Table 19 - Acquisition Points of Entry*

# Contract Value Drives Acquisition Strategy

| Contract Methods and Thresholds | | |
|---|---|---|
| **Threshold** | **Method** | **Notes** |
| < $10,000 | Micro-Purchase | *Not Advertised* |
| > $10,000<br>< $25,000 | Simplified Acquisition Procedures (SAP) (FAR Part 13) | *Not Advertised (sometimes posted locally)* Oral or Request for Quotation (RFQ) Reserved for small business Also found on GSA eBuy |
| > $25,000<br>< $250,000 | Simplified Acquisition Procedures (SAP) (FAR Part 13) | *Must be advertised in FEDBIZOPPS* *Non-GSA Schedule RFQ's in DLA DIBBS* Oral or Request for Quotation (RFQ) Reserved for small business |
| > $250,000 | Formal / Large Contract | *Must be advertised in FEDBIZOPPS* *Non-GSA Sched Solicitations in DLA DIBBS* Invitation for Bid (IFB) Request for Proposal (RFP) / or RFQ |

*Table 20 - Contract Methods and Thresholds*

# Most Common Contract Types

- **Three Most Common Contracts**
  - Fixed Price
  - Cost Reimbursement
  - Time and Material
- **You must understand level of risk and financial impact of each**
  - If you don't understand contract types – research and learn
- **According to FAR 16.104 – Government prefers Firm-Fixed-Price**
  - Reiterated by the White House throughout the years as part of various procurement overhauls

# Fixed Price Contract

- **Invoicing is event driven**
  - Payments for deliverables versus hours per labor category
- **Administrative burden and reporting is minimal**
- **Contractor assumes majority of risk**

- Contractor has maximum incentive to control costs
- **Used by government to** *separate* **cost from revenue**
  - If government fails to approve interim deliverable, your employees sit on the bench as non-billable
  - Compressed schedule = same revenue but lower expenses **(Higher Profits)**
  - Since you control materials and time management – *can build extra profit*
- **Pay special attention:**
  - Requirements must be well defined with detailed Statement of Work (SOW)
  - If Performance-Based, ensure Service Level Agreements (SLA) are clearly defined
  - Scope Creep is a common problem impacting contractors

# Time and Material (T&M) Contract

- **Periodic Invoicing (monthly, quarterly, etc.)**
- **Used only when the contracting officer determines** that it is not possible to accurately estimate the extent or duration of the work or to anticipate the costs with any reasonable degree of confidence
- **Revenue driven by number of labor hours**
- **Government is buying your direct labor versus a specific outcome**
  - Government typically specifies number of authorized hours per labor category
  - Contractor limited to specific numbers per labor category
  - No mix and match of hours and labor categories
- **Low Risk to Government**
  - Potential risk to Contractor – Government can interrupt project (stop work)

# Cost Reimbursement Contract

- **Periodic invoicing (monthly, quarterly, etc.)**
- **Heaviest administrative burden (detailed monthly reporting)**
- **Does not separate cost and revenue – Cost drives revenue**
  - If costs are reduced – *so is revenue*
  - Lost work is recouped through contract modifications and change orders
  - Unlike Time and Materiel (T&M), *labor mix can vary*
  - Compressed schedule = lower expenses and revenue **(Decreases Profits)**
- **Cost-Plus-Fixed-Fee**

- Reduction of costs increases profit

- Fee does not increase

- **Award-Fee or Incentive-Fee**

  - Reduction of costs may increase Fee and / or Profit

- **Financial Risk is limited to the Fee:**

  - Contractor limited to contract cost – not set number of hours to labor categories

# Contract Types - Summary

| | Contract Summary | | | | |
|---|---|---|---|---|---|
| | Invoicing | Contractor Risk | Financial Impact | Admin Burden | Reporting |
| **Fixed Price** | Event Driven "On Delivery" | **High** | • Separates Costs and Revenue<br>• Maximum incentive to control costs<br>• **Govt slow to approve deliverables: Employees become non-billable**<br>• Compressed schedule lowers expenses and increases profits | Minimal | Minimal |
| **Cost Reimburs** | Periodic "Monthly" | Medium | • Does not separate Cost and Revenue<br>• Work not performed = lost revenue. Requires contract mod to make up<br>• **If costs decrease, then revenue and profits decrease**<br>• **Compressed schedule lowers expenses and decreases revenue and profits** | Heavy | **Detailed Monthly Reporting** |
| **Time & Material** | Periodic "Monthly" | Low | • When CO can't estimate duration or anticipate costs<br>• **Revenue driven**<br>• Focus on "Labor" vs "Outcome" | Medium | Minimal |

*Table 21 - Summary Contract Types*

# Performance-Based Contracts

- **Links customer objectives to performance goals**
  - Requirements described as results, not methods
- **Performance measured against standards**
- **Includes Service Level Agreements and bonuses (not always both)**
- **Customer pays for performance**
  - Allows vendor to identify best method to achieve performance goals
- **Contracts focus on desired results versus specific tasks or process**
- **Statement of Work (SOW) replaced - Statement of Objectives (SOO)**
- **SOO becomes baseline for the Performance Work Statement (PWS)**
- **Value Proposition desired by the Government**
  - Develop innovative approaches
  - Increase efficiency
  - Reduce costs
  - Reduce risk
  - Reduce protests
  - Improve customer satisfaction
- **Force vendors to spend more time upfront on designing to requirements**

# Acquisition Vehicles

An acquisition vehicle is broadly defined as a method from which a company pursues and closes a sale. Some vehicles simply require that you apply for them, such as a GSA Multiple Award Schedule (MAS). Other vehicles, such as Indefinite Delivery Contracts (IDC) also known as IDIQs, MATOCs, SATOCs, GWACs, and MACs, require that you compete against other companies to win them.

Outside of these vehicles are other contract vehicles as outlined below. This is not an all inclusive list but covers the major ones.

| Acquisition Vehicles | |
| --- | --- |
| **GSA Schedule** | Most recognized contract vehicle |
| **Multiple Award Schedules (MAS)** MATOC, IDIQ, GWAC, BPA, etc.) | No government budget required Simplifies long-term acquisition |
| **Set-Aside Contract** | SB, 8(a), WOSB, EDWOSB, VOB, SDVOB, HUBZone |
| **Sole Source Contract** | Difficult without Niche and / or high differentiation |
| **Contracts held by your Partners** | Teaming Strategy |
| **Unsolicited Proposal** | Position for End of Fiscal Year Work Follow-On Work with current customers |
| **Public Procurement Contract** | Least Preferred (e.g. SAM.gov) |
| **Broad Agency Announcement** | R&D for Next Generation |
| **Small Business Innovative Research (SBIR)** | R&D for Small Business |

*Table 22 - Acquisition Vehicles*

# Types of Contracts

In government contracting there are many names and acronyms for various contracts. However, they all under one of two umbrellas. They are Definitive Contracts (DC) and Indefinite Delivery Contracts (IDC).

## Definitive Contract

Any contract that must be reported to SAM.gov's Data Bank other than an indefinite delivery vehicle. These are the most common contracts. There are no task orders, just a signed contract to provide supplies or a service, either one time or for a number of years. Multiple companies bid on the opportunity and only one company wins.

## Indefinite Delivery Contract (IDC)

An Indefinite Delivery Contract (IDC) is a vehicle that has been awarded to one or more entities to facilitate the delivery of supply and service orders. IDCs are almost always competed and can have one or more awardees. Take the technology acquisition from the National Institute of Health (NIH) called CIO-SP4. Over a thousand companies (teams of companies) submitted bids. The government will award 80+ contracts.

However, these awards do not generate revenue. Being an awardee on an IDC simply gives you a license to hunt. The government will release individual task orders over the period of the contract and only the 80+ awardees are allowed to submit proposals. Instead of competing against thousands of other companies, you are only competing against the 80+ that received an IDC contract.

## Common Types of Indefinite Delivery Contracts (IDC)

### 1) GSA Multiple Award Schedule (MAS) Contracts

Also referred to as GSA Schedule and Federal Supply Schedule (FSS) contracts, are often called indefinite delivery - indefinite quantity (IDIQ) contracts that are available for use by federal agencies and military commands worldwide. Under the MAS Program, GSA enters into government-wide contracts with commercial firms to provide over 11 million commercial supplies and services. Agencies place orders directly with MAS contractors and with some exceptions, the government is still required to compete these. Interagency agreements are not required when placing orders against MAS contracts.

### 2) Multi-Agency Contracts (MACS)

Task order or delivery order contracts established by one agency for use by government agencies to obtain a variety of supplies and services, with the exception of MACs for information technology that are established pursuant to the Clinger-Cohen Act.

## 3) Government-Wide Acquisition Contracts (GWACS)

GWACS are another type of IDC that is specifically awarded to *information technology* companies. GWACs are established by **a specific agency** for **government wide use**. Each GWAC is operated by an executive agent designated by the Office of Management and Budget (OMB) pursuant to section 5112(e) of the Clinger-Cohen Act.

## 4) Names for IDCs

Here are the most common names and acronyms for Indefinite Deliver Contracts. Don't let all of these confuse or scare you. For the most part, they are simply other ways of saying IDC.

- Blanket Purchase Agreement (BPA) (Can be DC or IDC)
- Indefinite Delivery Indefinite Quantity (IDIQ)
- Multiple Award Task Order Contract (MATOC)
- Single Award Task Order Contract (SATOC)
- Multiple Award Schedule (MAS) (GSA Schedule)
- Federal Supply Schedule (FSS) (Also a GSA Schedule)
- Best In Class (BIC)

# Enterprise GWAC Center

| Enterprise GWACs | | | |
|---|---|---|---|
| **GWAC** | **Description** | **Vendors** | **Period** |
| **8(a) STARS III** | • General Services Administration (GSA) GWAC<br>• Ceiling - $50 Billion<br>• Directed Orders (Set-Asides) up to $4 Million<br>• Supports Statutory Goal of 23% for Small Business<br>• 8(a) STARS III is a small business set-aside GWAC that provides flexible access to customized IT solutions from a large, diverse pool of 8(a) industry partners | 430 | 2021 – 2026<br><br>3 Year<br>Option to<br>**2029** |
| **ALLIANT 2 (A2)** | • General Services Administration (GSA) GWAC<br>• Ceiling - $50 Billion<br>• Alliant 2, a Best-in-Class GWAC that is preferred governmentwide solution, offers artificial intelligence (AI), distributed ledger technology (DLT), robotic process automation (RPA), and other types of emerging technologies. | 72 | 2018 – 2023<br><br>5 Year<br>Option to<br>**2028** |
| **VETS 2** | • General Services Administration (GSA) GWAC<br>• Ceiling - $5 Billion<br>• Supports Goal of 3% for Service Disabled (SDVOSB)<br>• The only GWAC set-aside exclusively for Service-Disabled, Veteran-Owned Small Businesses (SDVOSB) | 68 | 2018 – 2023<br><br>5 Year<br>Option to<br>**2028** |
| **CIO-SP4** | • National Institute of Health (NIH) GWAC<br>• Ceiling - $50 Billion<br>• Small and Large Business Awards | ~ 400 | 2022 – 2027<br><br>5 Year<br>Option to<br>**2032** |
| **POLARIS** | • General Services Administration (GSA) GWAC<br>• Replacement to ALLIANT Small Business<br>• RFP release in Fall 2021 | TBD | 2022 – 2027<br><br>5 Year<br>Option? |

*Table 23 - GSA Enterprise GWACs*

# GSA Multiple Award Schedule (MAS)

- **Government-preferred source for commercial products / services**
  - May have very short response time – may be wired for specific vendor
  - Simple
  - Rarely subject to protest
- **Not subject to "full and open" competitive procedures**
  - Do not have to widely advertise opportunities
  - Buyers can restrict competition (*you must be on their radar*)
- **Long-term contracts (5 – 20 years)**
- **No dollar limit on individual orders**
- **Does not have to be advertised in SAM.gov**
- **No guarantee of business (must market your capabilities)**
- **Why are Schedules Important?**
  - Shortens contracting cycle
  - Streamlines competition
  - Simplifies contracting officer's job
  - Utilizes commercial terms and conditions
  - Industrial Funding Fee (IFF) – 0.75% *
- **Must sell approximately $25,000 in the first two years**
  - Fail to sell and GSA may cancel your schedule
  - If you expend time and money to get on schedule – have someone dedicated to selling in the government market.
- **Enablers**
  - Blanket Purchase Agreements (BPA)
  - Contractor Teaming Agreement (CTA)

* The IFF is a fee paid by customers to cover GSA's cost of operating the Federal Supply Schedules program. The fee is a percentage of reported sales under Schedules contracts

# Do I Need a GSA Schedule?

- **No? – Subcontract via Teaming**

  - If you join a team (subcontract to a prime), you don't have to have a Schedule

  - This is how 90% of small businesses get their first several government contracts

  - Most opportunities on SAM.gov (>$25,000) do not require a GSA Schedule

  - Depending on your industry, you may not need a GSA Schedule

- **Yes?**

  - If you plan to stay in the Government market – you may need (or want) one

  - Depending on the agency, you may need to have a schedule

  - For some Indefinite Delivery Contracts (MATOCs, IDIQs, etc.), you may need a GSA Schedule first

  - You can not access GSA eBuy without a schedule

  - You do not need a schedule to bid on DLA's Internet Bid Board System (DIBBS) for supplies

- **Most small businesses team the first one or two years to obtain past-performance and then obtain and use their GSA Schedule to go after their own (Prime) contracts**

  - Recommend waiting until you're in year two of selling to the government before applying for a GSA Schedule so that it'll be ready in year three.

  - In general, it takes 9 to 12 months to submit your packet, negotiate pricing, and receive your schedule.

# GSA Schedule, eBuy, and Competition

While not well known, a regulation was published in the last several years that gives GSA Schedule holders a major advantage when submitting bids on GSA eBuy. GSA eBuy is an online system, similar to SAM.gov, that is ONLY accessible if you have a schedule.

Any RFP released via GSA eBuy, regardless of the number of bids, automatically meets the Federal Acquisition Regulations (FAR) for competition. If your company the is the only company to bid on a given procurement, simply using the eBuy platform satisfies competition requirements below and above the simplified acquisition threshold ($250,000).

# Step-by-Step Process For Figuring Out *If* You Need a Schedule

Whether or not you need a GSA Schedule is based on **how** the government buys what you sell. But it's more than that. It also depends on **how your target agencies** or military commands buy what you sell.

There is an entire industry for helping companies get on GSA Schedule. The GSA Schedule Application Service market is a multi-million dollar industry. However, many of them will say, "Look! You sell these services and the government buys $235 billion every year on GSA Schedule. You must have a schedule to succeed!"

Well, that's self-serving and doesn't take into account that you're not selling to the entire US Government. You're positioning with a small subset of the market based on your research. How you research your target market is explained elsewhere in the RSM Federal Ecosystem → Amazon's An Insider's Guide To Winning Government Contracts and the Federal Access Coaching and Training Platform.

Federal Access has *two* OUTSTANDING resources to help you make this decision before you spend a ton of time, money, and resources on getting a schedule.

*Figure 9 - Resources To Validate If You Need a GSA Schedule*

# You Have a GSA Schedule – Now What?

A GSA Schedule gives you a "License to Sell" to the Federal Government. So when do the orders start rolling in? The answer is they don't…unless you know how to position in the market with a strong business development strategy.

A GSA Schedule is a powerful method to override the barrier-to-entry in federal contracting, but there is still plenty of work to be done to start winning federal work.

This following sections provide the basic guidelines and recommendations for new GSA Schedule holders in their first two years. Your initial focus should be updating your website, uploading your schedule and price list to GSA Advantage and becoming familiar with eBuy.

When you decide to bid on your first eBuy solicitation, jump into the Federal Access Coaching and Training Platform. There is a resource on how to submit an eBuy bid. If you're not already a member, visit https://federal-access.com/manual

Once you understand the basic capabilities of GSA Advantage and eBuy, start taking advantage of the thousands of other tactics and strategies outlined in this Manual and other resources within the RSM Federal ecosystem.

# GSA Schedule – Hot Topics

- **Sales Threshold**
  - You are required to sell $25,000 in supplies or services in the first two years
  - You must maintain $25,000 each subsequent year of your contract

- **Government Credit Cards**
  - The government credit card program is called SmartPay ("Purchase or P-Card")
  - The Purchase Card often used for Micro-Purchases ≤ $10,000
  - Fast and preferred method of payment by Government
  - Decreases your invoicing and collection costs
  - Purchase Card transactions are generally tax exempt
  - Purchase Card is not applicable for discounts (but it happens. . .)

- **Maximum Order Threshold**
  - Your GSA Schedule identifies a maximum dollar threshold per order
  - You are obligated to accept orders under the maximum threshold
  - The threshold is NOT a ceiling; It means you are expected to provide additional discounts and / or more favorable terms if purchases exceed the threshold

- **Delivery time is critical – Deliver when you say you will**

- **Section 508 Compliance**
  - Required for information technology sales

- Ensures accessibility to people with disabilities

- For more information http://www.section508.gov

- Most solicitations require that validate and sometimes prove that you are 508 compliant. Most of our clients complete a 508 form / MS Excel spreadsheet, turn it into a PDF, and then post it to their website. However, it's a hidden URL so the only way to see it is if you have the URL. This URL is then used in the proposal or bid to allow government source selection teams to see it. Very easy!

- A copy of the template is in the Federal Access Coaching and Training Platform. Visit https://federal-access.com/manual

- **Buy America Act (BAA) and Trade Agreement Acts (TAA)**

  - Only provide US made/manufactured products / designated-country products

  - If you provide software, the code must be developed in the United States

  - Some companies will "re-code" their software in the US to meet this requirement but this is a slippery slope.

- **Prompt Payment Discount Terms**

  - Ability to accept Purchase Card must be identified at time of Schedule award

  - If your schedule does not authorize Purchase Card, you need a contract modification

## GSA Wants To Cancel Your GSA Schedule?

If you fail to sell $25,000 in the first two years or fail to maintain $25,000 in sales each year thereafter, GSA may send you a termination letter.

Do NOT get overly excited about this. All it takes is a strong response back to GSA about what actions you have taken, are currently taking, and will take to increase your sales.

A template on how to respond to GSA is in the Federal Access Coaching and Training Platform. It has a 100% success rate. So if you get a termination letter, don't freak out. Just jump into Federal Access and use our template to respond back to GSA.

## Your GSA Schedule Points of Contact

If you have a GSA Schedule, you are probably already familiar with your GSA points of contact. Don't hesitate to call them if you require assistance.

- **Procurement Contracting Officer (PCO)**

  - Awards your contract and handles day to day requirements

- **Administrative Contracting Officer (ACO)**

  - Assigned after your GSA Schedule is awarded

  - Keeps track of your company's Industrial Funding Fees (IFF)

  - Oversees your quarterly reports to GSA

- If you don't know who your ACO is, contact your PCO

- **Industrial Operations Analyst (IOA)**

    - Performs your Contractor Assistance Visits (CAV)

# GSA Schedule Contractor Assistance Visit (CAV)

- **Performed by the Industrial Operations Analyst (IOA)**

- **Purpose of the CAV**

    - Monitor contract compliance

    - Verifies health of company

    - Verifies you have the processes and reports in place to support your Schedule

    - Not an audit – he is there to help you

- **Timeline**

    - You will receive a CAV between 24 and 36 months into your base contract term

    - You will receive another CAV in the final 6 months of your base contract term

- **The Report Card**

    - Your Procurement Contracting Officer works with your Operations Analyst

    - PCO completes a report card after 24 months as a contract review

    - PCO completes another report card within the last 6 months of your base contract

    - Prepare for your report cards by having the right processes in place

# What is GSA Advantage?

GSA Advantage is one of the federal government's online shopping catalogs. An information and ordering system that provides federal customers with the ability to quickly search, compare, and order those GSA Schedule supplies and services that best meet their needs.

- **Advantages**

    - Provides greater market exposure

    - Participation is mandatory for all GSA Schedule holders

    - Free online training at vendor support center http://vsc.gsa.gov

    - More than one million customers access GSA Advantage every week

- **Government Agencies use GSA Advantage to:**

    - Search NAICS Codes, keywords, part numbers, supplier names, etc.

    - Research potential vendors through the vendor's websites

    - Compare features, prices, and delivery options

- Configure products and add accessories

- Place orders directly online through eBuy system

- Select convenient payment methods

- View history, track status, re-order, or cancel orders; and

- Meet agency environmental and other small business procurement goals

## GSA Advantage – Generating Your Price List

- **Formatting your price list**
    - Your GSA Schedule will outline the specific format to follow
    - If unsure, contact your Administrative Contracting Officer (ACO)
- **Basic Information included in your Price List:**
    - Contact information – convenient ways to contact you
    - Your Expertise and Strengths
    - What makes you unique for differentiation
    - Supplies and services under your GSA Schedule
    - Pricing for your products and services
    - Labor categories and descriptions
    - Geographic coverage (where you are authorized to sell)
    - Payment terms and Additional discounts from your list prices

## GSA Advantage – Tailoring Your Price List

Similar to selling to commercial clients, it is critical that you differentiate yourself, your company, and your company's supplies and services from your competition. There are hundreds of thousands of businesses that try to sell to the Federal Government.

The Price List is more than just a price list. It is another marketing opportunity to convince a contracting officer to purchase your supplies or services. If all you list are the supplies and pricing – that's all the government makes a decision on.

- **Recommendations**
    - Review your competitors "Contract Terms and Conditions" in the GSA eLibrary
    - Include a one-page "Capabilities Statement" within your price list
    - Make sure your corporate website is updated
    - Keep it simple and easy to read
- **Some ACOs will not allow you to "market" within your price list**

## Uploading your Schedule to GSA Advantage

For step-by-step instructions, visit the GSA Vendor Support Center (VSC)

- **Register at** https://vsc.gsa.gov/
- **Two Methods for Upload**
  - Schedules Input Program (SIP)
  - Electronic Data Interchange (EDI)
- **Schedules Input Program (SIP)**

  - Do NOT delete the software from your computer after upload
  - If you make modifications, you will have to reload SIP and all your data again
  - It happens ALL the time – companies have hundreds of line items and can't remember which computer they used to upload to SIP. They have to create the entire spreadsheet with all products all over again!
- **System for Award Management (SAM)**
  - Make sure that your corporate data is updated in SAM
- **Ensure there is a link to your company website**
- **Easy to find contact information**
- **Make sure you have detailed pictures / images of your products**
  - You are authorized ~4 images per product
- **Detailed Product Descriptions**
  - The government searches for products and services by NAICS and *key words*
  - Use generic terms that customers can understand and the keywords that the government searches by
  - Your descriptions should describe the product or service with the *value it provides*
  - Poor product descriptions = poor results
- **Once you load GSA Advantage – eBuy is available for bidding**

SIN = Special Item Number
NAICS = North American Industry Classification System

# What Is The GSA eBuy Portal?

eBuy is GSA's online portal for Request for Quotes (RFQ). Only vendors with a Multiple Award Schedule (MAS) may bid on these RFQs. Your GSA Schedule is a MAS contract. eBuy facilitates the request for, and submission of, quotes for a wide range of commercial services and products offered by sellers who have a GSA Schedule.

- **Advantages**
    - Notifies you of new government requirements for your products and services
    - Can save you money in locating government opportunities
    - Enables government to communicate requirements and quotes via the web
    - Helps you establish new business relationships
    - Efficient acquisition process
    - Increase sale's potential by making you aware of opportunities
    - Business opportunities sent directly to your email

- **Unique Buying Process**
    - Extremely fast (standard RFPs on SAM.gov can take months)
    - Time to respond can be as little as 2 to 5 days
    - No formal source selection process
    - Be prepared to respond quickly! Make sure your email alerts are scheduled.

## eBuy Techniques and Strategies

- **Question and Answers (Q&A)**
    - When bidders are putting together their proposals, they ask questions
    - Q&A's provide answers that can provide competitive advantage

- **The Contracting Officer didn't select my company for bidding**
    - You can still bid on the opportunity
    - Click "Watch This RFQ" to get emails when RFQ is modified and to get Q&A

- **Even if you don't bid an opportunity, you can review the RFQ and gain access to buyer contact information**

- **An RFQ number that ends with the letter "S"**
    - This is a State and Local Contract
    - You must have requested access to "Cooperative Purchasing" at the time of your GSA Schedule award to see these opportunities.
    - Applies only to GSA Schedules for technology and security services

- **When you Bid**
    - Even with product only buys, you may have to submit a proposal (it will tell you)

- Do not let your documents be larger than 5Mb in size

- Always upload a one page "Capabilities Statement" even if they don't ask for it!

- **Do you support multiple SINs or multiple GSA Schedules?**

  - Setup your email alerts by SIN to separate and have email alerts go to different employees or email accounts

- **Email versus Daily Login**

  - Setting up email alerts sends opportunities directly to your inbox

  - With all of your other daily requirements you can forget to login daily

  - Some RFQ's have a 2 to 5 day response (you need to maintain awareness)

  - eBuy email notices are sent-out every four hours

  - Create a "message rule" to have eBuy alerts filtered to a separate Outlook folder

  - Don't spend the entire day focusing on these alerts – setup a process where you check your eBuy alerts every morning with a cup of coffee

- **Invited To Bid**

  - Outstanding! Indicates your products and prices were successfully loaded into GSA Advantage and the contracting officer found your company and selected you to bid on the opportunity.

- **Do I Bid or Not?**

  - For the most part, if you receive an email inviting you to bid – you'll probably bid

  - Even contracting officers make mistakes – you may realize your capabilities do not match what they are looking for

- **A No-Bid Decision**

  - Make sure you notify the contracting officer you will not be bidding

  - It's common courtesy to notify a contracting officer that you won't be bidding if they specifically invited you to bid. You may not get another invite from that contracting officer again. It's just common business etiquette.

# New GSA Schedule? Update Your Website!

- **Government Buyers WILL visit your website**

  - Although you have a GSA Schedule, how mature is your business?

  - Do you have broken website links?

  - Does your website look professional?

  - Is your GSA Schedule number clearly visible?

  - Have a tailored GSA Schedule logo clearly visible on your homepage or government landing page

  - Clearly identify your socio-economic status on your government landing page, not your homepage; 8a, WOSB, VOSB, SDVOSB, HUBZone, etc.

  - Is your CAGE Code and DUNS Number / SAM Unique Entity ID easily found?

  - Is your contact information clearly visible?

  - Have a link to your GSA Schedule on GSA Advantage

Figure 10 - GSA Schedule Logo

# How Do I Review and Bid On an eBuy Opportunity?

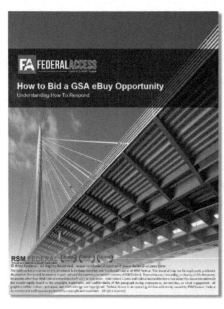

Figure 11 - How to Bid on GSA eBuy

## Need Help?

The Federal Access Coaching and Training Platform is packed full of excellent documents and templates including how to review and bid on a GSA Schedule eBuy opportunity.

# GSA Schedule – Economic Price Adjustment (EPA)

- **Defined**
    - This permits the increase or lowering of pricing during the life of the contract
    - It is outlined in your GSA Schedule and identified at time of award
    - Not automatically included in your GSA Schedule award - you have to ask

- **Price Modifications**
    - If schedule pricing was based on your commercial price list, with few exceptions, you are not authorized to make any price modifications in the first 12 months
    - No more than 3 price increases in any calendar year with few exceptions
    - There is a "percentage" ceiling each year that pricing can not exceed
    - Changes to any of the above requires a contract modification
    - GSA *rarely* allows you to increase pricing by more than 10% in a single year

- **Escalation Rate**
    - Identified in your Schedule – negotiated at time of award
    - Set to increase pricing once per year and does not require a contract modification
    - This is how your pricing keeps up with inflation

# Cooperative Purchasing and Disaster Recovery Purchasing

Cooperative Purchasing and Disaster Recovery Purchasing allows U.S. States to purchase off of GSA Schedules.

- **Cooperative Purchasing (COOP)**
    - Technology products and services to support State and Local requirements
    - To obtain Cooperative Purchasing, must be identified at time of Schedule submission
    - If not currently identified, requires contract modification (Contact your PCO)
    - If you are authorized to support State and Local, your schedule in GSA Advantage will have an image icon that says: **"COOP-PURCH"**
    - Prior to the GSA Schedule program consolidation in 2021, COOP only applied to Schedule 70 holders (Technology) and 84 (Security). Under the new consolidated schedule program, the following Special Item Numbers (SIN) are accessible by State governments:

        ➢ Electronic Commerce (SIN 54151ECOM)

        ➢ Leasing of new electronic equipment (SIN 532420L)

        ➢ Purchasing of New Electronic Equipment (SIN 33411)

> Maintenance of Equipment, Repair Services and/or Repair/Spare Parts (SIN 811212)

> Health IT Services (SIN 54151HEAL)

> Highly Adaptive Cybersecurity Services (HACS) (SIN 54151HACS)

> IT Professional Services (SIN 54151S)

> Software Licenses (SIN 511210)

> Software Maintenance Services (SIN 54151)

> Automated Contact Center Solutions (SIN 561422)

> Cloud and Cloud-Related IT Professional Services (SIN 518210C)

> Continuous Diagnostics & Mitigation (CDM) Tools (SIN 541519CDM)

> Earth Observation Solutions (EOS) (SIN 541370GEO)

> Identity, Credential and Access Management (ICAM) (SIN 541519ICAM)

> Public Key Infrastructure (PKI) Shared Services Provider (SSP) Program (SIN 541519PKI)

> Homeland Security Presidential Directive 12 Product and Service Components (SIN 541519IPIV)

> Training Courses (SIN 611420)

> Wireless Mobility Solutions (SIN 517312)

> Commercial Satellite Communications COMSATCOM Transponded Capacity (SIN 517410)

- **Disaster Recovery Purchasing (DR)**

  - Applies to all Schedules with products and services that support disaster recovery

  - If not currently identified, requires contract modification (Contact your PCO)

  - If your products and services are Disaster Recovery related, your schedule in the GSA Library will have an image icon that says: "**DISAST-PURCH**"

## Tracking Your GSA Schedule Sales

- **Track your GSA Sales**

  - Separate GSA Schedule sales from commercial sales

  - Separate Cooperative Purchasing and Disaster Recovery Purchasing sales

  - Your accounting system should be designed to isolate the different sales

  - For very small businesses, an Excel spreadsheet works fine

  - GSA Reports are now monthly

- **Monthly Report**

- The reporting system is called "72A Reporting System" (available online)
- You are required to report your sales each month
- GSA sends an email with a link for you to enter your sales numbers
- If you have no sales in a given quarter, you still need to report $0
- It is very fast and only takes a few minutes. . .*if you are tracking your sales*

- **Industrial Funding Fee (IFF)**
  - IFF fee is 0.75% of sales
  - IFF is computed from your monthly reports
  - IFF fees are due at the same time as your reports
  - Most companies pay their IFF via credit card or electronic Pay (ePay)

# Small Business Innovation Research (SBIR)

Small Business Innovation Research (SBIR) and Small Business Technology Transfer (STTR) funds billions of dollars every year in early-stage R&D projects with small technology companies.

The STTR Program provides early-stage R&D funding directly to small companies working cooperatively with researchers at universities and other research institutions.

## For Products – *Not Services*

- Your company retains intellectual property rights
- SBIRs and STTRs are a great way to "seed" your company's R&D

| 3 Phases for SBIR and STTR | | |
|---|---|---|
| **Funding Phase** | **SBIR** | **STTR** |
| **Phase 1**<br>Establish the technical merit, feasibility, and commercial potential | 6 Months<br>**$50K - $260K** | 12 Months<br>**$50K - $260K** |
| **Phase 2**<br>Project Development to Prototype | 2 Years<br>Up to **$1,700,000** | 2 Years<br>Up to **$1,700,000** |
| **Phase 3**<br>Commercialization | Commercialization of the technology in military and / or private sector markets with non SBIR / non STTR funds | |

*Table 24 - SBIR & STTR Phases*

# OMB Circular A-76 – Performance of Commercial Activities

Defines Federal Policy for determining whether re-occurring commercial activities should be performed by industry or performed by federal government employees.

*In other words, should the government outsource and privatize existing work?*

The Intent is to create a catalyst for competition, lower costs, and encourage next generation technology or improved process.

- **You are bidding against your competition** *and the Government*

- **Key Points**
    - Can be a very lengthy process
    - DoD assumptions – will have 20% - 30% savings regardless of who wins
    - Per DoD, 60% of competitions won by the government agency
    - Federal Agencies are not required to follow A-76 policy, but some do

- **Administration Overhead**
    - Government standard is          12% - 13%
    - Industry standard is          40%
    - Where are you going to make up the 27% difference to be competitive?

- **Your bid must be 10% lower than the Government's bid**
    - You will not know what the government bids

- **If the Government wins:**
    - The government business unit within the organization becomes a ***"Most Efficient Organization" (MEO)*** when it is restructured and realigned after winning an A-76 Competition

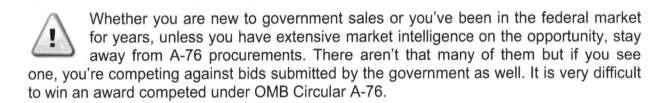 Whether you are new to government sales or you've been in the federal market for years, unless you have extensive market intelligence on the opportunity, stay away from A-76 procurements. There aren't that many of them but if you see one, you're competing against bids submitted by the government as well. It is very difficult to win an award competed under OMB Circular A-76.

# Chapter 4
# Branding, Differentiation, Shaping, and Positioning

# You Have 3,450* Competitors In The Federal Market

The key to winning government contracts is not only knowing who is buying but the ability to differentiate and communicate stronger value than your competition.

You also want to pose less risk than your competition. The government is very risk-adverse. Both the government buyer and your teaming partners want to deal with companies that pose low risk.

This chapter is designed to influence how you position your supplies and services verbally and in writing and how to communicate *value* for *competitive advantage*.

\* For Illustrative Purposes Only.

# 6 Steps – How To Position Your Capabilities

- What is your **brand**?
- What are your **competencies**? (Value and Benefit)
- What is your **niche**? (Less than 5% of companies have a true niche)
- How do you **differentiate**?
- What are your **core competencies**? (Competencies + Resources)
- How do you **position**, **tailor** and **shape** an *opportunity*?

# Value-Mapping

Value-mapping is asking yourself what does your company do, how do you differentiate and ghost the weaknesses of your competition, identify the quantifiable and qualifiable metrics for the value provided, and then marketing your value.

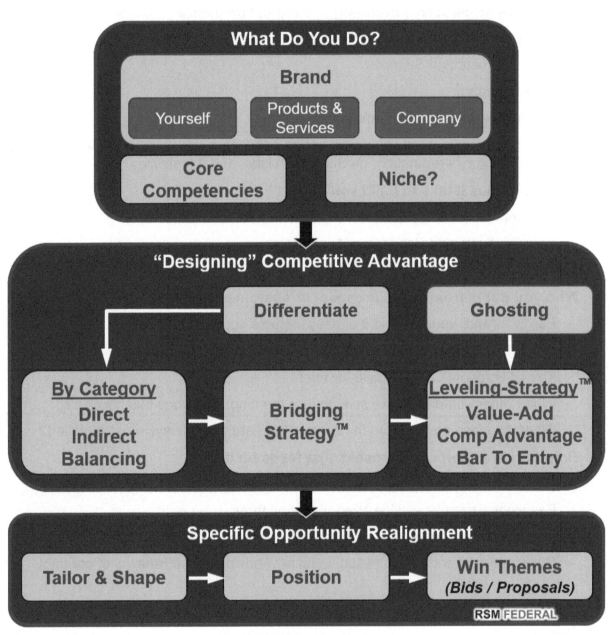

*Figure 12 - Value-Mapping Overview*

# Branding

Branding is a _conscious_ and _perpetually implemented activity_ to create an emotional and rational understanding which triggers a conscious or subconscious perception of you, your company, and your company's products and services.

- **The customer perceives branding in a logical sequence**
  - Yourself (Business Developer, Manager, Senior Engineer, etc.)
  - Your Products and Services
  - Your Company

- **Branding helps build trust and confidence**
  - Helps you create a psychological bridge between a customer's requirements and your company's reputation, products, services, and capabilities

- **How long does it take to build your brand?**
  - Yourself                              30 Seconds
  - Your Products and Services    1 – 3 Months
  - Your Company                       1 Year

- **Who you put in front of the prospect or customer is key**
  - Fail to "brand" yourself and it directly impacts your ability to sell

- **Brand differentiates similar products, services, and companies**
  - Think Microsoft, Coke, Oracle, or Intel
  - When other companies are selected for teaming, why does this happen?
  - When you lose an award to the competition, are they always more qualified?

- **Branding is a "perpetual process that feeds on itself"**
  - Poor customer service or project management impacts all three brands
  - Excellent customer service strengthens all three
  - Negative brand perception = Loss of contract
  - Positive brand perception = Additional new business and renewal of contract

# Branding Yourself

- **Professional Profile – All customer-facing employees**
- **Business Cards**
  - Don't have to be two sided with 27 colors and full bleed
  - Clear and high resolution company logo
  - Immediately recognizable company products or services
  - Not printed at home (no laser printed perforated cards)
- **JC Penney vs JoS A Banks**
  - If you look like a college student. . .
  - If your tie doesn't go with your shirt. . .
  - If your jacket isn't tailored. . .
  - If your skirt is above the knees
  - If your dress shoes are black sneakers because they're comfortable. . .
  - Perception is everything – You act how you look – spend a few extra dollars
- **Response Time**
  - Your boss' email can wait 24 hours
  - Your teaming partner's email can wait 24 hours
  - Your prospect's and customer's email gets a phone call within 6 hours

# Branding Your Products and Services

- **Marketing Collateral**
  - Simple to read
  - Corporate Capability Statement is accurate and professional
  - All marketing collateral has list of NAICS codes
- **Benefit and Value**
  - Don't lead with your features
  - When you talk to prospects, you are aligning the benefits of your solution to the prospect's requirements and problems (not your capabilities).
- **Very few products or services are truly unique or differentiated**
  - Communicating a strong corporate brand is one way to help differentiate

# Branding Your Company

- **Website**
  - Professional and Clean (doesn't look like 1980's website)
  - You have a government landing page
  - NAICS codes, DUNS, CAGE easy to find and accurate
  - If selling Micro-Purchase (<$10,000), ability to accept credit cards

- **Strong Transitional Capability**
  - Ability to mitigate the risk of transition when bidding to unseat an incumbent

- **Small Business Certifications (8a, WOSB, HUBZone, VOSB, SDVOSB, etc.)**
  - Don't be over-reliant on certifications!
  - Using socio-economic status as a crutch will do more harm than good
  - It's value and benefits of your capabilities, not your status, that wins contracts

- **Titles**
  - *Corporate titles are inflated*
  - Consider internal and external titles
  - Internal:    Senior Business Developer
  - External:    Account Vice President

*Senior Management*
*What do you care more about – closing a contract and building a revenue stream or the titles for your sales team?*

# What Is Differentiation

The following is an excerpt from a report on differentiation. "The process of distinguishing the differences of a product or service from others, to make it more attractive to a particular target market." This involves differentiating it from competitor's products as well as one's own product offerings.

Differentiation is the process of describing the differences between products or services, or the resulting list of differences. This is done in order to demonstrate *the unique aspects of your solution and create a sense of value.*

Differentiation primarily impacts performance through reducing directness of competition. As the solution or offering becomes more different, categorization becomes more difficult and hence draws fewer comparisons with its competition.

A successful differentiation strategy will move your product from competing based primarily on **price** to competing on non-price factors (such as *value*, prior experience, product characteristics, or distribution strategy).

\* Baker, Jonathon B., *Bureau of Economics Federal Trade Commission on Product Differentiation, Spring 1997*

- The objective of differentiation is to develop a position that potential customers see as valuable and solves a problem
- Differentiation:
    - Is a source of competitive advantage
    - Can be performed without modifying your product or service
    - Is a result of buyers and teaming partners perceiving a difference, creating perception reference functional aspects of the product or service, how it is distributed and marketed, or who buys it.

## Small Business Differentiation

- **Differentiation is a challenge for most small businesses**
    - 80% don't know how to differentiate their solutions
    - 60% know what they need to do but have not succeeded
    - 10% communicate real differentiation
- **Never differentiate until the prospect or teaming partner perceives that you are equal to your competition**
- **When you walk in the door, you're just another small business**
    - No immediate trust with the prospect or teaming partner
    - Perception that you are just like the other 50 small businesses that have called
- **How you position your solutions is based on stage of acquisition**
    - RFI, Sources Sought, RFP, RFQ
    - Relationship building – no formal acquisition initiated

- **Differentiators change over time**
  - Constantly reevaluate to confirm validity of your position
- **Proposal Tip – The most powerful discriminators focus on:**
  - Situational Awareness – the prospect's business, process, and systems
  - Individuals (primarily the prospect's employees but also your own)
  - Your Past Performance
- **Differentiators need to be constantly reviewed and updated**
  - Win a new contract? Have you "*Bridged*" your new capabilities?
  - Have you deployed an Earned Value Management System (EVMS)?
  - Is one of your senior engineers now ITIL certified? This includes engineers who are staff augmentation for a commercial company.
  - Have you moved from CMMI Level 1 to Level 2?
  - Did a large commercial company (such as Monsanto) just sign a large contract?
  - Have you recently received an Industrial Security Facility Clearance?

## Differentiation Based On Acquisition / Relationship Cycles

- **Acquisition Cycle**
  - Prospect has already engaged the market
  - RFI, Sources Sought, RFP, RFQ
  - Requirements and Scope may or may not be finalized
  - Your focus is to differentiate based on known requirements

- **Relationship Cycle**
  - Problems, Hot Buttons, and Pain exists, but prospect has not fully engaged
  - Has not moved the problem into the acquisition cycle
  - Only current contractors are aware of issues
  - Your focus is to build a relationship and *shape the requirements*

# Differentiation by Product or Service *

- **Types of Product Differentiation**
  - Differences in quality which are usually accompanied by differences in price
  - Differences in functional features or design
  - Ignorance of buyer needs regarding what they are purchasing
  - Sales promotion activities of sellers and, in particular, advertising
  - Differences in availability (e.g. timing and location)

- **Types of Service Differentiation**
  - Speed
  - Lower Risk (10 x more critical in Government Sales)
  - Stronger process
  - Differences in Project / Program Management methodology
  - Past performance

  - Understanding of customer's business, processes, and systems
  - Geographic location
  - Reputation

\* Baker, Jonathon B., *Bureau of Economics Federal Trade Commission on Product Differentiation, Spring 1997*

# Categories of Differentiation

- **Direct**
  - Easily Qualifiable and Quantifiable
  - Fairly easy to communicate and position
  - Communicate Value

- **Indirect**
  - Difficult to position
  - Trust is the most important
  - Position by "Telling a Story"

- **Balancing**
  - Socio-Economic Status
  - Corporate Certifications
  - Recognized certification, perhaps not yet mandated by government

- **A Differentiator can move between categories, e.g. CMMI Certification**

## Direct Differentiators

- Value versus Capability or Service
- Competencies and Past Performance
- Perceived / Actual Niche
- Key Personnel, Your Staff, SMEs
- Current Customers
- Staffing / Management Approach
- Teaming Partners
- Certifications
- CPARS / PPIRS Ratings
- Facility Clearance

## Indirect Differentiators

- Trust → You Can Do What You Say
- Agility, Flexibility, Innovation
- Hyper-Responsiveness
- Reputation

## Balancing Differentiators

- Socio-Economic Status
- Contract / Acquisition Vehicles
- CMMI, PMO
- Cyber CMMC                    **RSM** FEDERAL

*Table 25 - Categories of Differentiation*

# Differentiate Through Return On Investment (ROI)

- **ROI is** *notoriously difficult to calculate and position*
- **If you can't identify where the sales came from, you can't do ROI**
    - If you can't do ROI – how do you know money spent is not being wasted?
- **Must be able to measure success**
    - How many sales can you attribute to a specific marketing piece or campaign?
- **Requires that you understand the Prospect's:**
    - Requirements
    - Processes
    - Budget and budget cycle
- **ROI is built on two factors:**
    - Timeline for investment return
    - Prospect's tolerance for risk

## Six Categories of ROI & Communication Methods

- **Cost Reduction**
    - Cost of Ownership
    - Reduction in manpower (MDSA), software licenses, middleware, etc.
    - Decrease in design, development, or integration time
    - Lower cost for system maintenance
    - Consolidation of systems
    - Virtualization and Cloud Computing
    - Reduction in calls to the helpdesk
    - Reduction in inventory
- **Cost Avoidance**
    - Reuse of Enterprise assets
    - Replacement of Legacy systems to mitigate heavy maintenance requirements
    - Reduced overtime hours
    - Reduced FTEs or government employee turnover
    - Less equipment downtime

- **Non-Financial Graphical Event-Mapping** – *Useful for Social Media ROI*
    - Identify cost of acquisition for "Fans", prospects or patrons
    - Capture data points for:

> ➢ Number in affinity group / mailing list / etc.
> ➢ Magazine article correlated to spikes in visits
> ➢ Facebook coupon correlated to spikes in visits or sales
> ➢ Regional marketing effort correlated to type of product sale
– Develop graph and study data / marketing activities to identify cause and effect

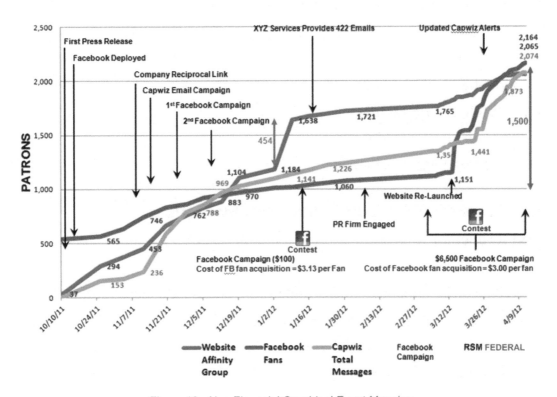

*Figure 13 - Non Financial Graphical Event Mapping*

- **Revenue Generation** (applicable but difficult to position for Public Sector)
  - Productivity improvements
  - Faster implementation to initiate Free Cash Flows
  - Increased orders
  - Increased market share

- **Soft / Indirect Benefits**
  - Keeping the customer out of The New York Times
  - Protection from negative Inspector General (IG) reports
  - Flexibility and Agility
  - Customer Satisfaction

- Maximizing return on human capital

- Business Innovation

- Responsiveness and Business Process Efficiencies

- Image and promotion for government employees

- **Administration to Operational Value™ (AOV) –** *Unique to Public Sector*
    - AOV is unique to Public Sector
    - Moving funds or capabilities from "The Tail to the Head"
        - ➤ Helping DoD move money from administration to Warfighters in the field
    - Speed of fund's redistribution to the Warfighter
    - Time-to-market for Warfighter or Federal employee critical systems
    - Ability to react to terrorist or other threats
    - Facilitating enterprise visibility (often used with buzzword "NextGen")

# Whitepapers, Best Practices, Case Studies

- **Clearly communicate your niche, core competencies, value & benefit**

- **Whitepapers target one or more "Value" messages**
  - Quality
  - Productivity
  - ROI or Cost Reduction
  - Customer Relations / Responsiveness
  - Value or Benefit

- **Two Types**
  - Generic:
    - ➢ Captures competencies, niche, differentiation, benefit, and value
  - Tailored:
    - ➢ Everything above but tailored to specific challenges and requirements of a specific prosect or customer in addition to ghosting the weaknesses of the competition

- **Whitepapers help you:**
  - Communicate the initial "equality" to your competition before you differentiate
  - Communicate **competitive advantage** that becomes part of your **"Brand"**
  - Shape, tailor, and frame "value and benefit" as part of **early engagement**
  - Validate that your capabilities are backed by best-practices
  - **Differentiate** from your competition
  - **Tailor your core competencies** to prospect's challenges and requirements
  - Bar-entry to competition by **ghosting** two or three of their weaknesses
  - Provide competitive advantage when prospect uses your **concepts in the RFP**
  - Clarify your capabilities from hundreds of similar offerings / companies

- **Management should ensure** that all Marketers and Business Developers have a checklist to ensure all key strategies are included and properly integrated

- **Recommendations for Tailored Whitepapers**
  - No more than two pages
  - Always communicate value and benefits before features
  - Structured for the specific contract or contract vehicle you want them to use

- Spend time making it highly professional and content rich
- Regardless of product or solution, discuss "continuity" and "stability"
- Use your prospects logo, graphical images of their processes, etc.
- Your prospect's name should appear more often than your company name

- **Design whitepapers as if you were asked to write an RFP**
  - Written so that it contains key requirements necessary to write an RFP
  - Supports potential sole-source awards (rare in today's market)

- **When possible, leave a whitepaper with your prospects**
  - *Tailored* to their specific requirements, challenges, or hot-buttons
  - Left onsite after a meeting or emailed (*followed by* regular *mail*) within 24 hours

# What Are Your Core Competencies?

The ability to clearly define your core competencies enables you to make a strong argument for your selection to perform a job requiring a specific capability.

- **A Core Competency meets three conditions**
  - Provides the customer with value and benefit
  - Not easily imitated by competition (otherwise, they are just competencies)
  - Can be widely leveraged across different markets and verticals
- **Most small businesses have trouble positioning their competencies**
- **Service Providers**
  - A fundamental knowledge, ability, skill or subject matter expertise that provides proven value and benefit
  - Product Providers
  - Value and benefit derived from the fundamental benefits, features, attributes, and capabilities of a product
- **Successfully market your core competencies:**
  - Customers will want you to bid on their opportunities
  - Customers will call you versus you calling them
  - You become a logical choice for a contract
  - In the GSA Schedule market, being solicited is critical to success
- **Successful sales professionals:**
  - Constantly reinforce core competencies (internally and externally)
  - Describe company, products, and services in terms of core competencies
  - Have a 45 Second "Elevator Speech" (Example in Federal Access)
  - Applies to all employees that face with the prospect or customer

- **Not every capability listed on your website is a core competency!**
  - *Most common problem that large partners have with small business*
  - Your website lists your NAICS codes and capabilities but rarely do small businesses communicate their core competencies

# What Is Your Niche?

In the Public Sector, a distinct niche market usually evolves when the potential or current demand for a product, service, or capability is not widely supported by commercial business within a specific geographic region; commonly the result of changes in government acquisition strategy or next-generation initiatives.

- Most small businesses with only Services do not have a niche

- BUT – you can position with differentiation

- Small business success comes from positioning your past performance and core competencies in a manner that differentiates your company from the competition

# Chapter 5
# Competency / Value-Mapping™

**RSM FEDERAL**
The Art and Science of Government Sales™

# Value-Mapping™

 Do **NOT** skip this section. This is one of the most important and valuable strategies in the entire Manual. Every one of our coaching clients is taken through this process by their RSM Federal coach.

*Value-Mapping is a step-by-step process for collecting contract, customer, and project data to improve differentiation and communication of competencies and value. This process supports all products, services, verticals, and industries*

Most companies position their competencies adhoc. Most don't communicate the value they provide. This includes small and large businesses. However, if you map your value properly, you will double the level of benefit and value that both prospects and teaming partners **perceive**.

Competency-Mapping is a method that forces you to evaluate and map the value and benefits of your products or services and differentiate them based on a specific prospect, that prospect's unique problems or challenges, and/or a specific opportunity.

| Value-Mapping™ |
| --- |
| Brand |
| Core Competencies |
| Niche |
| Differentiators |
| Position, Tailor, Shape |

*Table 27 - Value-Mapping*

Understanding Value-Mapping and learning how to map your past performance and value is one of the more complex tasks in business. This process is market agnostic. It applies to both commercial and federal markets. As a result, if you undertake this business process it will pay huge dividends in both commercial and government markets.

As you review this section on Value-Mapping, recognize that this Manual outlines the high-level process and the artifacts you need to successfully perform it. However, Value-Mapping is such an important element of successfully selling to the government that the entire RSM Federal Ecosystem has resources to help you.

- Book - *An Insider's Guide To Winning Government Contracts – Real World Strategies, Lessons, and Recommendations* → www.Amazon.com

- Book – *Game Changers for Government Contractors* → www.Amazon.com

- Federal Access Coaching and Training Platform → https://federal-access.com/manual

# Value-Mapping Overview

You'll find other resources on Value-Mapping throughout the Federal Access Coaching and Training Platform. However, these is the core instructions on how to approach and perform the mapping process. This process is so important that it makes the difference between success and failure in your government sales strategy. You must understand how to *map the value of your past performance.*

The purpose of this section is to provide instructions and guidance on facilitating increased awareness and generating a more detailed understanding of your past / current contracts and experience.

While the example provided below is specific to a technology vendor, *the process is industry agnostic.*

Many businesses, small and large, have problems communicating and differentiating their core competencies.  Many companies are challenged with:

- Communicating core competencies in the context of existing customers

- Building relevant and quality past performance documentation

- Shaping past performance to "cross-walk" into current prospect discussions or with current or future contract or RFP1 requirements

This document focuses on a process called Value-Mapping which has been directly responsible for facilitating billions of dollars in government contracts. This document will provide your Project / Program Managers, the Marketers, the Proposal Writers, and Business Developers with a better understanding of current contracts and how to strengthen your positioning for future business. Most businesses are surprised with the results of this process and the magnitude of their employee's activities.

The objective is to realign how you communicate with prospects and customers by improving the positioning of proposals, call plans, prospect meetings, how you approach conferences and trade shows, and how you shape your core competencies in response to new opportunities – all of which are communicated via "value and benefit," not your company's or employee's capabilities, products, or services. More important than collecting this information is the exercise of documenting it – which is why you need a strong past performance and contract database. When RSM Federal works with a company to map its competencies, the information is initially collected in Microsoft Excel.

Collecting and understanding this information is critical to accelerating revenue growth in any market or vertical.  Regardless of your sales focus, commercial or government, having information with this level of detail is key to identifying and communicating stronger differentiation and value. You will also need this information to strengthen your positioning

---

1 Request For Proposal (RFP)

with prospects as part of your overall Sales Plan, which we call the Market Sales Strategy (MSS – example provided in the Federal Access Coaching and Training Platform) and with other commercial and government vendors as part of a Programmatic Teaming Strategy (PTS – example also in Federal Access).

Your company may be ten years old with more than a dozen active contracts. However, if you have problems communicating the *value and benefit* (not the capabilities) that you provide to your customers, then you are impacting your ability to increase future revenue – with both current and future customers. You need to not only collect highly detailed information, but have a formal process to capture, document, and file with easy retrieval.

For some RFPs, you have less than two weeks from release to proposal submission (which is often the case with task orders under IDCs[2] – also known as IDIQ[3], GWAC[4], SATOC[5], MATOC[6], or MAC[7] contracts). You do not have time to strategize how your current contracts cross-walk or map to the prospect's requirements while focusing on writing the actual proposal.

Unless you are the Program Manager or Account Manager or you are involved in the daily or weekly support for a given contract, you will be surprised at how little you understand what your contracts entail or the activities that your employees perform. Although the actual contract and associated Statement of Work (SOW) may have excellent data and information, there is much more that you need to collect.

Many customers are hesitant or refuse to provide value-mapping information that you need to win new contracts. In this respect, you have to be cautious and critical of how you collect information. *But make no mistake – your competition is doing everything they can to collect this information.* The company that finds a way to collect data which the customer may not want to release, in a manner where the content and data does not violate regulation or irritate your clients, is the company that will win. Will your company win the next contract?

This is an internal exercise to facilitate differentiation and to provide current customers, prospects, teaming partners, and source selection committees with a solid perception of your capabilities and the value and benefit your products and services provide. The figure to the right outlines the value-mapping process flow and how your company's branding, competencies, and differentiation are positioned and realigned for competitive advantage.

---

[2] Indefinite Deliver Contract
[3] IDIQ – Indefinite Delivery Indefinite Quantity Vehicle
[4] Government Wide Acquisition Contract (specific to Information Technology)
[5] Single Award Task Order Contract
[6] MATOC – Multiple Award Task Order Contract
[7] Multiple Award Contract

Looking at this figure, the processes in the lower two blocks require real-world understanding of the *value of your past performance*. These process steps utilize the

information you will be collecting during the competency-mapping process. These tactics and strategies are covered extensively in this and other resources throughout the Federal Access Coaching and Training Platform.

For this exercise, the core activity is data collection. *The questions provided in this document should be used as a baseline and then **tailored** for your company, your specific industry, and the contracts your support.* Most companies provide these questions to their onsite employees to facilitate responses. If you have a senior employee at a customer location, you may

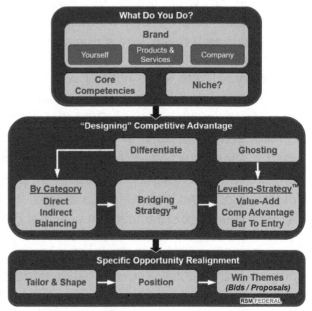

want to ask them to collect the information for the entire site. Some companies will contact every employee, by email, phone, electronic survey or a combination. How you collect this information is based on how your company best communicates with its employees.

 **Caution:** The data and information collected through Value-Mapping becomes business sensitive and will give your competition a competitive

*Figure 14 - Value Mapping Process*

advantage if obtained – which they are collecting today at your customer locations. It is important, as a general rule, that you have signed NDAs with your employees.

 **Caution:** One of the questions asks for your employees to identify the customer's challenges. Many onsite employees will attempt to shield and protect *your* client which is a culturally common response. Some of your employees may feel that although you pay their salary, they work for and owe their allegiance to the company, agency, or military command they support. This is normal. If this becomes an issue, there are several techniques you can use. The key technique is making **sure** your employees understand why you are doing this. You should send a short introductory note, either with the questionnaire or before in a separate message, or you may decide to do all of this by phone! How you communicate the importance of collecting this information is based on how your company best communicates with its employees. If necessary, contact RSM Federal for assistance.

 **Caution:** Once you start consolidating information, ***never send this information back into the field***. You can send feedback you receive from a specific employee back to that employee with comments and follow-up questions. You can also use that information to follow-up with other employees at the same customer

---

location. But never intermingle information between two different clients. Although this is common sense, we have seen this happen by accident. Although unlikely, you do not want one of your onsite employees to have a consolidated data-set which may "accidentally" or purposely be obtained by your competition. By discussing this possibility beforehand, you make sure it does not happen.

**Summary**. There is no right or wrong way to collect information and no two companies map their value the same way. This is a dynamic process which can and should be integrated into all facets of Operations, Business Development, Proposal Development, and Marketing. In fact, when you get your next contract, initiate this process several months after the contract has started. Value-Mapping is a *continuous process* to ensure you are always taking advantage of past performance and continually adding new differentiators and value. It guarantees that you'll understand how to communicate the value of your past contracts in a way that differentiates and wins the next contract.

You will be collecting a wealth of information that is used to increase actual and perceived company strengths. You will better understand who your customers are, what systems your employees support, the end users for those systems and most important, the value and benefits your customers receive from your products or services.

Again, this process is industry agnostic. We selected information technology for the example industry, but this applies to construction, electrical engineering, program management, marketing . . . every industry. Having this information is what enables the proposal, marketing, and business development teams to generate a differential competitive advantage during both acquisition and pre-acquisition phases.

These questions are not exclusive and should be regarded as a tutorial and starting point.

## Value-Mapping™ Discovery Process

One of the most important processes a company can perform, the following phases, activities, and deliverables are less complex than they may appear. At a high level, you are simply reviewing your past performance (your past work, past contracts, and / or past experience); documenting your processes and methodologies; and capturing quantifiable and qualifiable metrics, numbers, and percentages for value provided to your clients.

All of these activities and both examples and templates of the deliverables can be found in the Federal Access Coaching and Training Platform →
https://federal-access.com/manual

| Value-Mapping™ Discovery Process | | |
|---|---|---|
| **Phase** | **Activity** | **Deliverables** |
| **Plan** | Coordinate:<br>Management Oversight<br>Team Introduction<br>Resources<br>Discuss Competencies | Develop:<br>▲ Template → Competency-Matrix |
| **Discovery** | Review:<br>Past Performances<br>Statements of Work<br>Marketing Materiel<br>Website | Facilitate:<br>▲ CRM Questionnaire<br>▲ FTE Interviews |
| **Capture** | Capture:<br>Contract Scope<br>Methods and Process<br>Systems and Users<br>Value and Benefit | Develop:<br>▲ Competency Matrix<br>▲ Competency Data-Mart |
| **Analysis** | Analyze:<br>Competencies<br>Corporate Brand | |
| **Differentiation** | Value-Mapping:<br>Competencies<br>Bridging-Strategy™<br>Leveling-Strategy™ | Recommendations:<br>▲ Competencies<br>▲ Marketing Sales Strategy<br>▲ Marketing |

*Table 28 - Value-Mapping Discovery Process*

# Value-Mapping Steps

These steps are a baseline and your company should tailor the process to best fit your management style, the relationships you have with your customers, and the relationships with your employees.

| Phases 1-3 → Plan, Discovery, and Capture | |
|---|---|
| **Step 1** | **Identify Corporate Competencies – Create / Update Competency-Matrix**<br>• Collect list of current contracts<br>• Identify which products / services are performed on each contract |
| **Step 2** | **Review and tailor the CRM Questionnaire**<br>• CRM Questionnaire is attached later in the document<br>• Can be standardized / should be tailored for each customer |
| **Step 3** | **Create a spreadsheet to track employee responses:**<br>• Are you going to send the questionnaire to every employee?<br>• Send a standardized version to every employee? |
| **Step 4** | **Send questionnaires and communicate importance of project**<br>• If you plan to notify the customer – notify in person or over phone<br>• Provide clear purpose and value of collected information<br>• Explain that some will receive phone interviews |
| **Step 5** | **Filter incoming data into Value / Competency Data-Mart Matrix (.xls)**<br>• Review responses, identify follow-up questions<br>• Consolidate with SOW, monthly reports, account manager details<br>• Identify employees for follow-up and telephone interviews |
| **Step 6** | **Perform Phone Interviews** |
| **Step 7** | **Complete Documentation:**<br>• Competency Data-Mart Spreadsheet<br>• Competency-Matrix Spreadsheet |
| **Step 8** | **Analyze and Evaluate Data for Competencies and Differentiators** |
| **Step 9** | **Analyze and Evaluate Data For:**<br>• Value and benefits (Quantifiable metrics, numbers, and percentages)<br>• Identify / update differentiation points<br>• Bridge capabilities to increase actual and perceived differentiation<br>• Impact to your sales Market Sales Strategy (MSS)<br>• Impact to marketing mix and collateral |

*Table 29 - Value-Mapping Steps*

## Value-Mapping Deliverables and Outcomes

The below table outlines the various documentation and outcomes from the value-mapping process. The competency matrix and the competency datasets not only help you quantifiably communicate the value of your supplies and services, but also helps you, or perhaps new business developers at your company, quickly identify how competitive you will be on any given opportunity.

Think about it. An ability to review an opportunity in SAM.gov and be able to quickly search and filter across your past performances.

Examples of the client notification, employee notification, and CRM questionnaire are included later in this section. For examples of the competency matrix and competency datasets, they're too large and not easily formatted in book format. However, these and hundreds of other resources outlined in this book are available for download in the Federal Access Coaching and Training Platform. (There is only so much I can jam into a single book.)

FEDERALACCESS
ONLINE TEMPLATES

| Value-Mapping Documentation and Outcomes | |
|---|---|
| **Competency-Matrix** | List of customers and associated competencies for each contract |
| **CRM Questionnaire** | List of questions to help facilitate data collection |
| **Client Notification** | If applicable, meet with customers to convey purpose of collection |
| **Employee Notification** | Either before questionnaire or along with questionnaire. Corporate message to convey purpose of data collection, the importance of the data, the value of your employees to the company, and to mitigate potential pushback on providing this information to you. |
| **Competency Dataset** | Spreadsheet used to data-mine specific capabilities and competencies when you're reviewing new opportunities and RFPs. |

*Table 30 - Value-Mapping Deliverables*

## Caution: Deciding If You Need To Notify Your Clients:

You may decide to notify only a few of your customers, none of them, or all of them. The decision to notify a customer depends on the number of employees you plan to send the questionnaire to, the amount of information you plan to collect, how strong your relationships are with your employees, **and the status of your overall relationship with the customer.** What happens if one of your onsite employees approaches the customer with a copy of your questionnaire? What if you do not have a strong relationship with the customer? Think politically on this one.

The decision to notify your customers is dependent on the relationships you have with them. If you do not have a strong relationship, this is a client / account manager or senior management issue outside the scope of this document. If you believe a customer will have a negative perception of you collecting this data - do not notify them and adjust your questionnaire accordingly or just do verbally by phone. What you are doing is part of "business intelligence," a process that every successful company implements. Concerned about asking questions reference challenges, problems, or other onsite contractors? Then several of your questions may have to be asked orally in order to protect the political position of your company with the client.

## How To Notify Your Clients

Realignment Solution Methodology (RSM – where we get our company name from) is about positioning your company's brand, capabilities, and value in order to facilitate a competitive advantage in the market. The message below is *one example* of how to communicate your intent with current and past clients. You schedule a meeting to catch-up and discuss various topics with your client. During this session you mention the following:

*"We are initiating a corporate-wide program to better understand the support we provide to you. This program will enable our entire corporate staff to better understand and support your requirements and the requirements that our team is supporting. We plan to improve our understanding of your requirements, your systems, and your challenges. Over the next six weeks, John and Kathy will be talking with our employees and asking them questions to improve our understanding of how they support you and the value they provide. By talking with our employees, we will have a better understanding of how to support your current and future requirements."*

Imagine if you were this customer. They may have two or ten other vendors that support their operations. How many of these vendors simply call to ask, "Can we help you with that project? Can we get another two bodies? Any upcoming projects we can help you with? Are you ready to buy ten more widgets?" The answer is that many companies beg for positions, new sales, and new contracts. However, now you have met the client face to face, or via video, and communicated, "We don't simply want sales. We want to

understand your requirements, your challenges, and what *you* need to be successful."
I wouldn't have a problem with this! Most will not. *It's how you approach it.*

Also notice that you have not even told your client the primary purpose behind the data collection. *You have now strengthened your relationship with the customer and collected the information you need communicate quantifiable and qualifiable value.*

## Initial Questions for Corporate Project Discovery

The following questions are a baseline used by RSM Federal to better understand a company's operations and internal processes. An "Onsite Employee" is any full-time or part time employee who works for your company as a result of staff-augmentation or working under contract at a customer location or even at your corporate office. Your onsite employee may be called an FTE, a contractor, a consultant, or a field employee. Regardless, these questions apply to any employee who works for a client.

1) **Do you have signed NDAs for your employees?**

   - If you don't, double-check your employment contracts. Is there an NDA built into the contract you have every employee sign? (You may have a separate NDA for every employee). If not, have your legal or HR department add this to the next documentation update.

2) **Number of employees on each contract?**

   - This will help you plan your communication strategy with your onsite employees.

   - Includes past contracts already completed.

     - # Current Contracts and Employees

     - # Completed Contracts (Within last three years)

     - # Completed Contracts (More than three years ago)

3) **Type of contracts you support?**

   - Type of Product Sold

   - Type of Labor Categories? (IT, Administrative, Marketing, etc.)

4) **Any contracts supporting multiple geographic locations?**

   - If you're not sure, you will identify this information from the feedback you receive.

     - For example, you have a contract for a client in Chicago (with 235 client employees) but the Chicago office directly supports four branch or subordinate offices in St. Louis, Milwaukee, New York, and Tampa . . . and those offices, combined, have 4,578 employees.

– Most companies simply focus on the direct contract location in Chicago. But imagine the value and metrics you can communicate by including the other four locations? This is just the start of value mapping!

**5) Do you have a senior employee at each or some customer locations?**

- Some companies have "site coordinators, project managers, or other management level positions." If you have senior employees at some or all client locations, they can help you communicate and collect information. If you don't have any senior employees (you're most likely a subcontractor), most companies have a client or account manager who manages each customer account. Either way, your client or account managers can provide assistance during this process.

**6) Do you receive weekly or monthly reports from your employees?**

- If you receive these reports, they are important. These reports are used to add detail to the information collected during value-mapping. If you don't receive reports, another reason you are performing this exercise. You should also consider asking your senior employee on every contract to provide monthly updates (even if you're a subcontractor).

**7) How often do you meet with the Contracting Officer on each contract?**

**8) How often do you meet with your primary customer points of contact? (Not the contract officer)**

**9) Do you have copies of statements of work (SOW) for each contract?**

**10) What is your primary means of communication with your employees?**

**11) How often does average onsite employee hear from you? Is your communication by phone, email, newsletter, portal, other?**

## Employee Questionnaire

Use the following to create a list of questions for your employees. This is an example for an information technology company. You will need to tailor for your industry.

1) **Employee Name**

2) **Name of Company / Contract**

   - i.e. Scottrade, Blockbuster, Monsanto, Pepsi, US Army, etc.

3) **Provide a short description of your position (labor category) and your responsibilities.**

   - Key daily, weekly, and monthly responsibilities
   - You want this as detailed as possible

4) **Provide a short description of the value you personally provide to the client.**

   - Think in terms of time, money, resources, and other value
   - This question can be posed as, "Based on what you provide to the customer, do any of your daily or weekly activities create improvements in process for the client or for the client's customers? Do these improvements in process save the client money, time, or resources? Quantify and qualify these improvements with numbers, percentages, and metrics to the best of your ability."

5) **Do you work with other employees from our company?**

   - If your daily activities cause you to work with another employee from our company, please provide their name(s) and role.
   - This information is important because it allows you to map your employees to the projects and requirements at a given client location. You normally know the answers but you will sometimes be surprised with what you collect.

6) **Do you report directly to the client, another employee from our company, or do you report to an employee who works for another contractor?**

   - It is important to know who your onsite employees report to. You may be thinking, "Well that's not important...I know they report to Sally, our senior PM," but after a year, Sally may have task-detailed your employee to a client manager as part of a project that you're not even aware they're working on.
   - This helps us identify other onsite vendors (competition) and the potential "level of influence" your employees have for positioning on *future opportunities*. This helps the account or client manager gauge which employees are *most likely to have access to key information on future opportunities*.

7) **What other companies support the customer at this location? How many employees do they have?**

- If you do not have a strong relationship with your customers, pose this question by phone.

- This is one of the most important data points in the process. By knowing who your competition is, your account managers, as well as your marketers, can start to identify your competition's strengths and weaknesses as well as how your company's strengths and weaknesses compare. If you do not collect this information, recommend this be a new requirement for every account or project manager.

- This type of information is often identified over months or years and is rarely captured in writing. For the purpose of the value-mapping process, we need as accurate a baseline as possible on which other contractors are positioning for your current and future positions and contracts.

- These answers are important because if you're not doing this, you can be sure that your competition is!

8) Which <u>systems</u> and <u>processes</u> do you support? We need *as much detail as you can provide*. Think about the systems or processes you support and the value these systems provide. *(Remember, this example is for a technology contract)*

- Name all the systems or processes you directly support

- Acronym for each system or process (if applicable)

- What is the purpose of each system or process?

- What value or benefit does the client obtain from each system and process?

- What operating system, version, etc. does each system have?

- Do you support or access any databases? Which type and what version?

- Which of the above systems or processes access these databases?

- Do you support any other systems? Describe, types and versions.

- Are there any other systems you access as part of your daily or weekly activities?

- These answers are important. The questions above should be tailored for your company and industry.

9) **Who accesses these systems – both the client and their customers.**

- How many offices does the client have in the United States? Internationally?

- List total number of employees for the entire organization (regardless of systems you support)

- How many offices in the US or internationally access the systems you support

and where are they located?

- How many client employees access the systems you support? (by system)

- Does your client team or partner with any other organizations that jointly access these client systems? For example, you work for Anheuser Busch and supply chain / shipping is managed by ABC Shipping. They access your systems daily to obtain shipping data.

- Are there any other internal business units or external organizations or companies that access the data or applications on the systems you support?

- If your systems, applications, and/or data is accessible by the public, give a rough guess on how many people access the client's public-facing systems on a monthly or annual basis. Is public access national or global? What value does the public get from accessing these systems?

- These answers are important. Your ability to communicate "Enterprise" level capability and providing value and benefit *across geographical boundaries* improves the actual and perceptual maturity of your company. This is how small businesses become mid-size and how midsize becomes large.

## 10) Is the client discussing new technologies for future implementation or considering a change in how they manage technology today?

- If you do not have a strong relationship with your customers, you need to pose this question carefully or add this to the questions you will discuss with your account managers.

- One way to ask this question: "Over the last six or twelve months, describe one example where you took a great amount of pride in helping the customer fix a long-standing issue or where you helped the customer migrate to a new system or architecture."

- This is what provides your client managers with intelligence for prospecting and sales strategies.

## 11) Are you or the team you support planning to integrate current or future systems?

- Or, What future projects are you aware of that you anticipate you may be supporting?

- If you do not have a strong relationship with your customers, see recommendation in #10.

- This is what provides your client managers with intelligence for prospecting and sales strategies.

## 12) What other projects or changes in technology are you aware of which other teams, contractors, or vendors will be supporting in the future?

- This question is intended to identify the strengths and projects of your

competition. This allows you to review your strengths and weaknesses, ghost your competition's weaknesses, and eventually develop differentiation for future positions or contract opportunities.

- Regardless of your relationship with your customer, caution should be used in how you ask questions about other contractors. Most companies perform this question by phone.

13) **What are the current challenges and problems causing heartburn or difficulty?** It may only impact the team you work on, the client as a whole, or even your client's customers. What challenges or problems have been raised time and again that you or the client are trying to figure out the best means to resolve? If there are other contractors onsite, *are they experiencing any issues?*

- This is another important question. This goes to the basics of prospecting, business development, and sales. It also provides your client managers with insight on challenges they may not be aware of. This question supports your current contracts and helps you position for future contracts.

## What does a common response look like?

Example response to **Questions 8 and 9**: (example only)
Mary works at Ralston Purina and provides system and database administration for the FDA-PETS Database Channel System (FPDC). This is how she answered the questions:

"My name is Mary Williams and I am a system and database administrator working on the Ralston-Purina FDA team, responsible for the maintenance and operation of four servers and three databases."

- Two servers are Windows Server 2065 R2. With Windows Server, I use remote management through the ISS Manager as well as using Hyper-V with Live Migration to move virtual servers in the data center without causing outages or downtimes. These servers support FDA's external registration with drug companies.

- Two servers are IBM x9000 Servers. On the IBM servers, responsible for implementing mainframe ISV and OS software and implementation and administration of IBM's SMP/E software and IBM's SDSF product (ISV). One server supports FDA's internal registration validation process for internal software development and change management and the other supports our quality assurance in the development environment for the other three servers.

- Three Oracle Databases. One of the databases is Oracle 12c which supports the two Windows Servers and the other two are Oracle 11g which support the IBM servers. For database administration, I am responsible for managing automatic workload management, security, setting up virtual private databases, auditing, as well as daily, weekly, and monthly maintenance.

- Other duties include 24x7x365 operations and helpdesk support. Helpdesk software is Remedy. I help with backup and recovery planning and I'm on the CIO's team to support Hot-Site Disaster Recovery Exercises. Responsible for risk analysis on existing systems. I'm proud of the methodology I developed to mitigate risk which is now used as a baseline for every project at Ralston Purina.

- The systems I support are accessed by 85 Ralston employees on a daily basis. These 85 employees are located in four offices in Missouri, Iowa, Florida, and New York. However, the data housed in these systems support 2,000 Ralston employees on projects that rely on accessing our systems and information.

- Externally, our systems are accessed by FDA's Center for Veterinary Medicine (CVM) in Rockville, Maryland. More than 30 employees with CVM access our systems.

- Systems I access but don't directly support: MS Exchange, AutoCAD, etc. etc.

- The value we provide to Ralston and FDA is that whenever there are server upgrades or changes to technology, we ensure there are no outages and our systems are responsible for bringing 10 new drugs to market every year. The new architecture saves Ralston more than five million dollars every year (20% savings in cost). We have lowered the number of outages by 90% and have increased the accessibility by FDA and its employees to critical information by more than 40%. (Not all employees will have access to or know this information. But you'll be surprised at how many do and this type of value/benefit data is "Gold" for positioning on future contracts.)

## Final Notes

There is no right way for employees to respond. As you receive responses, focus on whether or not they have included the names for all systems or processes and the value and benefit those systems or processes provide to the client and to the client's customers. Remember, value is measured via quantifiable and qualifiable numbers, percentages, and metrics.

Yes, this example was specific to a technology company but the value-mapping process works for any company in any industry. If you're a product company, an architectural firm, a general contractor, or even an environmental remediation firm, use the above questions as a baseline and tailor for your market, supplies, and services!

You can decide to collect less or more information. Generally, we recommend providing a detailed questionnaire and in your instructions, let them know that if a question does not apply to them, simply leave it blank.

Some responses will be highly detailed. Other responses may be very basic because an employee is young and has an entry level position. But their response is just as critical as the more senior employees.

Finally, recognize that many of the questions will be via a questionnaire or survey and that some (or all) will be by telephone. You will find that after you receive the initial responses, you will need to schedule calls with some of your employees to ask follow-up and more detailed questions.

If you have any questions about this process, the questionnaire, or implementation, please contact RSM Federal. If you are a member of the Federal Access Coaching and Training Platform, simply log into Federal Access and send a note to the support desk.

# Chapter 6
# Differentiation – A Bridging Strategy

**RSM FEDERAL**
The Art and Science of Government Sales™

# Bridging Strategy
# For Communicating Differentiation

Due to the importance of value-mapping and this bridging strategy, the RSM Federal Ecosystem is packed with resources to help you accomplish these activities. These include books, podcasts, and the Federal Access Coaching and Training Platform.

Now that you have performed Value-Mapping, you are ready to take how you differentiate to a whole new level. While you don't have to complete value-mapping before you bridge, it makes it a thousand-times easier. If you haven't value-mapped, you likely don't have the quantifiable and qualifiable numbers, percentages, and metrics on every contract. If you don't have these numbers, it will make it *awfully difficult to bridge those numbers*. This section will include value-mapping examples for companies that have a couple government contracts and companies that have none and are just starting their journey.

- **Perform Value-Mapping *before* you start to bridge**
- **How do I differentiate when I only have commercial contracts?**
- **Now that I have a GSA Schedule – how do I market?**
- **6 Step Process**
  1) **Review scope of an upcoming RFP** – Prioritize key requirements
  2) **Research Prospect's Organization & Processes**
  3) **Research and outline your company's current contracts**
  4) **Update your Past Performances** (tailor to the new opportunity)
  5) **List potential Win-Themes** (initial review)
  6) **Tailor, Shape, and Position**
     - ➤ "Bridge" potential proposal Win Themes from current contracts
     - ➤ Shape and Position your message
- **Benefits**
  - – Your past performance documentation will become much stronger
  - – Your knowledge of current contracts will open more doors

## Bridging Strategy – No Government Contracts Yet

- This example: Company has **no** government contracts.

- This example is for companies that are in the process of bidding on their first government contract.

- You have an RFP for the Federal Emergency Management Agency (FEMA)

- You have past performance on three commercial contracts* that will enable you to bid as Prime (No past contracts with FEMA)

\* For most RFPs, the Government classifies a "Current Contract" as having been active in the last three (3) Years

*Figure 15 - Bridging Strategy - RFP Opportunity - Steps 1 and 2*

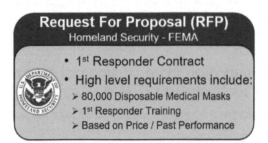

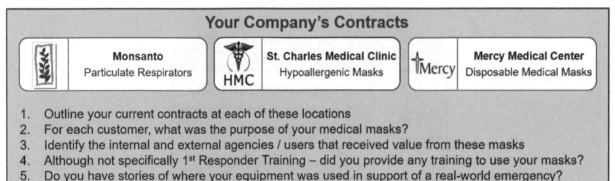

1. Outline your current contracts at each of these locations
2. For each customer, what was the purpose of your medical masks?
3. Identify the internal and external agencies / users that received value from these masks
4. Although not specifically 1st Responder Training – did you provide any training to use your masks?
5. Do you have stories of where your equipment was used in support of a real-world emergency?
6. Have you supported a city or state emergency exercise?
7. Do you have any employees in a prior job who supported an emergency exercise?

*Figure 16 - Bridging Strategy - Past Performance - Step 3*

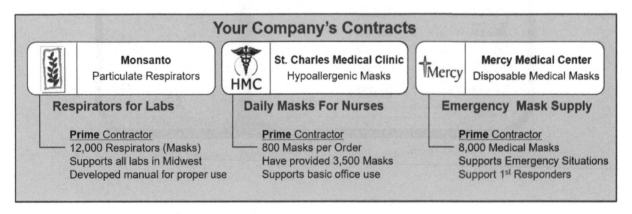

*Figure 17 - Bridging Strategy - Past Performance - Step 3*

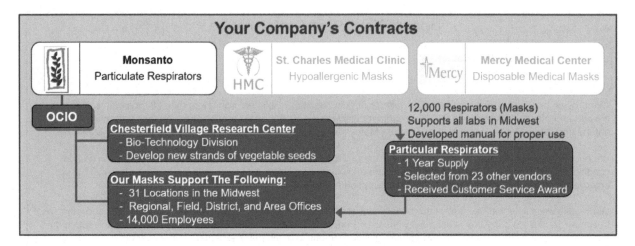

*Figure 18 - Bridging Strategy - Past Performance - Step 3*

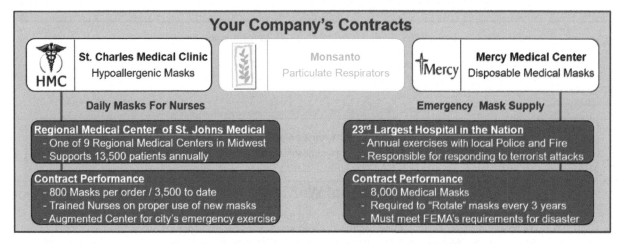

*Figure 19 - Bridging Strategy - Past Performance - Step 3*

## Update Your Past Performance

 **Mercy Medical Center**
Disposable Medical Masks

 Monsanto
Particulate Respirators

 St. Charles Medical Clinic
Hypoallergenic Masks

"We provide ongoing support to one of the nation's largest hospitals. Selected from more than **28** different vendors, we provide and maintain more than **8,000** disposable medical masks for **national emergencies**, **terrorist attacks**, and other natural disasters. We were also required to train Mercy Medical on how to maintain the masks during storage and use.

We have a climate controlled warehouse that ensures all medical and emergency supplies are maintained in optimum condition. Due to our strong supply chain and climate controlled environments, we rotate the hospitals supply of emergency masks every three years. We have supported Mercy Medical **since 1991**.

Our masks were selected because of our pricing, storage, and customer service. We team with other medical companies to ensure we always carry the safest masks based on current technology and medical standards. We not only rotate the **8,000 masks** every **three** years, but we perform this service onsite at the medical center. In the event of a natural disaster or terrorist attack, our supply chain can supply an additional **50,000** masks in under **14 hours**. Due to our network and supply chain, we are one of only two companies in the Midwest that can respond this quickly.

In 2009, as part of the City's annual **emergency preparedness exercise**, Mercy Medical asked that we participate to ensure communications and process were viable and functional. During this exercise, we surpassed the scope of our contract by coordinating for **65,000** masks when 1st Responders from neighboring cities entered the impacted area.

*Figure 20 - Bridging Strategy - Past Performance - Step 4*

 **Monsanto**
Particulate Respirators

 **St. Charles Medical Clinic**
Hypoallergenic Masks

Mercy **Mercy Medical Center**
Disposable Medical Masks

## Potential Win Themes

1. We will leverage our strengths in providing 80,000 medical mask via:
   a) We have the supply chain, climate controlled warehouses, and past performance
   b) We currently support daily and emergency usage for organizations in 5 states and more than 258 locations

2. We will leverage our strengths in "1st Responder Training" by taking the following actions:
   a) Mapping our Mercy Medical past performance for Emergency Exercises to 1st Responder requirement
   b) Mapping our storage and supply chain capabilities, both verbally and graphically (Design one or two charts) to create "proof" that we can support FEMA's requirement for 80,000 masks

*Figure 21 - Bridging Strategy - Win Themes - Step 5*

**RFP Requirements**
1 Provide 80,000 Medical Masks
2 Provide 1st Responder Training
3 Priority = 1) Price – 2) Past Performance

## Bridging – Putting It All Together

"We support local and dispersed medical centers and Fortune 500 Corporations in five states and in more than 258 geographic locations. We provide 1 multiple types of disposable and non-disposable respirators and medical masks in support of daily medical needs as well as anticipated 2 first responder requirements for natural disasters, national emergencies, and potential biological and chemical terrorist attacks.

On an annual basis, we provide more than 1 65,000 masks and respirators with 40% supporting the Monsanto Corporation (12,000), Mercy Medical the 23rd largest hospital in the United States (8,000), and the St. Charles Medical Center (3,500). For our three largest contracts combined, we were selected from 125 of the regions top vendors for the following reasons:

Proof Statements:
- Our supply chain provides immediate access to more than 1 500,000 masks.
- Our service and deployment team 2 trains Mercy Medical on how to use, store, and inspect all masks and respirators.
- We have supported county (St. Charles Medical) and city (Mercy Medical) 2 emergency preparedness exercises.
- We are experienced in onsite management (Mercy) and rotation of emergency mask supplies.
- In preparation for FEMA's contract, we have 1 positioned our supply chain to support 100,000 medical masks with the ability to access an additional 400,000 with delivery of 200,000 in under 24 hours and another 200,000 within 36 hours.
- We received the Monsanto "Pathfinder" award for superior customer service.

**Although your company may have played a minor role in the emergency preparedness exercises or provided only rudimentary training to the hospitals for use and storage of the masks, it's how you position and bridge your past performance that differentiates your company. Don't look at each of your individual contracts as separate past performances. The company's largest order has been for 12,000 masks and but with several calls their suppliers (we'll call it a supply chain in the proposal) can provide close to half a million. Without realizing it, when properly bridged and communicated, provides a solid value proposition for the FEMA's contract.**

*Figure 22 - Bridging Strategy - Outcome - Step 6*

# Bridging Strategy – You Have Government Contracts

- This example: Company has government contracts.

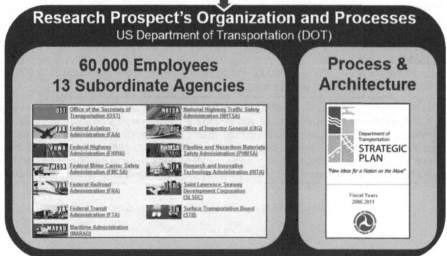

*Figure 23 - Bridging Strategy - RFP Opportunity - Steps 1 and 2*

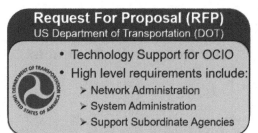

**Request For Proposal (RFP)**
US Department of Transportation (DOT)

- Technology Support for OCIO
- High level requirements include:
  - ➢ Network Administration
  - ➢ System Administration
  - ➢ Support Subordinate Agencies

**Your Company's Contracts**

|  **US Department of Labor** System Administration |  **Department of Treasury** Network Administration |  **Air Mobility Command** System Administration |

1. Outline the daily responsibilities for each of your employees.
2. What systems do you support?
3. Identify the internal and external agencies / users that access these systems
4. At each subordinate agency, how many employees access the systems?
5. Your government PM – who does she work for?

*Figure 24 - Bridging Strategy - Past Performance - Step 3*

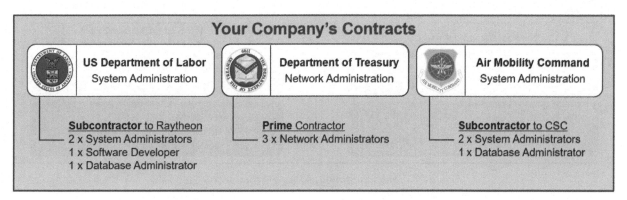

**Your Company's Contracts**

| **US Department of Labor** System Administration | **Department of Treasury** Network Administration | **Air Mobility Command** System Administration |

**Subcontractor** to Raytheon
- 2 x System Administrators
- 1 x Software Developer
- 1 x Database Administrator

**Prime** Contractor
- 3 x Network Administrators

**Subcontractor** to CSC
- 2 x System Administrators
- 1 x Database Administrator

*Figure 25 - Bridging Strategy - Past Performance - Step 3*

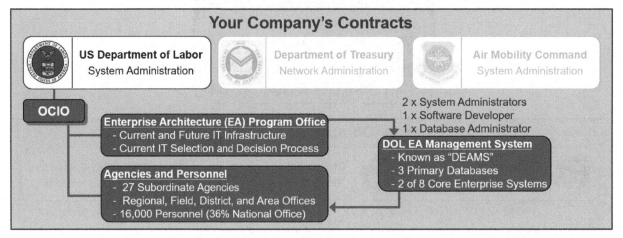

*Figure 26 - Bridging Strategy - Past Performance - Step 3*

*Figure 27 - Bridging Strategy - Past Performance - Step 3*

## Update Your Past Performance

|  **US Department of Labor**<br>System Administration |  Department of Treasury<br>Network Administration |  Air Mobility Command<br>System Administration |

"We provide system and database administration for the DOL Enterprise Architecture Program Office (EAPO) supporting DEAMS, the Enterprise Management System in addition to 2 Enterprise Solutions (AAFM & DOLSA) that supports all 27 subordinate agencies consisting of 16,000 employees.

As part of the current EA Deployment Plan, over the last six months, we supported the installation and deployment of DEAMS version 2.1 to 4,500 end-users in 240 geographically dispersed regions, in 38 States, supporting government users at the Occupational Safety & Health Administration (OSHA), the Employee Benefits Security Administration (EBSA) and the Employee Compensation Appeals Board (ECAB).

Our Database Administration supports the DEAMS Oracle 10g database and with integration, testing, and deployment activities alongside our software developers and system administrators.

We provides Tier 2 End User Support when agency problems require subject matter expertise (SME) on both software and system issues. Software development utilizes the IBM Rational Unified process (RUP) Suite. Our employees support Functional Qualification Testing (FQT), System Compatibility Testing (SCT), System Integration Testing (SIT), and Support User Acceptance Testing (UAT).

Our team also creates and maintains the DOL project libraries, repositories of project metrics, and testing documentation.

*Figure 28 - Bridging Strategy - Past Performance - Step 4*

|  **US Department of Labor**<br>System Administration |  **Department of Treasury**<br>Network Administration |  **Air Mobility Command**<br>System Administration |

## Potential Win Themes

1. We will leverage our strengths in "Multi-Location Network Management" by taking the following actions:
    a) Mapping our DOL past performance into the Multi-Disciplined Staffing Approach
    b) Positioning our ability to communicate and resolve network issues across geographically dispersed regions

2. We will leverage our strengths in "Supporting all subordinate agencies" by taking the following actions:
    a) Mapping our DOL past performance where we touch or manage IT systems in all 27 subordinate agencies
    b) Mapping our Treasury past performance where we manage system and network operations with support to not only Treasury, but the FBI and Secret Service as well.

*Figure 29 - Bridging Strategy - Win Themes - Step 5*

## Bridging Strategy – Putting It All Together

"We provide ② system and database administration for the DOL Enterprise Architecture Program Office (EAPO) supporting DEAMS, an Enterprise Management System in addition to 2 Enterprise Solutions (AAFM & DOLSA) that provides enterprise level awareness and real-time support to the OCIO's office and ③ all 27 subordinate agencies consisting of 16,000 employees. We support the Department of the Treasury (DOTreas), providing ① network administration for the Financial Crimes Enforcement Network (FinCEN) in addition to supporting ① network operations for the Technical Services and Solutions Division and the DOTreas OCIO office. We provide network management for 300 DOTreas personnel and ③ supporting agencies which include the FBI and Secret Service.

③ Every contract we hold with the federal government contains a government workforce which is geographically dispersed with ① ② network or system administration support at multiple locations for subordinate and sister agencies. Combined, our Performance Based Contracts with the Air Mobility Command and the Department of Labor supports more than 24,000 government employees, at 41 subordinate agencies, with network and system access at approximately ③ *254* geographic locations. As a result of successfully managing the extensive networks and systems for our current customers, we have developed a strong Multi-Disciplined Staffing Approach™ (MDSA) which minimizes down-time and provides each of our customer's with recognized agility, flexibility, innovation, and responsiveness. We built these capabilities into our MDSA approach for each contract and successfully decreased the prior incumbent's overtime by 48%; decreased system and network downtime by 83%; and contractor turnover has dropped from 36% down to 8%. We are well known for our relationship management approach and for being strong partners with our government customers.

**Most small businesses have one or more contracts where they provide these services with a geographically dispersed user base – but don't realize it! As a result, most small businesses do not successfully differentiate. However, by "*Bridging*" past performance and competencies across multiple contracts and customers, you develop and communicate an "*Increased level of capability*" that provides clear "*value and benefit*" to your prospect. It is also a method to increase the "perceived" maturity of your company. This supports your prospects in addition to other companies as part your Programmatic Teaming Strategy™ (PTS)**

*Figure 30 - Bridging Strategy - Outcome - Step 6*

# Bridging–Strategy – Summary

- You MUST understand your current contracts and past performance
- Most small businesses that do not have a government contract or who primarily support the private sector with staff augmentation have difficulty with starting this process.
- If you perform staff augmentation for a private sector corporation:
  - Your employees do much more than you think they do for the client
  - If you can't outline your current contracts in this level of detail, you need to perform Competency-Mapping in the previous chapter.
- Regardless of your supplies or services, you can not properly position without this level of detail.
- Since the results of competency-mapping are critical to all corporate marketing and sales activities, if you need help getting started, please contact RSM Federal.
- There is no limit to what you can Bridge
  - Systems and Infrastructure
  - Any Product, Service, or Bundled Solution
  - Processes or Methodology
  - Subject Matter Expertise
  - How you successfully managed "unanticipated events" at multiple locations
  - Any RFP requirement
- Desired End State
  - Development or Refinement of differentiators, actual *or perceived*, which project value and benefit with a *potential* competitive advantage.
- Next Steps
  - Identify and evaluate your competition's weaknesses and *Ghost* them *
  - Utilize the Leveling–StrategyTM to confirm areas of competitive advantage and finalize draft Win-Themes

* Ghosting – Process of influencing requirements in the RFP which are your strengths and your competition's weaknesses

# Chapter 7
# Differentiation – Leveling Strategy

**RSM FEDERAL**
The Art and Science of Government Sales™

# Overview Leveling Strategy

- **Before you communicate differentiation,** you need to understand your competition's capabilities as relates to a specific opportunity and to a specific prospect.

- **Desired End State – Win Themes that:**

  - Provide value and benefit (not features or capabilities); Highlight competitive advantage; and differentiate, actual / *perceived*, which bars-entry to competition

- **Steps to Leveling Your Capabilities**

  - What value and benefit do you provide?

  - How do your capabilities differentiate based on value and benefits?

  - How do you position for competitive advantage?

  - How do you bar-entry to your competition?

- **Use the tools we've already discussed:**

  - Competency–Mapping

  - Bridging-Strategy

# Leveling Strategy Graphical Overview

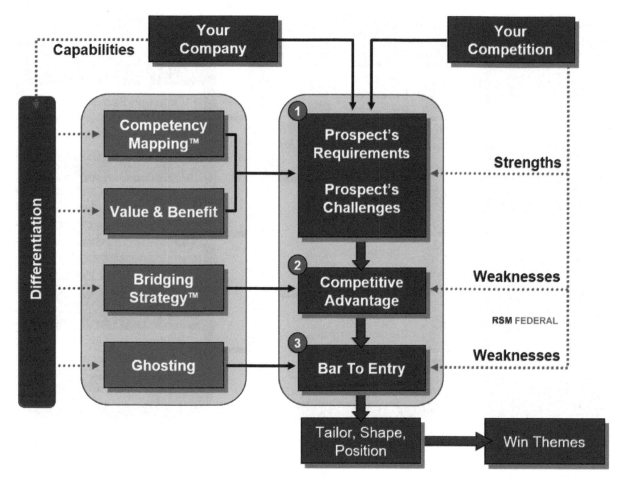

*Figure 31 - Leveling Strategy*

# Leveling Strategy – Bringing It All Together

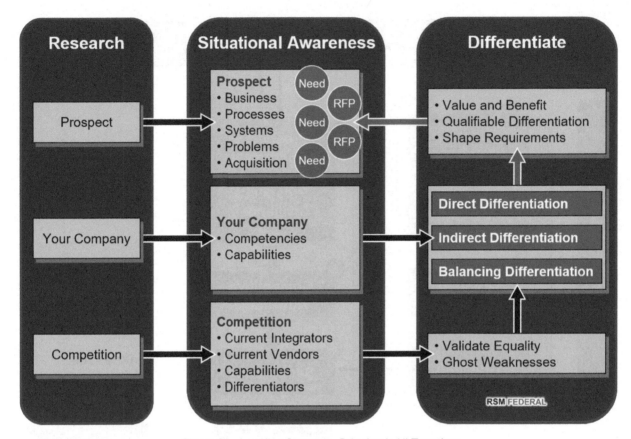

*Figure 32 - Leveling Strategy - Bringing It All Together*

# Chapter 8
# Marketing

**RSM FEDERAL**
The Art and Science of Government Sales™

# Marketing Activities Must Map To Revenue

I've worked with thousands of companies and many of the small and mid-size businesses spend money on marketing without having specific and measurable outcomes.

- **Do not expend cash on your Marketing-Mix without the following:**
  - Ability to measure the success of all advertising activities
  - If you can not communicate how an ad or promotion will increase revenue, do not authorize or expend the funds
- **If you are a Business Developer**
  - Recognize that every request for marketing materials involves corporate cash-flow
  - Be able to explain how you will:
    - ➤ Measure success at a trade-show
    - ➤ Measure success for a newspaper ad
    - ➤ Measure success for a whitepaper or case study
- **The days of Marketing being "Magic" are over.**
  - Every dollar spent on marketing must have metrics tied to revenue

# Evaluating ROI and Cost of Marketing

How do you know if the money you are spending is responsible for winning contracts? The majority of your marketing dollars should be for industry days, conference and event travel, online presence, and teaming travel costs.

| Measure Marketing ROI | | | |
|---|---|---|---|
| **Medium** | **Spend** | **Sales** | **ROI** |
| Viral Marketing (Social Networking) | ● $500 | ? | ? |
| Trade Show Publications | $2,000 | ? | ? |
| Trade Show Booth | $3,000 | ? | ? |
| Online CRM | $2,500 | ? | ? |
| Email Marketing | ● $1,000 | ? | ? |
| Free Education Campaigns | ● $500 | ? | ? |
| Search Engines | ▲ $500 | ? | ? |
| Media Ads | ▲ $550 | ? | ? |
| Radio Ads | $250 | ? | ? |

*Figure 33 - Measuring Marketing ROI*

- ● If no external spend, calculate based on hourly rates of your employees
- ▲ With time and experience, you'll be able to find dozens of FREE placements

# Marketing Collateral

If you have two or three standard marketing slicks which you give to every prospect, regardless of market, vertical, or challenges, you are not positioning or differentiating. *You are hindering your sales process.*

- **You need several presentations**
  - Yes, you need standardized slicks as a baseline
  - But you need to tailor your capability statements / presentations for every prospect
- The most valuable are those which are tailored

## What You Need For Marketing

The table that follows outlines the most common marketing slicks or products that are utilized by government contractors. When you've been learning about the government market for only a week, you will already know about the capability statement or "Cap Statement."

When you look at the table, nothing is absolute. Some companies will adjust the page counts or content. More important, is making sure you understand that generic marketing material, while valuable, is much less valuable than tailored marketing materials.

There are situations when generic marketing is acceptable. For example, your standard capability statement that you can download off your website is perfectly fine without being tailored. You don't know who will download it.

When you are scheduled to meet a government prospect, in person or virtually, or you have a meeting with a new potential teaming partner, or you want to get onto the team for a specific Prime, you do not want to use generic marketing slicks. You want to have the meeting first, go back to the office, and spend five or ten minutes tailoring your capability statement based on your discussion and knowing exactly what they are looking for.

## Marketing Collateral – Tactics and Strategies

| Phase | Document | Type | Tailored | Audience | Time & Value |
|---|---|---|---|---|---|
| **All Acquisition Phases** (9%, 1%, 45%, 45%) | Corporate Capabilities Brief | | Not Tailored | Everyone | **2 – 4 Hours**<br>• Easiest – do it once and you're done<br>• Most common and *least beneficial*<br>• Not tailored to reqt's, prospects, or partners |
| | Capability Statement | | Not Tailored | Everyone | **2 – 4 Hours**<br>• Uploaded with every GSA eBuy bid<br>• Added to your Price List in GSA Advantage |
| **Acquisition Phase** (9%, 1%) | Capabilities Statement | | Tailored | Prospects | **30 Minutes – 1 Hour**<br>• For Sources Sought, RFIs and Proposals<br>• Part of your Documentation Library<br>• Do it once and then edit for future opportunities |
| **Pre-Acquisition** (45%, 45%) | Opportunity Capabilities Brief | | Tailored | Prospects Partners SB Office | **30 Minutes**<br>• The power-horse of all MS PowerPoints<br>• *Most useful* capabilities brief<br>• *Tailored* to specific requirements of a specific agency<br>• *Maps* to your Teaming Partner's gaps |
| **Pre-Acquisition** (45%, 45%) | Introduction & Capability Statement™ (ICS) | | Tailored | Teaming Partners | **2 – 4 Hours – Five to seven page mini-proposal**<br>• Completely Maps value and benefit of competencies to prospects requirements<br>• Maps to your Partner's gaps<br>• Teaming – 90%+ success rate<br>• Followed by Sell The Prime™ |

*Table 31 - Marketing Collateral Tactics and Strategies*

# Capability Statement

If you are a small business, the capability statement is a cornerstone of your marketing world. A capability statement is simply a one or two page marketing slick that is recognized and expected in the government market.

Figure 34 - Example Capability Statements

## Look and Feel

Like everything else in business, everyone has an opinion. It's no different in the government space. Talk to any small business counselor, specialist, non-profit, or paid consultant and they will all provide you with fairly similar feedback. However, every one of them will have a different approach.

The example capability statement to the right is just one of many possible looks. Every company will be different based on what they do, their brand, color scheme, and how they communicate their value.

There are close to a dozen examples and templates in the Federal Access Coaching and Training Platform. So if you're new to government sales, one more reason to join Federal Access →

<u>federal-access.com/manual</u>

## What Goes Into a Capability Statement?

There are several core sections in a capability statement. Over time, you will understand the basics and what goes into each section. Simply downloading all the templates in Federal Access will speed-up the process. However, to make this Manual as comprehensive as possible, here are the individual sections that you will have in your capability statement.

- **Corporate Overview**

    - Imagine your 45 second pitch squeezed into a one paragraph overview.

    - Make sure your overview discusses the value you provide, not products, features, or services.

- **Your Past Performance (Commercial, State, Local, Federal)**

    - The average person will only look at your capability statement for six seconds. This includes potential teaming partners and government buyers and program managers.

    - The easiest way to communicate your past performance is with a map of the United States with logos for your past and current customers. If you only have six seconds, the map and logos jump off the document.

    - However, you may have enough clients that you want to simply bulletize in text.

- **Product or Services**

- Don't list "Project Management" as a core service unless you support Project Management Organizations (PMOs) and you help clients with their project management.

- Most small businesses list project management as a core service. Don't do this unless that's your primary service. In the government market, EVERY Prime contractor is responsible for the project management of their contracts. As a result, you will NEVER get a project management position on a contract unless you are the Prime.

- **Certifications (Corporate and Employees)**

- **Contract Vehicles (IDCs, IDIQs, MACs, GSA Schedule, etc.)**

- **Acquisition Codes**
  - NAICS Codes
  - PSC Codes

- **DUNS / SAM Unique Identifier and CAGE Code**

- **Size and Socio-Economic Status**

  - If you are small and / or have been certified 8a (minority or socially disadvantaged), Woman-Owned Small Business (WOSB), Veteran Owned or Service Disabled Veteran Owned Small Business (VOSB / SDVOSB), HUBZone, etc. → Do NOT put these on top of your capability statement. That's not the value you provide! It's just a status.

  - Place your socio-economic statuses and certifications at the bottom.

  - I also recommend you consider NOT using certification logos. There is much more to this and it's discussed throughout the resources in Federal Access.

  - At a high level, you will never win a contract or sole-source because you are minority, woman, or Veteran owned. Therefore, focus on the value of your products or services.

- **Other Corporate Data (Awards and Recognition**

  - Absolute least important section on your capability statement

# Chapter 9
# Who Buys What You Sell?

**RSM FEDERAL**
The Art and Science of Government Sales™

# Who Buys What You Sell?

Let's take a pause. The next two chapters are about business development, sales, and creating your own Market Sales Strategy (MSS). But none of those tactics and strategies will provide a winning formula **unless** you know who buys what you sell.

Shotgun sales is not a viable strategy, whether government or commercial. You probably already know that. But figuring out how to target the right agencies and military commands can be a daunting task, even if you know where to find the data!

Propensity is a process of reviewing government contract actions over a period of time. Propensity is identifying who buys what you sell, how much they buy, and how often they buy it. From a business perspective, *how can you possibly target the federal market* or develop a strong corporate sales strategy without having this information?

Identifying propensity takes me 1.5 hours to teach, in front of the computer, with several supporting documents. I can't do that in the format of a manual. However, I can point you in the right direction on where to get access to the training materials.

## Procurement Technical Assistance Centers (PTAC)

Every State in the country has one or more PTAC offices. PTACs are funded part by the Department of Defense and part by your local university. Their services are free to any company that wants to pursue government contracts. Just call them. Earlier, I mentioned that I have a 1.5 hour training video on how to find this information. Most of the PTACs are able to help you perform this process! In fact, every PTAC office has access to my training video via partners.

Because of all the resources that the Federal Access Coaching and Training Platform provides; and because I've referred to it throughout this Manual, you probably already have access to it! But if you still haven't registered for Federal Access, just recognize that you can get free help on performing this process from your local PTAC.

**Association of Procurement Technical Assistance Centers**
www.aptac-us.org

**Federal Access Coaching and Training Platform**
www.federal-access.com/manual

# It's In The Details

There are three systems that provide the majority of historical contract data from previous procurements:

- Data Bank in the System For Award Management (SAM)
- USASpending.gov
- DLA's Internet Bid Board System (DIBBS)

It's important to understand what each of these systems provides in terms of historical contract data and functionality.

Let's start with SAM.gov's Data Bank. This is the primary repository for the last twenty years of contract data, both products and services. If you're familiar with or used the Federal Procurement Data System (FPDS), SAM.gov's Data Bank replaced FPDS in October 2020. While FPDS is still accessible, contract data after October 2020 is no longer entered. As a result, you need to be using the Data Bank. The Data Bank includes more than 300 fields of data and is the primary repository for all contract actions for federal agencies and DoD.

Next is USASpending.gov. Also managed by the government, it's much easier to use because it has a simple user interface. You select boxes, add keywords, add NAICS codes, and you have what you want. However, *USASpending.gov does NOT include all the fields from SAM.gov's Data Bank – only about two thirds*. As a result, while it will be much easier to get started with USASpending.gov, I highly urge you to learn how to setup SAM.gov's Data Bank. Regardless, you CAN identify who buys what you sell, how much, and how often with USASpending.gov. As you get more proficient, you need to learn the Data Bank. One other key difference is that USASpending.gov includes subcontract data. SAM.gov's Data Bank does not. In otherwords, you can look up a contrractor's DUNS number or SAM Unique Identifier and see who they've subcontracted to. The subcontract data is only as good as the information entered into it. Quite a few contracts don't have the associated subcontracting data. It's a huge system! Just recognize none of the data in any of these systems are perfect. But these systems have enough of the data to make strong corporate business decisions.

The third system is DLA's Internet Bid Board System (DIBBS). Like SAM's Data Bank and USASpending.gov, you can find historical contract data for both products and services. But DIBBS is primarily for product. Also, unlike the first two systems, which holds data for the last 20 years, DIBBS only keeps data for the last three to four months.

The rest of this chapter will be examples of the contract data you need to be looking at and how to setup your searches in SAM.gov's Data Bank.

# Pivot Tables

When you download data from USASpending.gov or SAM.gov's Data Bank, you will likely be downloading data for the last three years (that's what I do). This likely includes several hundred thousand to millions of fields of data. There is nothing you can do with this data unless you understand how to run pivot tables and you know which fields you need to pull from the system. Like anything else in business, the first time is painful. There's a reason why I developed an hour and a half training video where you see my computer screen and watch how I do it.

Again, this is one of the most important steps in developing a strong sales strategy.

## Examples of Historical Contract Data

**Raw Data - Hundreds of Thousands to Millions of Data Fields**
Need to understand Microsoft Excel Pivot Tables

| Contracting Department Name | Contracting Office ID | Contracting Office Name | Contracting Agency Name | Date Signed | NAICS Code | NAICS Description | Product or Service Code | Award or IDV Type | Prepared By | Action Obligation |
|---|---|---|---|---|---|---|---|---|---|---|
| DEPT OF DEFENSE | W912GB | W25D FEST NAU1 EI | DEPT OF THE ARMY | 11/16/2016 | 541330 | ENGINEERING SERVICES | C211 | DELIVERY ORDER | DAYON.T.SANTOS.W | $5,811.00 |
| DEPT OF DEFENSE | W912GB | W25D FEST NAU1 EI | DEPT OF THE ARMY | 9/21/2017 | 541330 | ENGINEERING SERVICES | C211 | DELIVERY ORDER | DAYON.T.SANTOS.W | $0.00 |
| DEPT OF DEFENSE | W912GB | W25D FEST NAU1 EI | DEPT OF THE ARMY | 11/1/2017 | 541330 | ENGINEERING SERVICES | C211 | DELIVERY ORDER | DAYON.T.SANTOS.W | ($629,120.00) |
| DEPT OF DEFENSE | W912GB | W25D FEST NAU1 EI | DEPT OF THE ARMY | 1/28/2019 | 541330 | ENGINEERING SERVICES | C211 | DELIVERY ORDER | DAYON.T.SANTOS.W | $0.00 |
| HOMELAND SECURITY, DEPARTMENT OF | 70FA60 | MITIGATION SECTIO | FEDERAL EMERGENCY MAN/ | 12/10/2017 | 541330 | ENGINEERING SERVICES | C212 | DELIVERY ORDER | PATRICE.FRENCH@/ | $0.00 |
| HOMELAND SECURITY, DEPARTMENT OF | 70FA60 | MITIGATION SECTIO | FEDERAL EMERGENCY MAN/ | 2/27/2018 | 541330 | ENGINEERING SERVICES | C212 | DELIVERY ORDER | PATRICE.FRENCH@/ | $0.00 |
| GENERAL SERVICES ADMINISTRATION | 47PM01 | PBS NCR CAPITAL CC | PUBLIC BUILDINGS SERVICE | 8/30/2018 | 236220 | COMMERCIAL AND INSTITUTION/ | R408 | DELIVERY ORDER | 11.TAMMY.AREVAL | $47,786.00 |
| GENERAL SERVICES ADMINISTRATION | 47PM01 | PBS NCR CAPITAL CC | PUBLIC BUILDINGS SERVICE | 9/14/2018 | 236220 | COMMERCIAL AND INSTITUTION/ | R408 | DELIVERY ORDER | 11.MARY.PINEDA.G | $0.00 |
| GENERAL SERVICES ADMINISTRATION | 47PM01 | PBS NCR CAPITAL CC | PUBLIC BUILDINGS SERVICE | 10/9/2018 | 236220 | COMMERCIAL AND INSTITUTION/ | R408 | DELIVERY ORDER | 11.TAMMY.AREVAL | $0.00 |
| GENERAL SERVICES ADMINISTRATION | 47PM01 | PBS NCR CAPITAL CC | PUBLIC BUILDINGS SERVICE | 12/27/2018 | 236220 | COMMERCIAL AND INSTITUTION/ | R408 | DELIVERY ORDER | 11.CHING.HUNG.GS | $6,500.00 |
| GENERAL SERVICES ADMINISTRATION | 47PM01 | PBS NCR CAPITAL CC | PUBLIC BUILDINGS SERVICE | 1/29/2019 | 236220 | COMMERCIAL AND INSTITUTION/ | R408 | DELIVERY ORDER | 11.TAMMY.AREVAL | $9,000.00 |
| GENERAL SERVICES ADMINISTRATION | 47PM01 | PBS NCR CAPITAL CC | PUBLIC BUILDINGS SERVICE | 2/28/2019 | 236220 | COMMERCIAL AND INSTITUTION/ | R408 | DELIVERY ORDER | 11.TAMMY.AREVAL | $0.00 |
| GENERAL SERVICES ADMINISTRATION | 47PM01 | PBS NCR CAPITAL CC | PUBLIC BUILDINGS SERVICE | 4/25/2019 | 236220 | COMMERCIAL AND INSTITUTION/ | R408 | DELIVERY ORDER | 11.TAMMY.AREVAL | $800.00 |
| GENERAL SERVICES ADMINISTRATION | 47PM01 | PBS NCR CAPITAL CC | PUBLIC BUILDINGS SERVICE | 7/31/2019 | 236220 | COMMERCIAL AND INSTITUTION/ | R408 | DELIVERY ORDER | 11.TAMMY.AREVAL | $0.00 |
| GENERAL SERVICES ADMINISTRATION | 47PM01 | PBS NCR CAPITAL CC | PUBLIC BUILDINGS SERVICE | 8/26/2019 | 236220 | COMMERCIAL AND INSTITUTION/ | R408 | DELIVERY ORDER | 11.TAMMY.AREVAL | $289,226.00 |
| GENERAL SERVICES ADMINISTRATION | 47PM02 | PBS NCR CAPITAL CC | PUBLIC BUILDINGS SERVICE | 1/18/2017 | 236220 | COMMERCIAL AND INSTITUTION/ | R408 | DELIVERY ORDER | 11.TAMMY.AREVAL | $44,000.00 |
| GENERAL SERVICES ADMINISTRATION | 47PM02 | PBS NCR CAPITAL CC | PUBLIC BUILDINGS SERVICE | 5/17/2017 | 236220 | COMMERCIAL AND INSTITUTION/ | R408 | DELIVERY ORDER | 11.TAMMY.AREVAL | $53,458.00 |
| GENERAL SERVICES ADMINISTRATION | 47PM02 | PBS NCR CAPITAL CC | PUBLIC BUILDINGS SERVICE | 5/25/2017 | 236220 | COMMERCIAL AND INSTITUTION/ | R408 | DELIVERY ORDER | 11.TAMMY.AREVAL | $98,000.00 |
| GENERAL SERVICES ADMINISTRATION | 47PM02 | PBS NCR CAPITAL CC | PUBLIC BUILDINGS SERVICE | 9/1/2017 | 236220 | COMMERCIAL AND INSTITUTION/ | R408 | DELIVERY ORDER | 11.TAMMY.AREVAL | ($73,438.00) |
| GENERAL SERVICES ADMINISTRATION | 47PM02 | PBS NCR CAPITAL CC | PUBLIC BUILDINGS SERVICE | 9/5/2017 | 236220 | COMMERCIAL AND INSTITUTION/ | R408 | DELIVERY ORDER | 11.TAMMY.AREVAL | $20,000.00 |
| GENERAL SERVICES ADMINISTRATION | 47PM02 | PBS NCR CAPITAL CC | PUBLIC BUILDINGS SERVICE | 12/12/2017 | 236220 | COMMERCIAL AND INSTITUTION/ | R408 | DELIVERY ORDER | 11.MARY.PINEDA.G | $300,000.00 |
| GENERAL SERVICES ADMINISTRATION | 47PM02 | PBS NCR CAPITAL CC | PUBLIC BUILDINGS SERVICE | 1/30/2018 | 236220 | COMMERCIAL AND INSTITUTION/ | R408 | DELIVERY ORDER | 11.TAMMY.AREVAL | $164,019.20 |
| GENERAL SERVICES ADMINISTRATION | 47PM02 | PBS NCR CAPITAL CC | PUBLIC BUILDINGS SERVICE | 3/29/2018 | 236220 | COMMERCIAL AND INSTITUTION/ | R408 | DELIVERY ORDER | 11.TAMMY.AREVAL | $39,000.00 |
| GENERAL SERVICES ADMINISTRATION | 47PM02 | PBS NCR CAPITAL CC | PUBLIC BUILDINGS SERVICE | 4/19/2018 | 236220 | COMMERCIAL AND INSTITUTION/ | R408 | DELIVERY ORDER | 11.TAMMY.AREVAL | $14,000.00 |

## Contracting Offices That Buy What You Sell (City & State)

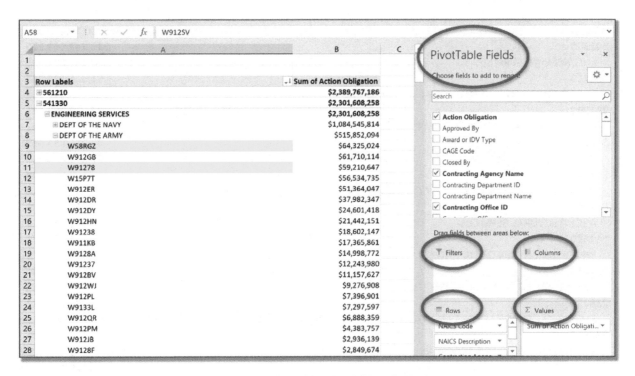

*Figure 35 - SAM Data Bank Pivot Table 1*

# Which Are Your Strongest NAICS Codes?

| Row Labels | Sum of Action Obligation |
|---|---|
| ⊟ 541330 | $10,147,881,225 |
| ENGINEERING SERVICES | $10,147,881,225 |
| ⊟ 236220 | $8,516,172,738 |
| COMMERCIAL AND INSTITUTIONAL BUILDING CONSTRUCTION | $8,516,172,738 |
| ⊟ 237990 | $2,677,099,231 |
| OTHER HEAVY AND CIVIL ENGINEERING CONSTRUCTION | $2,677,099,231 |
| ⊟ 562910 | $2,271,894,459 |
| REMEDIATION SERVICES | $2,271,894,459 |
| ⊟ 237310 | $608,931,614 |
| HIGHWAY, STREET, AND BRIDGE CONSTRUCTION | $608,931,614 |
| ⊟ 541310 | $491,971,026 |
| ARCHITECTURAL SERVICES | $491,971,026 |
| ⊟ 541620 | $478,521,579 |
| ENVIRONMENTAL CONSULTING SERVICES | $478,521,579 |
| ⊟ 236210 | $396,379,643 |
| INDUSTRIAL BUILDING CONSTRUCTION | $396,379,643 |
| ⊟ 238210 | $288,598,712 |
| ELECTRICAL CONTRACTORS AND OTHER WIRING INSTALLATION CONTRACTORS | $288,598,712 |
| ⊟ 238910 | $193,817,806 |
| SITE PREPARATION CONTRACTORS | $193,817,806 |
| ⊟ 237130 | $166,148,077 |
| POWER AND COMMUNICATION LINE AND RELATED STRUCTURES CONSTRUCTION | $166,148,077 |
| ⊟ 237110 | $122,185,993 |
| WATER AND SEWER LINE AND RELATED STRUCTURES CONSTRUCTION | $122,185,993 |
| ⊟ 213112 | $116,855,158 |
| SUPPORT ACTIVITIES FOR OIL AND GAS OPERATIONS | $116,855,158 |
| ⊞ (blank) | |
| Grand Total | $26,476,457,262 |

*Figure 36 - SAM Data Bank Pivot Table 2*

## Which Are Your Strongest Product Service Codes (PSC)?

| Row Labels | Sum of Action Obligation |
|---|---|
| R425 | $2,677,916,177 |
| F999 | $1,146,986,061 |
| Y1JZ | $1,058,191,910 |
| C211 | $980,560,348 |
| 1510 | $945,919,009 |
| Y199 | $798,070,995 |
| AZ16 | $784,925,419 |
| Y1DA | $755,643,004 |
| 1680 | $576,699,002 |
| R414 | $522,596,181 |
| Y211 | $516,352,204 |
| F108 | $511,418,288 |
| J069 | $446,141,268 |
| C219 | $437,994,549 |
| AZ15 | $405,338,730 |
| Z2DA | $360,667,241 |
| Y1PZ | $351,013,325 |
| Y299 | $339,880,235 |
| Y1AA | $335,184,542 |
| Y111 | $313,268,974 |

*Figure 37 - SAM Data Bank Pivot Table 3*

## Which Agencies or Commands Should You Target?

| Row Labels | Sum of Action Obligation |
|---|---|
| ⊕ DEPT OF THE ARMY | $11,817,006,371 |
| ⊕ DEPT OF THE AIR FORCE | $4,921,220,583 |
| ⊕ DEPT OF THE NAVY | $3,267,894,024 |
| ⊕ VETERANS AFFAIRS, DEPARTMENT OF | $1,530,638,318 |
| ⊕ ENERGY, DEPARTMENT OF | $1,255,443,869 |
| ⊕ NATIONAL AERONAUTICS AND SPACE ADMINISTRATION | $876,043,462 |
| ⊕ FEDERAL AVIATION ADMINISTRATION | $511,869,080 |
| ⊕ PUBLIC BUILDINGS SERVICE | $511,552,349 |
| ⊕ ENVIRONMENTAL PROTECTION AGENCY | $466,338,464 |
| ⊕ U.S. COAST GUARD | $159,789,381 |
| ⊕ FEDERAL HIGHWAY ADMINISTRATION | $111,996,629 |
| ⊕ DEFENSE MICROELECTRONICS ACTIVITY (DMEA) | $107,959,334 |
| ⊕ FEDERAL EMERGENCY MANAGEMENT AGENCY | $98,345,509 |
| ⊕ FEDERAL LAW ENFORCEMENT TRAINING CENTER | $88,272,699 |
| ⊕ INTERNATIONAL BOUNDARY AND WATER COMMISSION: U.S.-MEXICO | $71,639,288 |
| ⊕ DEFENSE COMMISSARY AGENCY (DECA) | $63,230,942 |
| ⊕ FEDERAL PRISON SYSTEM | $59,276,111 |
| ⊕ NATIONAL PARK SERVICE | $54,482,707 |
| ⊕ BUREAU OF INDIAN AFFAIRS | $51,716,904 |
| ⊕ MARITIME ADMINISTRATION | $49,735,169 |
| ⊕ FEDERAL ACQUISITION SERVICE | $48,524,012 |
| ⊕ NATURAL RESOURCES CONSERVATION SERVICE | $38,817,257 |
| ⊕ U.S. SPECIAL OPERATIONS COMMAND (USSOCOM) | $37,820,111 |
| ⊕ FOREST SERVICE | $34,714,522 |
| ⊕ U.S. CUSTOMS AND BORDER PROTECTION | $33,146,415 |
| ⊕ U.S. FISH AND WILDLIFE SERVICE | $26,414,984 |
| ⊕ BUREAU OF RECLAMATION | $24,099,027 |
| ⊕ AGRICULTURAL RESEARCH SERVICE | $21,467,934 |
| ⊕ EMPLOYMENT AND TRAINING ADMINISTRATION | $16,953,813 |
| ⊕ GEOLOGICAL SURVEY | $16,479,400 |
| ⊕ OFFICE OF ASST SECRETARY FOR HEALTH EXCEPT NATIONAL CENTERS | $15,445,675 |
| ⊕ FOOD AND DRUG ADMINISTRATION | $13,216,568 |

*Figure 38 - SAM Data Bank Pivot Table 4*

## Which Subordinate Agencies Should You Target?

| By Agency and Subordinate Agency | Sum of Dollars Obligated |
|---|---|
| ⊟LABOR, DEPARTMENT OF | **$14,282,993** |
| OFFICE OF THE ASSISTANT SECRETARY FOR ADMINISTRATION AND MANAGEMENT | $7,850,788 |
| OFFICE OF PUBLIC AFFAIRS | $5,730,605 |
| OCCUPATIONAL SAFETY AND HEALTH ADMINISTRATION | $401,600 |
| EMPLOYMENT AND TRAINING ADMINISTRATION | $300,000 |
| ⊟HEALTH AND HUMAN SERVICES, DEPARTMENT OF | **$11,143,216** |
| OFFICE OF THE ASSISTANT SECRETARY FOR ADMINISTRATION (ASA) | $5,785,025 |
| NATIONAL INSTITUTES OF HEALTH | $4,410,863 |
| AGENCY FOR HEALTHCARE RESEARCH AND QUALITY | $400,000 |
| CENTERS FOR DISEASE CONTROL AND PREVENTION | $397,352 |
| FOOD AND DRUG ADMINISTRATION | $149,976 |
| ⊟AGRICULTURE, DEPARTMENT OF | **$8,768,280** |
| USDA, OFFICE OF COMMUNICATION | $3,107,627 |
| FOOD AND NUTRITION SERVICE | $2,925,547 |
| AGRICULTURAL RESEARCH SERVICE | $1,083,463 |
| USDA, OFFICE OF THE CHIEF INFORMATION OFFICER | $790,321 |
| NATURAL RESOURCES CONSERVATION SERVICE | $396,121 |
| AGRICULTURAL MARKETING SERVICE | $335,085 |
| NATIONAL INSTITUTE OF FOOD AND AGRICULTURE | $89,310 |
| FOREST SERVICE | $40,806 |
| USDA, OFFICE OF THE CHIEF FINANCIAL OFFICER | $0 |
| ⊟INTERIOR, DEPARTMENT OF THE | **$8,138,193** |
| US GEOLOGICAL SURVEY | $3,281,591 |
| U.S. FISH AND WILDLIFE SERVICE | $1,599,436 |
| DEPARTMENTAL OFFICES | $1,297,976 |
| NATIONAL PARK SERVICE | $475,438 |
| BUREAU OF LAND MANAGEMENT | $453,283 |
| BUREAU OF INDIAN AFFAIRS AND BUREAU OF INDIAN EDUCATION | $284,901 |
| BUREAU OF INDIAN AFFAIRS | $284,576 |
| BUREAU OF RECLAMATION | $283,461 |
| BUREAU OF OCEAN ENERGY MANAGEMENT | $80,935 |
| BUREAU OF SAFETY AND ENVIRONMENTAL ENFORCEMENT | $80,755 |
| OFFICE OF THE INSPECTOR GENERAL | $15,840 |
| OFFICE OF THE SECRETARY OF THE INTERIOR | $0 |
| ⊟VETERANS AFFAIRS, DEPARTMENT OF | **$4,795,653** |

*Figure 39 - SAM Data Bank Pivot Table 5*

## Number of Bids Submitted For Past Contracts

| Number Bids by Contract # | Sum of Dollars Obligated |
|---|---|
| ⊟VETERANS AFFAIRS, DEPARTMENT OF | $4,795,653 |
| ⊟VA11816F1198 | $4,798,434 |
| 1 ← | $4,798,434 |
| ⊟VA25515C0176 | -$2,782 |
| 5 ← | -$2,782 |
| ⊟ENVIRONMENTAL PROTECTION AGENCY | $3,273,829 |
| ⊟0406 | $15,000 |
| 2 | $15,000 |
| ⊟EPB15H00049 | $177 |
| 4 | $177 |
| ⊟EPB16H00020 | $355,917 |
| 3 | $355,917 |
| ⊟EPG12H00332 | -$1,680 |
| 9 | -$1,680 |
| ⊟EPG13H00626 | -$16 |
| 8 | -$16 |
| ⊟EPG15H01173 | $2,904,431 |
| 4 | $2,904,431 |

*Figure 40 - SAM Data Bank Pivot Table 6*

## Type of Contract | Competition Type | Place of Performance

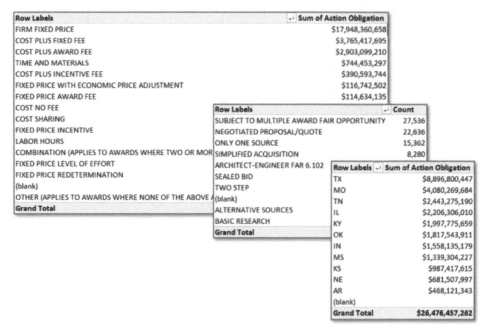

*Figure 41 - SAM Data Bank Pivot Table 7*

## Identifying Potential Teaming Partners – Small and Large Business

| Row Labels | Sum of Dollars Obligated |
|---|---|
| ⊟ DEPT OF DEFENSE | $183,763,518 |
| ⊟ DEPT OF THE NAVY | $63,205,797 |
| ⊟ OTHER THAN SMALL BUSINESS | $27,213,799 |
| SCIENCE APPLICATIONS INTERNATIONAL CORPORATION | $18,321,378 |
| (blank) | $6,295,090 |
| CACI INC FEDERAL | $1,410,077 |
| INSIGHT PUBLIC SECTOR, INC | $886,218 |
| BOOZ ALLEN HAMILTON INC. | $267,732 |
| DIGITAL EQUIPMENT CORPORATION | $20,054 |
| TECHNOLOGY LEARNING GROUP, INC. | $13,250 |
| ⊟ SMALL BUSINESS | $35,991,998 |
| (blank) | $34,625,386 |
| MANAGEMENT TECHNOLOGY, INC. | $571,869 |
| PROFESSIONAL SOFTWARE ENGINEERING, INC. | $351,840 |
| REALITY TECHNOLOGY, INC | $236,539 |
| MILVETS SYSTEMS TECHNOLOGY, INC. | $109,680 |
| SOFTWARE INFORMATION RESOURCE | $77,370 |
| ESVA | $11,413 |
| ALAMO CITY ENGINEERING SERVICES, INC. | $7,900 |
| ⊟ DEPT OF THE ARMY | $61,796,301 |
| ⊟ OTHER THAN SMALL BUSINESS | $30,516,049 |
| (blank) | $14,985,544 |
| GENERAL DYNAMICS INFORMATION TECHNOLOGY, INC. | $13,766,205 |

*Figure 42 - SAM Data Bank Pivot Table 8*

## Contracting Officer Contact Information

| Row Labels | Sum of Dollars Obligated |
|---|---|
| ⊟ VETERANS AFFAIRS, DEPARTMENT OF | **$40,315,002** |
| ⊟ VETERANS AFFAIRS, DEPARTMENT OF | **$40,315,002** |
| ⊟ PCAC HEALTH INFORMATION (36C776) | $31,269,673 |
| ⊟ 36C776 | **$31,269,673** |
| LAMONTE.JONES.776@VA.GOV | $19,031,282 |
| KAYLAN.GROVE.776E@VA.GOV | $4,009,446 |
| ROBERT.BLASKO.776E@VA.GOV | $3,811,930 |
| LAURIE.WALKER.776@VA.GOV | $1,989,109 |
| WILLIAM.HENKEL.776@VA.GOV | $1,177,971 |
| MATTHEW.KLEMPAY.776@VA.GOV | $678,600 |
| CLAYTON.SMITH.776@VA.GOV | $517,221 |
| CLEMENT.UDEANI.776@VA.GOV | $148,655 |
| ADEITRA.JIMMISON.776@VA.GOV | $31,691 |
| KYMBERLY.MORGAN.776@VA.GOV | $0 |
| WALTER.THOMPSON.776@VA.GOV | -$344 |
| CHARLES.HOLMES.776@VA.GOV | -$8,100 |
| MICHAEL.RAYNACK.776@VA.GOV | -$117,788 |
| ⊟ DEPT OF DEFENSE | **$32,412,390** |
| ⊞ DEFENSE HUMAN RESOURCES ACTIVITY | **$25,810,674** |
| ⊞ DEPT OF DEFENSE | **$4,343,093** |
| ⊞ DEPT OF THE NAVY | **$1,306,920** |
| ⊞ DEPT OF THE ARMY | **$485,873** |
| ⊞ DEFENSE COMMISSARY AGENCY (DECA) | **$456,305** |
| ⊞ DEPT OF THE AIR FORCE | **$9,525** |
| ⊟ COMMERCE, DEPARTMENT OF | **$12,487,033** |
| ⊞ INTERNATIONAL TRADE ADMINISTRATION | **$11,845,173** |
| ⊞ US CENSUS BUREAU | **$479,220** |

*Figure 43 - SAM Data Bank Pivot Table 9*

# Setting Up SAM.gov's Data Bank Query

There is a process to accessing and taking advantage of historical contract data in SAM.gov's Data Bank. These are two very distinct activities. First, you have to setup your query in the Data Bank. The second is running pivot tables to make sense of the data. Again, none of this is hard - but it's a lot easier if you watch the video outlined at the start of this chapter.

When you first access the Adhoc Award section of the Data Bank, you will not have any searches. You have to create the first one. This becomes your master search query. You then use the master search query for everything.

Below is the guidance and recommendations we provide to the companies we coach and for our Federal Access members.

**Adhoc Award / IDV Information Report**
Report Setup

**Read This First**

When you first setup your master query report, don't set the time for one, three, or five years. Set it for one week! The Data Bank likes to time-out just when you've spent a half-hour finding data fields, adding them, and trying to run them! Don't run the query for years when first setting up the query. If you get too many results, it times out and it won't save your work. So... set the time span for one week. Add 10 fields. Run it. Save it. Add another 10 fields. Run it. Save it. Do it over and over until you have all 123 fields saved in your query! Then you can run the report for as far back as you want!

# Step 1

## Enter Start and End Dates

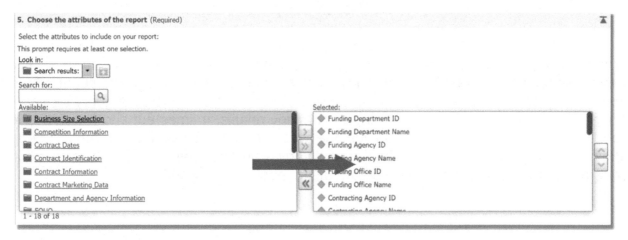

**1. Start Date for Date Signed** (Required)

Please Enter a Start Date for Date Signed

This prompt requires a value between 10/31/2007 and 10/31/2019.

10/1/2018

**2. End Date for Date Signed** (Required)

Please Enter an End Date for Date Signed

This prompt requires a value between 10/1/2018 and 10/1/2030.

10/31/2019

*Figure 44 - AdHoc Query Setup - Step 1*

# Step 2

## Choose Report Fields

If this is your first time, plan on it taking an hour to find and add all the attributes / fields.

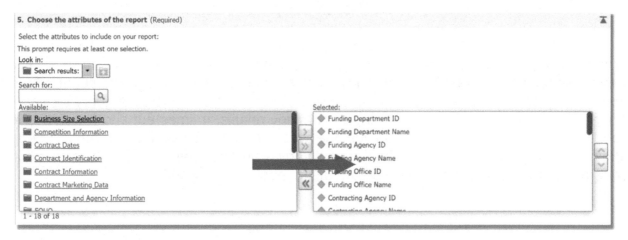

**5. Choose the attributes of the report** (Required)

Select the attributes to include on your report:
This prompt requires at least one selection.

Look in:
Search results:

Search for:

Available:
- Business Size Selection
- Competition Information
- Contract Dates
- Contract Identification
- Contract Information
- Contract Marketing Data
- Department and Agency Information

1 - 18 of 18

Selected:
- Funding Department ID
- Funding Department Name
- Funding Agency ID
- Funding Agency Name
- Funding Office ID
- Funding Office Name
- Contracting Agency ID
- Contracting Agency Name

*Figure 45 - AdHoc Query Setup - Step 2*

The following is a list of the fields that are a baseline for your query. You will find that the more fields you have, the more information and intelligence you have at your fingertips.

## Attributes / Fields

Funding Department ID
Funding Department Name
Funding Agency ID
Funding Agency Name
Funding Office ID
Funding Office Name
Contracting Agency ID
Contracting Agency Name
Contracting Office ID
Contracting Office Name
Contracting Department ID
Contracting Department Name
Major Command Code
Major Command ID
Major Command Name
Parent Macom Code
Sub Command 1 Code
Sub Command 1 ID
Sub Command 1 Name
Sub Command 2 Code
Sub Command 2 ID
Sub Command 2 Name
Clinger Cohen Act Code
Clinger Cohen Act Description
NAICS Code
NAICS Description
Product or Service Code
Product or Service Description
Contracting Officer's Business Size Determination
Contracting Office Business Size Determination Description
Evaluated Preference
IDV Contracting Officer Business Size Selection
IDV Contracting Officer Business Size Selection Description
Evaluated Preference
Evaluated Preference Description
Extent Competed Code
Extent Competed Description
Number of Offers Received
Other Than Full and Open Competition
Simplified Procedures for Certain Commercial Items
Simplified Procedures for Certain Commercial Items Description
Solicitation Procedures
Type of Set Aside
Date Signed
PIID
Modification Number

Solicitation ID
Major Program
National Interest Action
National Interest Description
Purchase Card As Payment Method Code
Purchase Card As Payment Method Description
Type of Contract Pricing
Type of Contract Pricing Description
Type of IDC
Performance Based Service Acquisition Code
Performance Based Service Acquisition Description
Ordering Procedure
Principal Place of Performance City Name
Principal Place of Performance State Code
Description of Requirement
Multiple Or Single Award IDV
IDV NAICS Code
IDV NAICS Description
IDV Number Of Offers
IDV Type of Set Aside Code
IDV Type of Set Aside Description
IDV Contracting Agency Name
IDV Contracting Officers Business Size Selection
IDV Department ID
IDV Department Name
IDV Major Program Code
IDV Multiple Or Single Award IDV
IDV NAICS Code
IDV NAICS Description
IDV Type Of IDC
IDV Type Of IDC Description
Period of Performance Start Date
Last Date to Order
Completion Date
Approved By
Closed By
Created Via
Last Modified By
Prepared By
Vendor Name
Global DUNS Number
Global Vendor Name
CAGE Code
Doing Business As Name
Contractor Name
Vendor Address Line 1
Vendor Address Line 2
Vendor Address Line 3

Vendor Address City
Vendor Address State
Vendor Address Zip Code
Number of Actions
Vendor DUNS Number
Vendor Phone Number
Is Vendor Business Type - 8A Joint Venture
Is Vendor Business Type - 8A Program Participant
Is Vendor Business Type - Alaskan Native Corporation Owned Firm
Is Vendor Business Type - Alaskan Native Servicing Institution
Is Vendor Business Type - American Indian
Is Vendor Business Type - Asian-Pacific American Owned
Is Vendor Business Type - Black American Owned
Is Vendor Business Type - DoT Certified Disadvantaged Business Enterprise
Is Vendor Business Type - Educational Institution
Is Vendor Business Type - Emerging Small Business
Is Vendor Business Type - Economically Disadvantaged Women Owned Small Business
Is Vendor Business Type - HUBZone Firm
Is Vendor Business Type - HUBZone Joint Venture
Is Vendor Business Type - Native American Owned
Is Vendor Business Type - Tribally Owned
Is Vendor Business Type - Planning Commission
Is Vendor Business Type - Service Disabled Veteran Owned Business
Is Vendor Business Type - Veteran Owned Business
Is Vendor Business Type - Women Owned Small Business
Labor Standards Code
Email Address
Labor Standards Description

# Step 3

## Choose Report Metrics
Select "Dollars Obligated"

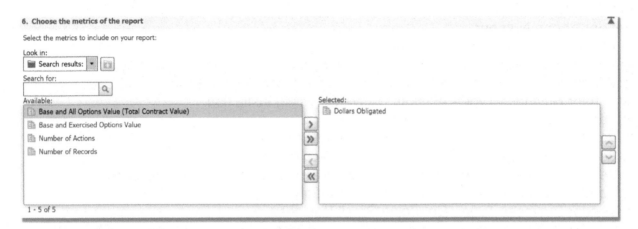

*Figure 46 - AdHoc Query Setup - Step 3*

# Step 4

Qualify Attributes – This is where you filter fields; such as NAICS Code, Contracting Office ID, DUNS Number, etc.

In this example, we are researching NAICS 541330

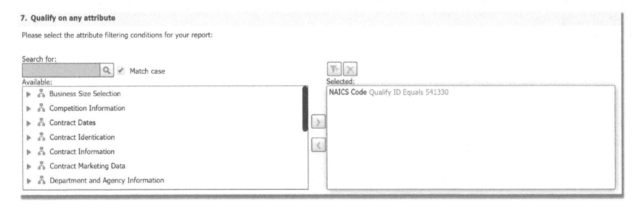

*Figure 47 - AdHoc Query Setup - Step 4*

# Step 5

Click the button for Run Report
- The report will show:
- Last 3 Fiscal Years (if that was your timeframe)
- 123 Attributes For Every Contract Action (Data Fields)
- Only Contracts with NAICS 541330 (selected)

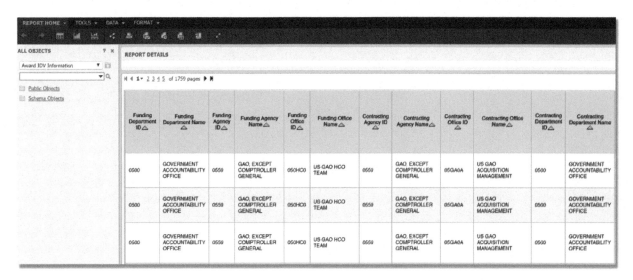

*Figure 48 - AdHoc Query Setup - Step 5*

# Step 6

Export to Microsoft Excel and run your pivot tables

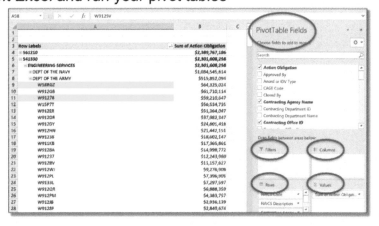

*Figure 49 - AdHoc Query Setup - Step 6*

# Chapter 10
# Business Development and Sales

**RSM FEDERAL**
The Art and Science of Government Sales™

# Don't Be Like The Rest

Before we jump into tactics and strategies, let's look first at several surveys and polls that were given to government decision makers.

## What Vendors Should Start Doing?

These lessons apply to all industries – not just technology.

- **Information Week conducted a survey of 350 IT Professionals in the Federal government**

    - Survey results clearly show that today's IT vendors are not perceived as being focused on customers, their requirements, or their needs

    - Understanding the results of this survey is an excellent primer for this Module

- **Market Data helps you position and tailor your capabilities**

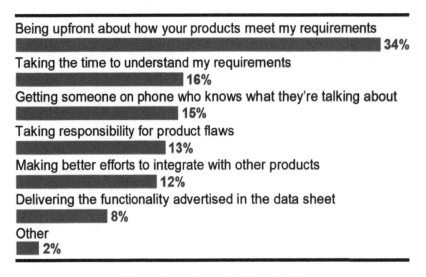

Being upfront about how your products meet my requirements
**34%**
Taking the time to understand my requirements
**16%**
Getting someone on phone who knows what they're talking about
**15%**
Taking responsibility for product flaws
**13%**
Making better efforts to integrate with other products
**12%**
Delivering the functionality advertised in the data sheet
**8%**
Other
**2%**

*Figure 50 - Information Week Poll 1*

# Qualities you want in your most-trusted technology vendor?

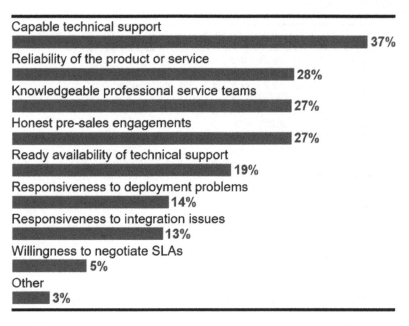

*Figure 51 - Information Week Poll 2*

# 72% Vendors Fail To Keep Promise – *24% Lied*

**Key Features promised in your last major product release were:**

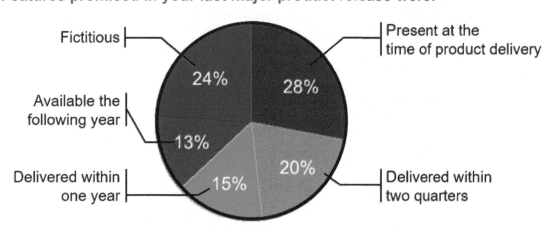

*Figure 52 - Information Week Poll 3*

# 50% Don't Believe You Are Focused On Their Requirements

## What should vendors start doing?

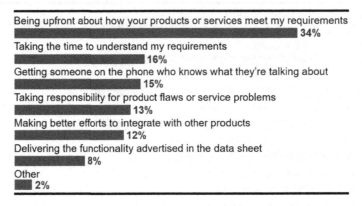

*Figure 53 - Information Week Poll 4*

# 51% Want Vendors To Be More Customer Focused

## What should vendors stop doing?

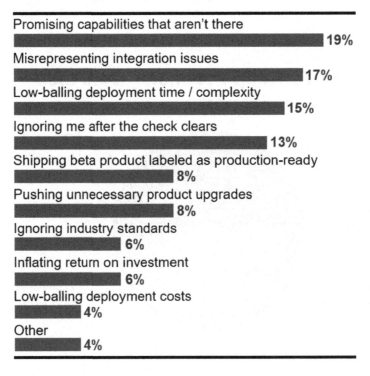

*Figure 54 - Information Week Poll 5*

# 6 Common Challenges For Small Business

- Not every prospect is qualified to be a customer
- Bidding without prior meeting to communicate value and benefit
- Bidding without knowing the customer
- Bidding without knowing the competition
- Bidding without having done the up-front work
- Believing your own press releases

## Don't Simply Search For Opportunities – *Understand Them*

- Information enables you to map capabilities to value statements
- People buy from people they know – relationship management
- Develop your own approach – what works and what does not
- Buyers care about their salary and promotions (minimal risk)
- Get in the "Gossip Chain"

---

*Prospects don't want you to sell to them. . .
They want to buy something from you."*

---

# Business Development - Desired End-State

Realignment Solution Methodology (RSM) Sales defines Business Development as those activities that make up the Market Sales Strategy where you:

- Collect Information on your Prospects
- Position that information against the value and benefit of your solutions
- Tailor your capabilities / solutions and differentiate
- Send that information back into the market to build the perception (actual or perceived) of you as the subject matter expert (SME) for a specific agency, specific prospect, specific program, and specific challenges and problems currently faced by that program.
- Differentiate, build competitive advantage and close more contracts to increase revenue.

# Business Development Versus Sales

- **Business Development**
  - Strategic
  - 6 Months to 2 Years
  - Focus on Budget, procurement, acquisition forecasts, and relationships
  - Focus on identifying challenges you can fix
  - Capture management
  - Responding to RFIs and Sources Sought
  - Prospecting
    - ➤ A strategic activity – the foundation for business development
    - ➤ Prospecting is **not** Sales

- **Sales**
  - Tactical
  - Solidifying Relationships
  - Current Quarter up to 1 Year
  - Responding to RFQs and RFPs (that you knew about in pre-acquisition)

# The Pipeline Calculator

This is an awesome tool for your toolbox. You can use it for the company as a whole and / or for each of your business developers. It's interesting that our Clients and Federal Access Members rarely ask the question, "How many opportunities do I need in my pipeline?" Instead, they focus on the revenue that want to make. Yet, you can't achieve your revenue (unless you get lucky) without knowing how many opportunities you need to engage.

This calculator is available in the Federal Access Coaching and Training Platform. When you look at the fields on the left, you immediately understand how valuable this is for any company.

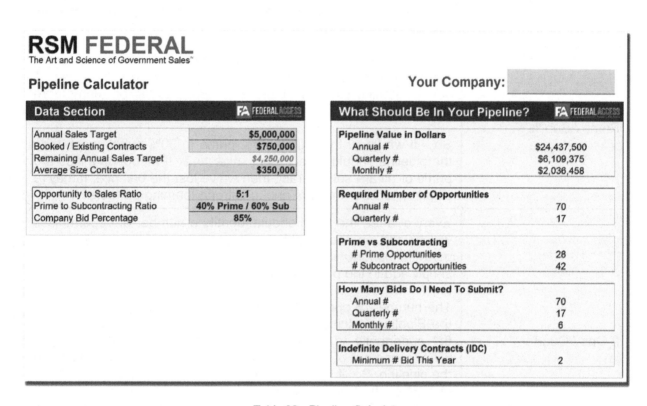

*Table 32 - Pipeline Calculator*

# Business Development Metrics

My team is often asked about sales metrics. Which metrics should we be using? Which metrics can we use in our employment agreements with our sales professionals? Here are the most common metrics that our clients use.

| Primary Business Development Metrics | |
|---|---|
| Quota | How much is the BDM required to sell this year? |
| Strategic Targets | Every BDM should have one to three strategic targets. These are targets identified by the company based on identifying who buys what you sell, how much, and how often.<br><br>These are the agencies or commands they are responsible for building relationships with over the next 12 months with the intent to flow this down into tactical pipeline opportunities. |
| Teaming Stable | This is more a company target than individual BDM targets. But if the company doesn't have a strong teaming stable of companies, you can assign requirements to a BDM to identify and build specific relationships. |
| Prime / Sub % | Every company decides at the beginning of the year what percentage of contracts will be prime versus subcontracting. A strong teaming strategy allows a company to bid on many more opportunities than they can bid by themselves.<br><br>So – if we know the ratio is 70% prime to 30% subcontract, then the pipeline should reflect this… *over time*. If all opportunities are prime or all are subcontract, then we've lost the balance. If they're all prime, do we not have enough strong teaming partners? |
| # Ops / Quarter | Every quarter, the BDM should identify a number of opportunities which land on the pipeline. *Very important - these are strong qualified opportunities* - not something we find on SAM.gov and simply add to the pipeline.<br><br>The number of opportunities, per quarter, is based on the Pipeline Calculator. For example, if we assume a 5:1 opportunity to sales ratio, then we plan on only winning one out of every 5 opportunities that we bid on  the pipeline. So, if the BDM needs to win four contracts at $2M each, they will need a minimum of 20 contracts over the period of a year. Assuming strong sales practices, this means they need at least five opportunities per quarter. The Pipeline Calculator is in the Federal Access Coaching and Training Platform. |
| Proposals Submitted per Month / Quarter | Similar to the prior metric. The average companies needs to submit at least 2.5 proposals per month. But don't let this discourage you! These proposal submissions can be as a prime or subcontractor! Since most small businesses don't have the bandwidth to write 2+ solid proposals or bids per month, you make up for it by getting on teams. |
| PWIN | # bids won versus bids submitted |

*Table 33 - Primary Business Development Metrics*

| Secondary Business Development Metrics | |
| --- | --- |
| Time Spent on Proposals | Hours for all employees |
| Time Spent on Graphics | |
| Length of Proposals | |
| Opportunities | By Territory and Annual Target List |
| Teaming Partners | Teaming Statistics |
| Customer Expansion | New Revenue / Original Contract Price<br>Goal 10%  (100,000 : 1,000,000) |
| New Clients to Retention | New Accounts / Retention Accounts<br>Goal 20%  (2 : 10) |
| New to Retention Booking | Goal 50%  (500,000 : 1,000,000)<br>2 Contracts, worth $500K, new accounts |
| Business Developer Yield | Bookings / Total Number Sales Team |
| Option Years | # Options Years Remaining / Total Option Years |

*Table 34 - Secondary Business Development Metrics*

# How Long Does It Take To Get a Contract?

- **No Right Answer.** **Depends on how fast you implement the tactics and strategies in this manual and educate yourself**

- **For more complicated / large-value RFPs, 12 to 24 month cycle**

- **Government requires 7 to 20 "Touches"**

  - Commercial sales is 7 to 10 "Touches"

  - If you touch the prospect twice a month – you accelerate your cycle to 10 Months

  - Focus is on communicating your value

  - Focus is educating the prospect

- **Persistence and Focus**

- **Accelerate your cycle: Target opportunities _before_ acquisition phase**

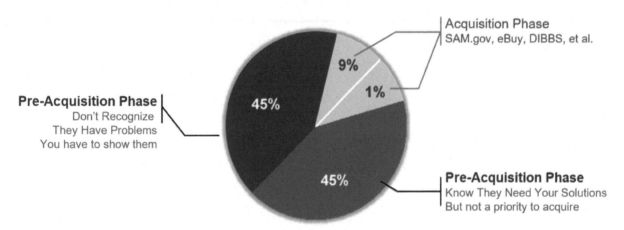

*Figure 55 - Pre-Acquisition Focus*

# Hiring Business Developers

- **Average  (90% of Professionals)**
  - Plenty of activity and perception of being "in-tune" with prospects and customers
  - Common focus on the tactical sale with little strategic direction
  - Focused on selling your products or services instead of selling "value"
  - Few repeatable processes or different approaches for each opportunity
  - Reactive (target opportunities in the acquisition phase)
  - In a crowded room, they only talk to people they know
  - Increase annual revenue by small percentage or not at all

- **Stars  (9% of Professionals)**
  - Experts in either strategic business development (prospecting and capture management) or tactical sales – but not both
  - Very strong when working with their opposite (Strategy & Tactical BDMs)
  - Proactive
  - In a crowded room, they talk to people they don't know
  - Increase annual revenue by 10% to 50%

- **Superstars  (1% of Professionals)**
  - Have both strategic understanding of business development and the tactical sales acumen for approaching, positioning, and closing the deal
  - Proactive
  - In a crowded room, they talk to everyone and get everyone's contact information
  - They double annual revenue

# Hiring – Ego and Attitude

- **Average often says:**
  - We can't be competitive on price
  - Our solutions aren't competitive
  - The prospect didn't make the requirements clear
  - I spend as much time on reports and documentation as actual sales
  - We're like the other companies – no real differentiation for us to stand-out
  - I don't have a security clearance to get into the office
  - I don't have a pass to get onto the base
  - I don't have the marketing materials I need
- **Stars and Superstars can sell anything to anyone**
  - Refuse to accept "No" until they make the sale  (but smooth and diplomatic)
  - Their prospects say "I've never been targeted like this"
  - Complete and total tenacious mentality
  - Have the cocky ego and attitude you need
  - **They are Often difficult to manage** (that's the challenge you must bear)

# Hiring Stars and Superstars

Hiring the right sales people is not as simple as knowing what you want and then interviewing a half dozen people. There are very specific questions you need to ask. The general points below will get you started.

For a complete PowerPoint packet (that I use for webinars) with all the questions you need to ask, visit the Federal Access Coaching and Training Platform.

- **General points:**
  - One of the more common requests we get for helping business owners
  - You must learn how to profile them (before you start hiring)
  - Hire "Average" and it will cost $60,000 - $80,000 *to replace them*
  - You don't interview for superstars like other positions *(different techniques)*
  - Federal Access can help your company ask the right questions

- **What to look for**
  - The right personality and profile
  - Formal sales training

- Possesses aptitude for mapping strategic initiatives to tactical activities
- Qualifiable and quantifiable success (proven successful history of sales)
- Strong and current network and / or Strong relationship skills

- **You have to decide. . .**
  - Are you willing to spend for the top talent to increase revenue?
  - Design the right compensation package with key performance indicators (KPIs) and even a small business with $500,000 revenue can afford a $125,000 business developer.

# Business Development Refresher

- **Don't lead with your product or service**
  - Build a relationship and create trust
  - When it's time to sell – sell the value and benefit, not your solutions

- **Don't let yourself be a "single face to industry"**
  - This is counter-intuitive (perception of job security; your importance)
  - Customer wants to know a team is behind you (unless you're startup)
  - Partners and Teammates want to know a mature company is behind you

- **Don't just focus on your NAICS codes!**
  - You will miss opportunities you can support (subcontracting)
  - You will miss opportunities to build relationships for teaming
- **Do not shotgun – target specific opportunities within an organization**

# Sales and Capture Competencies

*Figure 56 - Business Development and Sales Competencies*

## The Sales Triangle

- **3 Key Functions**

  - Capture Management      *Strategic*
  - Sales      *Tactical*
  - Pipeline Management      *Metrics*

- **3 Objectives**

  - Repeatable Processes
  - Communicating Value and Benefit
  - Creating Visibility and Quantifiable Metrics

- **1 Strategy – "Position Best Value"**

  - All Encompassing – Relationship Management
  - Your number one goal is to "make money" (notice this is at the bottom)

# Prospecting

- **You need a Customer Relationship Management (CRM) System**
    - Who are the decision makers?
    - Who are the influencers? (senior management, commanders, SES, etc.)
    - Who are the contracting officers?
    - Who are the program managers?
    - Who are the end-users?

- **Identify and validate who has the authority to evaluate or purchase**

- **Understand**
    - Where they are now (current contracts)
    - Where they want to be (in acquisition or just vision)
    - How your products and services provide value / benefit
    - Do they have a plan to get there or need your help with the vision
    - You can do all of these even if you only provide staff augmentation services!

- **What are their priorities?**

# The 5 Myths Of Prospecting*

- **Prospecting is Sales**
    - Prospecting is a separate function from sales
    - Prospecting is discarding unqualified leads – retaining quality ones

- **Prospecting is a numbers game**
    - Quality supersedes quantity
    - Identify prospects that have a motive and propensity to buy

- **Scripts are for kids**
    - Scripts provide the framework for a successful campaign *(repeatable process)*
    - Allow you to test which key benefits or differentiators influence your prospects

- **Prospecting takes time**
    - Takes only an email or phone call to get information from current customers
    - Takes only a few minutes to perform initial qualification

- **Setting-up another call to discuss interest**
  - Most people will say yes to the next call rather than say no to your solution
  - If they are hesitant, it's because you are selling your product and service instead of value
    * Zahorsky, Darrell, 5 Myths of Prospecting

# Collect Information That *Improves* Your Positioning

- **Agency Information**
  - Identify Organization, Stakeholders, Decision Makers
  - Identify programs you want to target
  - Identify vendors currently supporting these programs
  - Identify status and perception of existing work
  - Identify preferred contract vehicles

- **Prospect Information**
  - Identify Mission, Vision, Requirements
  - Identify prospect personnel who award the contracts
  - Identify problems, challenges, and pain points for both PM, COR, and COTR

- **Opportunity Information**
  - Identify recompetition and new opportunity timelines
  - Identify preferred contract vehicles
  - Which vendors are likely to compete
  - Likely evaluation factors  (you will know this through your relationship)
  - Prospect's agenda driving opportunity (you will know this through your relationship)

- **Think long term – 6 to 24 months**

PM – Program Manager
COR – Contracting Officer Representative
COTR – Contracting Officer Technical Representative

## Prospecting Takes Uninterrupted Time

- This is one area that differentiates successful Business Developers

- Select a time every day and notify your colleagues you are unavailable

- Put your prospecting times on your Calendar

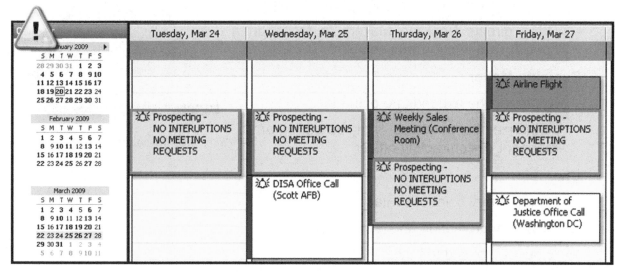

Figure 57 - Time-Blocking for Prospecting

# Identifying Buyers and End Users

- **Buyers**

  - Source selection decisions

  - Conduit to end users

  - Who you contact for acquisition information, RFPs, etc.

  - Includes Program Managers and Contract Officers

- **End Users**

  - Have the "need" and outline the requirements

  - Have the money

  - Control source selection

  - Accept delivery

- **Use "Official Buyers" to find the End Users**

# Are You Targeting The Right Individuals?

- **Influencer**

  - Senior Officials, Senior Executive Service (SES), General Officers, Colonels

  - Service or Pentagon level Program Managers

  - Often directs Decision Makers to focus on a specific requirement (not solution)

- **Decision Maker**

  - Approves the expenditure of funds

  - Authorizes the purchase - may be a program manager or contracting officer

- **Champion**

  - Your primary point of contact

  - Driven by promotion and recognition

  - Is not authorized to buy

  - Will introduce you to the Decision Maker

*Figure 58 - Prospect Authority Levels 1*

# Adversaries – Neutralize Them

Any individual that won't let you speak to the Champion or Decision Maker is an "Adversary." You have four options:

- **Sell them – Make them a Champion**

- **Neutralize Them**

  - Position your value to minimize their involvement

- **Eliminate Them**

  - Go over their head (burning a bridge)

- **Be "Average" and do nothing (not smart)**

*Figure 59  - Prospect Authority Levels 2*

# Research Agency or Command's Website

- The Contracting Organization
- Office of Small Disadvantaged Business Utilization (OSDBU) or Office of Small Business Programs (OSBP) → OSBP = Department of Defense and OSDBU = Federal Agencies
- "Doing Business With" section
- Names of buyers and phone numbers
- Organizational charts
- Budget information
- Procurement forecasts
- Active contract listings and historical contract data
- Public bids

# Other Sources of Government Requirements

- **Research Appropriations (when, where, how much)**
- **Inspector General (IG) Reports**
- **Congressional Bill's such as H.R. 1 Stimulus Bill**
  - The Library of Congress, THOMAS, https://www.congress.gov/
- **Base Realignment and Closure (BRAC) Reports**
  - Transition of DoD Commands
  - All contracts are revised or recompetition
- **Online PowerPoint Presentations**
  - Agency updates presented at Trade Shows
  - Strong and valuable information you may not find anywhere else

# Bookmark File of Key Government Websites

One more reason to register on the Federal Access Coaching and Training Platform is a bookmark file that you upload directly into your Internet browser. This file is updated several times a year when the government changes URLs and websites.

- The key websites that your competition uses for government sales

- Product and service related government websites

- Everything you need to know about NAICS, PSC, FSC, Size Status, etc.

- Government websites with all the key data, information, and intelligence on contracts

- Every website for agency and command small business offices

- Every agency's forecasted opportunities

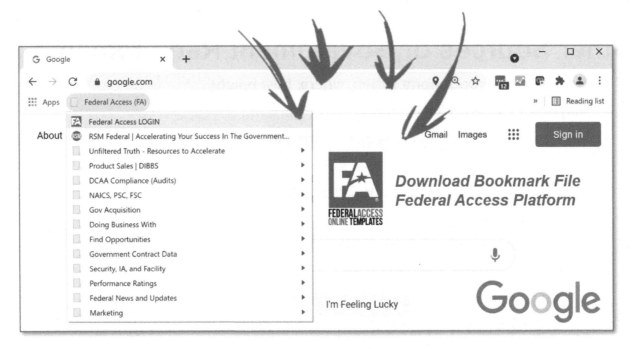

*Figure 60 - Federal Access Bookmark File*

# The Approach To Small Business Offices

## Statutory Goals For Small Business

- **Mandated by FAR\* Part 19 "Small Business Programs"**
- **Agencies and DoD follow the FAR to varying degrees**
    - Not all meet their small business obligations
    - Some agencies utilize one set-aside more than others
- **SBA Goals are not necessarily DoD or Agency Goals**
- **Primary SBA set-aside categories:**
    - Small Business
    - Small Disadvantaged Business (SDB) – Includes 8(a)
    - Woman Owned Small Business (WOSB)
    - Historically Underutilized Business Zone (HUBZone)
    - Service Disabled Veteran Owned (SDVOSB) and Veteran Owned (VOSB)

| Federal Agency Small Business Statutory Goals | | |
|---|---|---|
| **Percentage** | **Set-Aside** | **Certification Authority** |
| 23% | Small Business (SB) | NAICS Thresholds |
| 5% | Small Disadvantaged Business (SDB) 8(a) | Through SBA |
| 5% | Woman-Owned Small Business (WOSB); and Economically Disadvantaged Woman Owned Small Business (EDWOSB) | Through SBA |
| 0% | Veteran-Owned Small Business (VOSB) | Through VA Transfers to SBA in January 2023 |
| 3% | Service-Disabled Veteran-Owned Small Business (SDVOSB) | Through VA Transfers to SBA in January 2023 |
| 3% | Historically Underutilized Business Zone (HUBZone) | Through SBA |

*Table 35 - Small Business Percentages*

# Your Approach to a Small Business Office

- **The value of any specific office is hit or miss**
    - Very few are able to facilitate set-asides on behalf of small business
    - Identify if they have "influence" to facilitate small business Contracts
- **Talking with Small Business Office:**
    - Focus on the government / prospect – not your products and services
    - What are the current issues / requirements or who would know?
    - Excellent source of information on points of contact
    - Excellent source of information on type of programs you can support
    - Provide copy of your Capability Statement
- **You must identify if they have "influence" to facilitate SB Contracts**
- *Excellent* **source of information on points of contact**
- **Some are excellent at facilitating set-asides – but think this through:**
    - If you hear of a Sources Sought (SS) or RFI, get involved immediately
    - SS and RFIs are part of the pre-acquisition phase
    - Government may or may not have an idea of which vendors can support
- **You still position for that set-aside:**
    - Work on building a relationship with the prospect, regardless of the opportunity
    - Your objective is to shape future opportunities
    - You want to shape and position before opportunities enter acquisition

# Interacting With Office of Small Business Programs (OSBP)

- **Schedule a Meeting**
    - Focus 100% on the Service or Agency (they will want to focus on you)
    - Use OSBP to help build and manage content in your CRM
    - The OSBP is not a buyer or end-user – just a facilitator
- **Provide Copy of Tailored Opportunity Capabilities Brief**
    - First 2 slides are NAICS Codes, Socio-Economic Statuses, and Capabilities
    - Final 6 to 8 slides are mapping value and benefit to agency's requirements
    - Provide updated copy every six months
    - When possible, do not provide tailored brief until after meeting with a prospect

| Opportunity Capabilities Brief | | | | |
|---|---|---|---|---|
| **Phase** | **Document** | **Type** | **Audience** | **Value** |
| 45% Pre-Acquisition 45% | Opportunity Capabilities Brief | | Prospects Partners SB Offices | **30 Minutes**<br><br>The power-horse of all MS PowerPoints<br><br>***Most useful*** capabilities brief<br><br>***Tailored*** to specific requirements of a specific agency |

*Table 36 - OSBP Opportunity Capabilities Brief*

# Getting Onsite / Field Employees To Support Sales

- **These are your onsite employees supporting current contracts**
- **One of the most difficult challenges for any business**
  - Onsite employees have access to customer management and challanges
  - Misperception – Non-Sales employees are not "wired" to "support" BD
- **Hire employees (Non Business Developers) with experience in:**
  - Capture Management
  - Requirements Collection
  - Scope Definition
  - Other Pre-Design Support  (very common for engineers)
- **The Solution – Position during hiring phase**
  - Target labor categories for site leaders, site coordinators, other senior positions
  - From the labor rate, identify annual salary range
  - Subtract $3,000 - $5,000 from that range
  - At end of salary negotiation, add a "reporting" requirement to job description
  - Inform individual that "you will add $4,000 to their salary" for weekly reports
  - Facilitated before offer letter is provided to candidate
- **The Solution – Quid-Pro-Quo**
  - Build a requirement into job description and map to salary

> "Mr. Layfer, we would like to add an additional requirement to this position's job description. Outside of the customer's requirements, we would like a weekly report, separate from any other reporting, that captures information on other projects being supported by other vendors, the customer's future direction, current problems or challenges facing the customer on your contract or other contracts, new architectural or IT related methodologies, and discussions about future potential projects or contracts.
>
> As a growing company, we recognize the importance of what *you will see and hear*. This type of information will help our company grow and remain competitive.
>
> Because this information is important to our corporate strategy, we are going to add $4,000 to your annual salary."

*Figure 61 - Email Example For Convincing Onsite Employees*

# Prospecting Methods

Sell in the government market for just a couple of weeks and you'll have more recommendations than you can count. You may start with the Procurement Technical Assistance Center; talk with the Director of a small business office for on of the agencies or militry commands; talk with colleagues, non-profits, and paid consultants. Everyone gives you some form of what you see in the graphic below.

Each of these prospecting methods provides some level of value. But the question is, "Which ones provide the most value and will help me win contracts faster than the rest?"

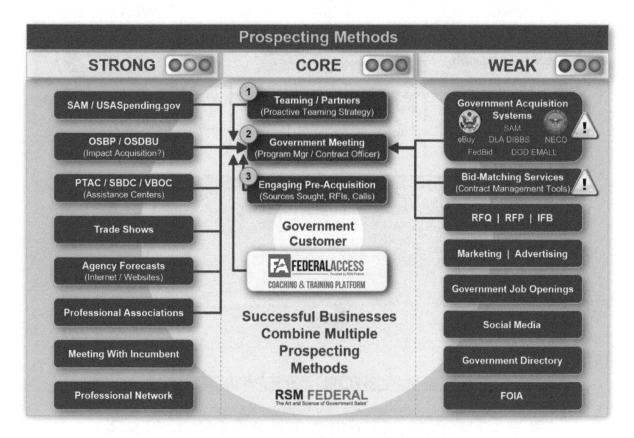

*Figure 62 - Prospecting Methods*

If the only methods you use are in the Weak column, you will not likely win many contracts or consistently win contracts. If you use the Strong methods, you may win one or two contracts but will not consistently win contracts. If you want to accelerate your sales, you must focus on the Core methods. Notice that most of the other methods map into these three. You must spend 80% of your time focused in pre-acquisition (before it's released on SAM.gov; you must speak with government employees; and the majority of companies must have a strong programmatic teaming strategy.

## Tactics and Strategies for Core Prospecting Methods

This manual is designed to be the most comprehensive educational deskside reference on the market. However, I can't put an hour long webinar of content into text. If you want to understand each of these prospecting methods, there is an excellent one hour video in Federal Access Coaching and Training Platform, from a live conference training event, that will walk you through each one.

*Figure 63 - Prospecting Training Video*

## 80% of Businesses Focus On Unqualified Opportunities *

- **Target opportunities which align with your strongest offerings**
    - Where you clearly understand or plan to understand the prospect's needs
- **Target agencies which are likely buyers of your solutions**
    - Discard all others – "Shotgun Sales" are rarely successful
- **Number of organizations you target is based on your team**
    - Only three to five major organizations per business developer
    - Each organization will have multiple subordinate agencies and opportunities
    - You target three to five in order to build the necessary relationships

* RSM Federal Study, February 2017 (updated)

## SAM.gov Only 10% of All Government Opportunities

 As discussed earlier in the Manual, most small businesses spend 80% of their time identifying opportunities in the acquisition phase (RFP already released). In fact, 90% of opportunities listed in SAM.gov and other systems are already in acquisition phase.

However, 90% of all market and sales opportunities are not on SAM.gov. Think of this from a business perspective, not a government sales perspective. The only time you see an opportunity for bid is after it's moved into the acquisition phase. As a result, 90% of your opportunities should be engaged pre-acquisition!

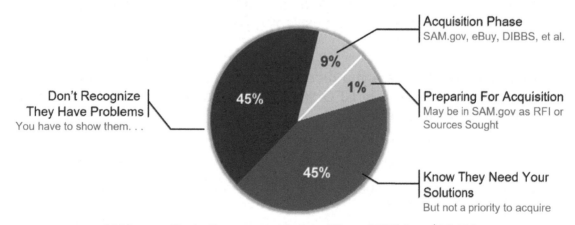

SAM.gov – Single Government Point of Entry (GPE) for >$25,000

*Figure 64 - SAM.gov Only 10% of Opportunities*

# Ghosting Requirements

You will often hear my team talking about ghosting throughout RSM Federal's ecosystem. We discuss it on our podcasts, in books, and it's tailored into the templates and strategies on the Federal Access Coaching and Training Platform.

Ghosting is one of the most powerful strategies you can use in government (and commercial) sales. One of the most comprehensive chapters in the book *An Insider's Guide to Winning Government Contracts* is on Ghosting. Rather than repeat that chapter, I'm going to provide the high-level overview. To read real-world examples of how you implement ghosting, head over to Amazon for the Insider's Guide.

## Overview

Ghosting has quite a few connotations. Our clients and members use a ghosting strategy that I developed in 2001.

Ghosting is based on the general business principle of positioning a company's value inside the prospect's decision cycle in order to influence an acquisition. There are four sub-activities:

1) Ghosting is positioning the value of your capabilities and differentiators in order to *marginalize your competition*.

2) Ghosting is an activity you perform in order to *bar-entry or decrease the perceived effectiveness* of your competition.

3) Ghosting is a process of taking your competition's weaknesses, tailoring your competencies to compensate, and positioning your strengths to *build a competitive advantage*.

4) Ghosting is a process where you *recommend information and value* that you want to have included in the RFP or RFQ. You do this in order to provide your company with a competitive advantage.

If we boil this down, there are two types of Ghosting:

1) Positioning your value, capabilities, differentiators, and past performance to marginalize your competition.

2) Positioning your competition's weaknesses though your strengths.

# Ghosting / Shaping Requirements

Example email following a discussion with a buyer or decision maker in order to ghost requirements that make you more competitive and to influence the RFP and acquisition.

---

John Breeze     Sent: November 14, 20xx   10:15am      **Pre-RFP Phase**

To: rjones@dhs.gov
Subject: Follow-Up

| Your Differentiators |
| --- |
| Manage Multiple Sites |
| Performance Based Contracts |
| Earned Value Management |
| Top Secret Facility Clearance |

Dear Mr Jones,

I wanted to thank you again for discussing the future acquisition for the DHS Network Operations Center. You were very helpful in outlining each of the anticipated task areas. Based on our meeting, we would like to confirm the four task area groups (TAGs) envisioned for the RFP:

Planned
Task Area Group 1: Enterprise Network Service Desk
Task Area Group 2: Desktop Remote Administration
Task Area Group 3: Software Support
Task Area Group 4: Network Connectivity

Based on our understanding of DHS' requirements, we also recommend three additional capabilities:

Recommendation 1: Recommend that one or two of the past performances require that the prime have experience managing multiple sites under a performance based contract. Having managed multiple sites will ensure less down-time and improve DHS's current problems with communication.

Recommendation 2: From the standpoint of a dispersed network management team, providing best value to DHS can be measured and tracked via Earned Value Management (EVM). The ability to capture these metrics will mitigate DHS' current problems with scope creep and related expenditures.

Recommendation 3: You indicated a Secret Facility Clearance would be necessary to mange this contract. However, several of your networks outside this effort are Top Secret. From our experience with DoD, being able to communicate with other network administrators would provide immense value for current and future challenges and upgrades. In 2008, you experienced two outages as a result of this communication silo.

Sincerely,
John

---

# The First Call

- First words might be "Maybe you can help me. . .I'm looking for. . ."
- Be confident - no hesitation
- Seek to quickly build rapport
- Match and mirror the volume and speed of their voice
- Be genuine, be yourself
- Ask several questions the prospect knows the answers to
- Build trust. Be brutally honest. Set accurate expectations.
- Address prospects formally until asked to use their first names

# Focus on Prospect - Not Your Capabilities

- **Discuss value & benefit of your solutions but *focus* on the Prospect**
  - Have you met the prospect?
  - Have you performed "Early Engagement?" (before RFPs are released)
  - Understand the incumbents strengths and weaknesses?
  - Understand the customer's challenges, problems, issues?
  - Understand the customer's strategic direction and vision?
- **Once you *understand* the customer:**
  - You've already *branded* yourself personally
  - *Differentiate* your competencies specifically to the prospects opportunities
  - *Shape* the requirements
  - *Ghost* the weaknesses of the competition
  - *Position* the *value* of your solutions

# Meeting with a Prospect

- You're not meeting the prospect to sell your solutions
- Your focus is understanding organization, requirements, and challenges
- Your focus is building rapport and collecting intelligence
- Once you have a better understanding, you start mapping to your solutions
- Don't start with the features you provide, *even if they ask for them*!

- Ensure your initial "Elevator Speech" includes benefit statements
- Your 45 Second Pitch should be tailored to the prospect
- What is your "Wow Factor"?

# "The Most Powerful Sales Question"

## Scenario

You're on a call or in a face to face meeting with Ms. Janice Smith, a Program Manager for one of the Divisions in the Army's XVIII Airborne Corps.

The discussion is going well, you've asked the right questions, and you now understand one of their core challenges which you believe your company can resolve.

### *What do you say?*

Most business developers say, *"That's what we do!"*

Which is exactly what the other one hundred companies told her.

## Response

"Ms. Smith,

**1** **we solved this problem or one very similar . . .**

**2** **for Anthem Blue Cross / Blue Shield**

**3** **at their national resource delivery division**

**4** **in Chicago**

**5** **8 months ago**

**6** **If we can get on your schedule in the next couple weeks, we'll bring our project manager who managed the project to explain how we did it . . .**

**7** *Would that be fair?*

---

# How Well Do You Understand Your Prospect?

Over the next several pages we are going to discuss how well you know or should know your prospects and customers.

| | How Well Do You Know and Understand Your Prospect? |
|---|---|
| 1 | Fill out a "Bulls-Eye" Decision Support Template (DST)<br>*Although the Bulls-Eye can be downloaded from Federal Access, we strongly recommend Zoho, HubSpot, or Salesforce* |
| 2 | Identify prospect's key players and their roles |
| 3 | Identify prospect's programs you want to target |
| 4 | Identify current vendors / contractors supporting these programs |
| 5 | What is the prospect's mission and requirements |
| 6 | What are the prospect's "hot-buttons" and "pain points" |
| 7 | What contract vehicle does the prospect prefer |
| 8 | What are the likely evaluation factors |
| 9 | What is the prospect's agenda underlying a specific opportunity |
| 10 | What is the prospect's budget for a specific opportunity |
| 11 | Does the prospect have a "propensity" to use small business? |
| 12 | What are the prospects priorities? |

*Table 37 - How Well Do You Understand Your Prospect?*

# Components of Customer Relationship Management *

- **Front Office Operations**
  - Direct interaction with prospect or customer (meetings, phone, email)
  - Business Development, Sales, Management
- **Back Office Operations**
  - Operations that affect activities of the front office
  - Billing, Marketing, Finance, Recruiting, Proposal
- **Business Relationships**
  - Interactions with other companies or partners

- External network supports both front and bck office operations

- **Data Analysis**
  - Analyze key CRM data to plan target-marketing campaigns
  - Conceive business strategies
  - Judge success of market penetration (number and type of customers, revenue)

\* http://en.wikipedia.org/wiki/Customer_Relationship_Management

# What Is Your Customer Relationship Management Plan?

- **If you don't have one - your competition will take your current business**
  - Customer didn't exercise the option year
  - Early contract recompetition
  - The RFP for the recompetition has requirements *you've never seen*

- **What is a Customer Relationship Management Plan?**
  - Combination of policies, processes, and strategies
  - Unifies customer interactions
  - Provides a means to track customer information
  - Involves use of technology to attract new and profitable customers
  - Used to form tighter bonds with existing customers
  - Use of marketing to augment revenue producing activities

- **A CRM:**
  - Protects your current contracts
  - Keeps you focused to win new business

- **Educate and provide value outside the requirements of your contract**
  - Similar activities as the ones you will perform as part of your Market Sales Strategy
  - This is what positions your company to get new contracts
  - Monthly, quarterly, and annual education campaigns

- **Hyper-Responsiveness**
  - There is always one phone number they can reach 24 x 7 x 365

- When a customer emails, you may call (vs email) to confirm receipt
- If there is a problem - your focus is the customer, not your company

- **Consistent Relationship-Building Activities**
  - Build rapport outside the workplace
  - Identify their hobbies and extra-curricular activities
  - Invite them to a social event as long as you don't pay (5 C.F.R. 2635)

# Third Party CRM Systems

- **Every company needs a CRM solution**
  - Entrepreneurs, Startups, Small Businesses
  - Prospect information easily tracked, maintained, and organized
- **Why is CRM Important?**
  - Business developer quits and you have no idea who she has been talking to
  - No contact information for pipeline opportunities
  - Ensure that business developers are targeting the right organizations
  - You get a call six months later and you can't remember the specifics

- **Sampling of CRM Solutions ***
  - Salesforce
  - Zoho
  - HubSpot
  - InfusionSoft
  - CapsuleCRM
  - WORKetc
  - Microsoft Dynamics
  - SugarCRM (Open Source)
  - BridgeCRM
  - ACT

* Listed systems are not recommendations

# How Do You Manage Prospect & Customer Information?

## Daily Capture Management

- **Which do you use?**
    - Customer Relationship Management (CRM) Software (e.g. Zoho)
    - Microsoft Outlook
    - Excel Spreadsheets
    - Sticky Notes

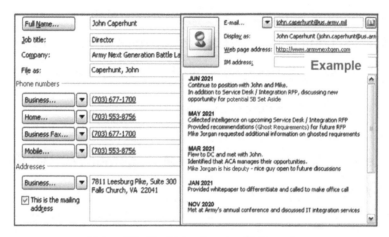

*Figure 65 - Capturing Prospect Information*

# The Bulls-Eye Decision Support System (BDSS)

## Overview

- **The following pages outline the Bulls-Eye Decision Support System**

- **If you can afford a CRM System – *Pay For One***

- **If you can not afford one, the Bulls-Eye provides similar capabilities and helps you think more critically about what types of information you should research and have on-hand**

- **The Bulls-Eye Decision Support System (BDSS):**

  - Provides historical background on opportunity status

  - Synchronizes contact information with specific opportunities

  - Outlines prospect initiatives, strategies, and priorities

  *It does not matter what system you use. . .*
  *Just ensure you have a system that collects the information you need*

- **The BDSS is a Customer Relationship Management (CRM) System**

- **The Bulls-Eye ensures that you:**

  - No Goldfish Syndrome = "Oh! Look a castle! Oh Look a castle! (Opportunity)"

  - Identify decision makers, influencers, program managers and contract officers

  - Understand the agency's goals, vision, and strategy

  - Identify budget and which subordinate agencies have the money

  - Identify which small and large Primes have contracts

- **The Bulls-Eye is a tool that supports:**

  - Market Sales Strategy
  - Prospecting
  - Teaming

- **Where Do You Start?**

  - Identify your Annual Target List (Strategic)

## The RSM Federal Ecosystem

There is another resource in the GovCon Ecosystem called *An Insider's Guide To Winning Government Contracts* that I also wrote. You'll find it on Amazon. This Manual is a Deskside Reference, not meant to be read cover to cover. The objective of this Manual is to provide you with a comprehensive understanding of government sales and force you to think about the business processes your company must use to successfully and consistently win government contracts.

An Insider's Guide provides the mental aspect; how you should approach the market! And then you have the Federal Access Coaching and Training Platform with the templates and step-by-step strategies you need to execute the concepts in this Manual and the book the Insider's Guide.

What is not covered in these resources is then covered in the Podcast Game Changers for Government Contracts on iTunes and Soundcloud.

Finally, what if you don't learn this way? What if you want a coach to simplify the process? Then you work with one of our certified coaches.

When you combine all of these resources, you have the most comprehensive coaching and training ecosystem in federal space. It's why our clients and Federal Access members have won billions of dollars in government contracts.

*Figure 66 - RSM Ecosystem Resources*

# Annual Strategic Target List

This is the first step in developing any sales strategy. How do you identify your targets? You figure it out by checking the "Propensity" with federal agencies and military commands for what you sell.

*Propensity*
*Who buys what you sell, how much, and how often*

In order to perform Propensity, you must pull millions of fields of data from USASpending.gov or SAM.gov's Data Bank. It's not hard. You simply have to learn how to do it.

The remainder of this section on the Bullseye decision support system is an example of what one looks like using Microsoft Excel. It'll look much different using a third party CRM. But I'm showing you the MS Excel version because you'll be able to immediately understand what it looks like, the information you have to collect, and how to works together.

| Annual Strategic Business Development Targets | | |
|---|---|---|
| # | Agency | Prime or Subcontracting Strategy |
| 1 | Department of Homeland Security (DHS) | **Indirect** (subcontract) |
| 2 | US Department of Agriculture (USDA) | **Hybrid** (prime and subcontract) |
| 3 | US Transportation Command (USTRANSCOM) | **Direct** (prime) |
| 4 | Air Mobility Command (AMC) | **Hybrid** (prime and subcontract) |
| 5 | Internal Revenue Service (IRS) | **Direct** (prime) |

*Table 38 - Annual Target List*

These Five Targets have more than 27 major agencies or commands. You have to also select a focus within the major agencies.

# Panel A – Overview

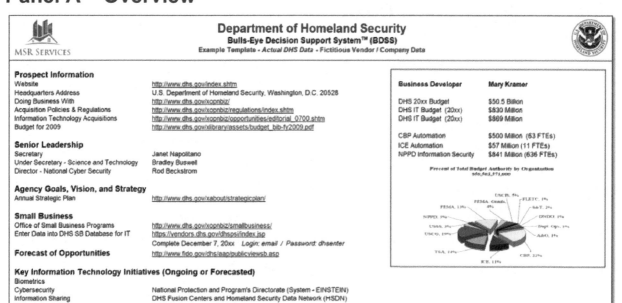

### Department of Homeland Security
Bulls-Eye Decision Support System™ (BDSS)
Example Template - *Actual DHS Data* - *Fictitious Vendor / Company Data*

**MSR SERVICES**

**Prospect Information**

| | |
|---|---|
| Website | http://www.dhs.gov/index.shtm |
| Headquarters Address | U.S. Department of Homeland Security, Washington, D.C. 20528 |
| Doing Business With | http://www.dhs.gov/xopnbiz/ |
| Acquisition Policies & Regulations | http://www.dhs.gov/xopnbiz/regulations/index.shtm |
| Information Technology Acquisitions | http://www.dhs.gov/xopnbiz/opportunities/editorial_0700.shtm |
| Budget for 2009 | http://www.dhs.gov/xlibrary/assets/budget_bib-fy2009.pdf |

**Senior Leadership**

| | |
|---|---|
| Secretary | Janet Napolitano |
| Under Secretary - Science and Technology | Bradley Buswell |
| Director - National Cyber Security | Rod Beckstrom |

**Agency Goals, Vision, and Strategy**

| | |
|---|---|
| Annual Strategic Plan | http://www.dhs.gov/xabout/strategicplan/ |

**Small Business**

| | |
|---|---|
| Office of Small Business Programs | http://www.dhs.gov/xopnbiz/smallbusiness/ |
| Enter Data into DHS SB Database for IT | https://vendors.dhs.gov/dhspsi/index.jsp |
| | Complete December 7, 20xx  *Login: email / Password: dhsenter* |

**Forecast of Opportunities**  http://www.fido.gov/dhs/aap/publicviewsb.asp

**Key Information Technology Initiatives (Ongoing or Forecasted)**

| | |
|---|---|
| Biometrics | |
| Cybersecurity | National Protection and Program's Directorate (System - EINSTEIN) |
| Information Sharing | DHS Fusion Centers and Homeland Security Data Network (HSDN) |
| Network Consolidation | 1,780 Networks consolidated |

| **Business Developer** | **Mary Kramer** |
|---|---|
| DHS 20xx Budget | $50.5 Billion |
| DHS IT Budget (20xx) | $830 Million |
| DHS IT Budget (20xx) | $869 Million |
| CBP Automation | $500 Million (63 FTEs) |
| ICE Automation | $57 Million (11 FTEs) |
| NPPD Information Security | $841 Million (636 FTEs) |

*Percent of Total Budget Authority by Organization*

*Figure 67 - Bulls Eye Panel A*

# Panel B – Agency Priorities and Initiatives

**Annual Initiatives for Five Agency Priorities (Datamined for IT initiatives and Qualification)**

**1. Protect our Nation from dangerous people**

| | | |
|---|---|---|
| Western Hemisphere Travel Initiative (WHTI) | $107 Million for Infrastructure and Technology | Customs and Border Patrol (CBP) |
| E-Verify Initiative | $100 Million for automated system | Citizenship and Immigration Services (ICE) |
| Modernization of IT Systems | $57 Million for automation modernization | Citizenship and Immigration Services (ICE) |
| SBInet for Border Security | $775 Million and 15 FTEs | Customs and Border Patrol (CBP) |
| Cyber Crime | $5.7 Million and 20 FTEs | Citizenship and Immigration Services (ICE) |

**2. Protect our National from dangerous goods**

**3. Protect Critical Infrastructure**

| | | |
|---|---|---|
| Security Management | $7.1 Million and 19 FTEs | Citizenship and Immigration Services (ICE) |
| Co-Location of ICE Facilities | $12.3 Million and 1 FTE | Citizenship and Immigration Services (ICE) |
| Modernize & Integrate FEMA IT Systems | $20.7 Million and 0 FTE | Federal Emergency Management Agency (FEMA) |
| US-CERT | $81.3 Million and 23 FTEs | National Protection and Programs Directorate (NPPD) |
| Control Systems Security Program | $6 Million and 1 FTE | National Protection and Programs Directorate (NPPD) |
| Next Generation Networks | $34.9 Million and 0 FTE | National Protection and Programs Directorate (NPPD) |

**4. Build a nimble effective emergency response system and culture of preparedness**

| | | |
|---|---|---|
| Vision - Shape the Workforce | $64.5 Million for Workforce Program | Federal Emergency Management Agency (FEMA) |
| DHS Grant Programs | $2.2 Billion for State and Local | Homeland Security (DHS) |

**5. Strengthen and unify DHS Operations and Managemnt**

| | | |
|---|---|---|
| Transformational and Systems Consolidation | $15.5 Million to integrate financial systems | DHS CFO |
| Analysis & Operations (A&O) | State & Local Fusion Center (SLFC) Program | Homeland Security (DHS) |
| National Operations Center (NOC) | Improved data infusion, consolidated data repository | DHS Office of Operations Coordination (OPS) |

*Figure 68 - Bulls Eye Panel B*

# Panel C – Organization Chart

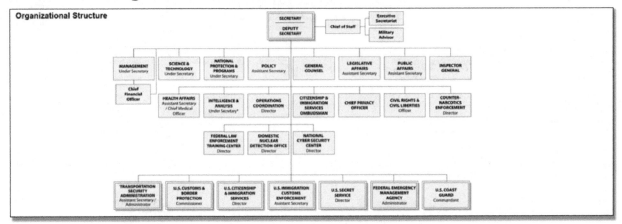

*Figure 69 - Bulls Eye Panel C*

# Panel D – Points of Contact

| Organization | Contact | Phone | Email | Address |
|---|---|---|---|---|
| **Headquarters, Department of Homeland Security** | | | | * Fictitious |
| OSDBU - Main Number | | (202) 447-xxxx | | |
| OSDBU - Office of Procurement | | | | |
| SB Specialist | Trish Wyatt | (202) 447-xxxx | patricia.wyatt@dhs.gov | 245 Murray Drive SW (Bldg. 410), Room: 3523-28, Washington, DC 20528 |
| SB Specialist | Faye Jones | (202) 447-xxxx | faye.jones@dhs.gov | 245 Murray Drive SW (Bldg. 410), Room: 3523-28, Washington, DC 20528 |
| SB Advisor | Mary Ellen Dorsey | (202) 447-xxxx | maryellen.dorsey@dhs.gov | 245 Murray Drive SW (Bldg. 410), Washington, DC 20528 |
| Mentor Protégé Program | Angela Williams | (202) 447-xxxx | angela.williams@dhs.gov | 245 Murray Drive SW (Bldg. 410), Washington, DC 20528 |
| SBA Procurement Rep for DHS | Bernard Durham | (202) 447-xxxx | bernard.durham@hq.dhs.gov | 245 Murray Drive SW (Bldg. 410), Washington, DC 20528 |
| WOSB Advocate | Wendy Hill | (202) 447-xxxx | wendy.hill@dhs.gov | 245 Murray Drive SW (Bldg. 410), Washington, DC 20528 |
| VOSB Outreach Director | Dan Sturdivant | (202) 447-xxxx | dan.sturdivant@dhs.gov | 245 Murray Drive SW (Bldg. 410), Washington, DC 20528 |
| SBIR Program Director | Lisa Sobolewski | (202) 447-xxxx | elissa.sobolewski@dhs.gov | DHS S&T/HSARPA/SBIR, Attn: (Lisa Sobolewski), Washington, DC 20528 |
| Contracting Officer | | | | |
| | | | | |
| **Large System Integrators with Strong Presence \*** | | | | * Fictitious |
| SAIC | DHS Capture Manager and Program Manager | | | |
| | John Smith | (202) xxx-xxxx | jsmith@saic.com | 11251 Roger Bacon Drive MS R-4-1, Reston, Virginia 20190 |
| Northrup Grumman | DHS Capture Manager and Program Manager | | | |
| | Mary Jones | (202) xxx-xxxx | mjones@ngc.com | 7575 Colshire Dr, Mc Lean, VA 22102-7508 |
| Lockheed Martin | DHS Capture Manager and Program Manager | | | |
| | James Martin | (202) xxx-xxxx | jmartin@lmc.com | 1725 Jefferson Davis Highway Suite 403 Arlington, VA 22202 |
| | | | | |
| **Small Businesses with Strong Presence** | | | | |
| BI Methods | Vice President of Operations and Business Development | | | |
| | Jango Unwalla | (703) 889-8500 | junwalla@bimethods.com | 12310 Pinecrest Road, Suite 202, Reston, VA 20191 |
| CSSS | Senior Business Development Manager | | | |
| | Teri Lesicko | (202) 639-5103 | tlesicko@csss.net | 729 15th St. NW, Suite 600, Washington, DC 20005 |
| Global Systems Technologies | Director Business Development | | | |
| | Ozzie Gerald | (215) 579-8200 | ozzieg@gstpa.com | 109 Floral Vale Blvd, Yardley, PA 19067 |

*Figure 70 - Bulls Eye Panel D*

# Panel E – Targeted Subordinate Agencies or Commands

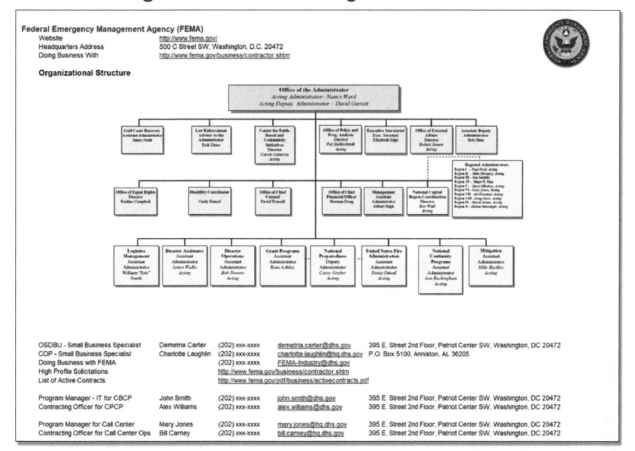

Figure 71 - Bulls Eye Panel E

# Panel F – Problems and Challenges Identified During Meetings

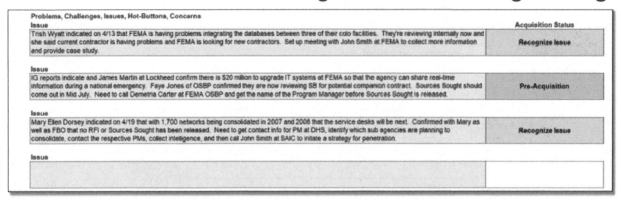

| Problems, Challenges, Issues, Hot-Buttons, Concerns | |
| --- | --- |
| **Issue** | **Acquisition Status** |
| Trish Wyatt indicated on 4/13 that FEMA is having problems integrating the databases between three of their colo facilities. They're reviewing internally now and she said current contractor is having problems and FEMA is looking for new contractors. Set up meeting with John Smith at FEMA to collect more information and provide case study. | **Recognize Issue** |
| **Issue** | |
| IG reports indicate and James Martin at Lockheed confirm there is $20 million to upgrade IT systems at FEMA so that the agency can share real-time information during a national emergency. Faye Jones of OSBP confirmed they are now reviewing SB for potential companion contract. Sources Sought should come out in Mid July. Need to call Demetria Carter at FEMA OSBP and get the name of the Program Manager before Sources Sought is released. | **Pre-Acquisition** |
| **Issue** | |
| Mary Ellen Dorsey indicated on 4/19 that with 1,700 networks being consolidated in 2007 and 2008 that the service desks will be next. Confirmed with Mary as well as FBO that no RFI or Sources Sought has been released. Need to get contact info for PM at DHS, identify which sub agencies are planning to consolidate, contact the respective PMs, collect intelligence, and then call John Smith at SAIC to initate a strategy for penetration. | **Recognize Issue** |
| **Issue** | |
| | |

*Figure 72 - Bulls Eye Panel F*

# Panel G – Draft Win Themes

May or may not be specific to an RFP.

**Draft Win Themes**
- Ongoing process during Market Penetration Strategy
- *Transferred to Proposal Team Plan when RFP is released*

| | Prospect Objectives | Approach | Value and Benefit | Proof |
| --- | --- | --- | --- | --- |
| 1 | Provide experienced contractors to minimize change orders for surge or unanticipated events | Multi-Disciplined Staffing Approach (MDSA) | Cross-Functional Capabilities<br>Alternates and Backup<br>Save overtime $$$ | AFMC<br>USACOE<br>St. Louis Orthopedic Authority |
| 2 | Consolidate network operations from five to one site for centralized operations and management under a Performance-Based Contract | Communicate National versus Regional using two performance-based contracts with DISA in California and St. Louis | Experience managing centralized network operations<br>Successfully manage multiple sites across the country today<br>Already perform work at 4 of 5 geographical locations | AFMC<br>AMC<br>Department of Transportation |
| 3 | Close interaction with the OCIO's office for current and future IT planning requirements | Have two government and two commercial contracts where we work with and provide value to the CIO | Strong competency in helping CIOs manage IT direction | Department of Labor<br>HUD<br>St. Louis Orthopedic Authority<br>Regional Lumber Associates |
| 4 | | | | |
| 5 | | | | |

*Figure 73 - Bulls Eye Panel G*

# System For Award Management (SAM.gov) - How Should I Use SAM?

- **You need to know about opportunities *before* they list on SAM**

    - Identify opportunities as part of your Market Sales Strategy (MSS)

    - It is okay to bid on various opportunities when you see it for the first time on SAM. These are tactical opportunities. But you still need to focus your business development processes on pre-acquisition activities.

    - If a teaming partner asks you to team - find out when they first heard of the opportunity. Only SAM and no other market intelligence on the opportunity?

    - There is no firm rule here. However, if every RFP you bid on has no intelligence other than what you see in SAM, chances are you haven't won many contracts.

- **Strategic Information For Future Opportunities**

    - SAM (just like SAM's Data Bank - discussed later) is an excellent source of information to educate yourself about the market and agencies.

- **SAM is all opportunities > $25,000**

| What You Can Find on SAM.gov (Sampling) |
| --- |
| Which agencies have a propensity to release RFPs with your NAICS codes |
| Agency Contracting, Program Management, and other key contact information |
| Which agencies have a propensity for using small business |
| Which agencies use draft solicitation for RFPs during acquisition |
| Which agencies release solicitations for work in your State |
| Examples of current RFPs to create proposal templates for future opportunities |
| The type of acquisition strategies common to a specific agency |

*Table 39 - Information on SAM.gov*

# Identifying and Qualifying Opportunities

At some point in time, every organization your company targets will need your products or services. *"No . . . simply means Not Now"*

- **Identifying opportunities – Easiest activity**
- **Qualifying opportunities – Greatest challenge**
  - Feel overwhelmed
  - Spend enormous amount of time on losing proposals
  - Intimidated by the government market or other companies
  - Fail to understand the government's acquisition process and methodology
- **Process and Methodology**
  - Understand key tactics required to *position* the *value* of your solutions
  - Proven tactics to take advantage of *qualified* opportunities
- **Prospecting - all activities that get you in front of the prospect**
  - Documentation and marketing collateral do not replace the necessity for face to face meetings and talking on the phone

# 50% New Business From Current Customers

- **Poor customer service and you go out of business**
  - Includes your helpdesk, managers, PMs, and BDMs
- **Strong customer service can increase revenue by 50%**
  - Easier and Faster than new prospects
  - Upsell and Cross-Sell
- **Provide a valuable Case-Study every quarter**
- **Cite them on your website as a market leader**
- **Invite them to sit with you on trade-show panels**
- **Treat them like your company depends on them; It does!**
- **Don't get comfortable – Maintain start-up company mentality**

# How Well Do You Know Your Current Customers?

Understanding your current contracts and customers ensures that you understand the value your company, products, and services provide. This is why we perform the Value-Mapping process.

| | How Well Do You Know Your Current Customers? |
|---|---|
| 1 | Daily responsibilities for each employee |
| 2 | Name all systems / platforms / programs your employees work on or support |
| 3 | Name all systems and programs that are impacted by your contract |
| 4 | List all internal customers / users who access or use data from systems / platforms |
| 5 | List all external customers / users who access or use data from systems / platforms |
| 6 | Identify the federal programs which these systems / programs support |
| 7 | Which networks do your employees work on (NIPR, SIPR, JWICS, etc.) |
| 8 | Which contract vehicles are most utilized at each location |
| 9 | What are your customers requirements over the next 12 months |
| 10 | What problems do they have, regardless of your specific contract |
| 11 | Does the prospect have a "propensity" to use small business or specific set-asides |

*Table 40 - How Well Do You Understand Your Customers*

# The Cold Request To Bid

Nothing feels better than getting a call from a contracting officer asking you to bid or write a proposal. Most companies drop everything they're doing because the government came to them! Not to take away from the potential value of winning that opportunity, but you must understand business strategy and the federal acquisition process and regulations.

We know that there is generally a rule of two. At least two companies need to submit a proposal. Yes, there are exceptions, such as the one for GSA Schedules where the government utilizes the eBuy system. For generally, they need two proposals.

What if the program manager went to the contracting officer and said, "Hey, I want this company to work this project. We've contracted with them before and they have what I need. Do me a favor? Call one or two other companies and get some bids so we meet the competition requirements." You then receive one of those calls or emails. In this example, that call you received doesn't appear as awesome as it first did.

I'm not saying this happens often. But this is one example of why you need to ask some questions. Let's be realistic. The government wants you to jump, to drop what you're doing, and spend the time, money, and manpower on an opportunity you've never heard about until that call. From a business perspective, no matter what the regulations say, you should attempt to force the contracting officer to answer certain questions. All throughout this Manual and the other resources, templates, and strategies across RSM Federal's ecosystem, we consistently focus on pre-acquisition activities. Why? Because that's how you successfully and consistently win contracts.

The call from the contracting officer is likely after the RFP has been released. Consider why you are willing to treat this opportunity differently from any other opportunity from the perspective of a bid – no bid decision. I'm not saying don't engage it. I'm saying make sure you, to the best of your ability, that you have a chance of being competitive!

- **Customer or prospect asks you to bid on an *unexpected* RFP**

    - Is the procurement decision already made?

    - Ask how many companies were invited to bid? *If they won't say – they may have called several dozen companies*. Now consider your competitive position.


- **Always ask the contracting officer to allow you to speak with the manager**

    - If they so no and you identify that there's not enough information for you to be competitive, then decline, via email, to the contracting officer.

    - Why would you bid on an opportunity where you have no relationship?

    - Why would you bid without influencing the prospects vision or requirements?

    - Say to the CO, "Unrealistic for your company to bid with lack of information"

    - Exception: But if you have a relationship, then bid!

- **If the RFP has not been released:**
  - Immediately ask for a meeting with the government program manager to ascertain:
    - ➢ Challenges, problems, requirements
    - ➢ Prospect vision, objectives, strategy
    - ➢ Outline your company's value and benefits for competitive advantage
    - ➢ Ghost your competition's weaknesses to minimize their advantage
  - If you can not get a meeting – you have to evaluate your competitive position

---

John Breeze          Sent: November 14, 20xx  10:15am          **Pre-RFP Phase**

To: rsmith@dhs.gov
Subject: Meeting with Program Manager

Ms. Smith,

Thank you for the opportunity to submit a proposal for the DHS Network Operations Center. It is our practice that we only respond to RFPs where we have the opportunity to speak with the assigned program manager or a member of his or her team. This provides us with an opportunity to understand the direction, challenges, and project vision. As a result, DHS will receive a strong proposal followed by a more successful implementation.

If you will introduce me to the Program Manager or his team, prior to RFP release, we will invest the time and resources to respond to the RFP.

In the interim, enclosed is our Opportunity Capability Brief which cross-walks our competencies and past performance to our understanding of the requirements as outlined in the Sources Sought. Thank you again and if you have any questions, please don't hesitate to call.

Sincerely,

John

*Figure 74 - Email Response to Cold Request to Bid*

# Your Sales Pipeline

There are entire books dedicated to managing a sales pipeline. In this chapter, we're going to cover the basic principles that I recommend you focus on. Interestingly, these principles are market agnostic. You may be learning them for government sales but they are just as applicable to commercial sales.

- **Hitting and exceeding your quota requires pipeline management**

- **Pipeline Overview**
  - The key to any pipeline is the consistency of your metrics and milestones
  - In general, a well managed pipeline yields an average of 20% to 25% revenue
    - Pipeline = $1,000,000    $200,000 to $250,000 revenue
    - Pipeline = $8,000,000    $1,600,000 to $2,000,000 revenue

- **Opportunity Pipeline**

| Tactics vs Strategic Opportunities | | |
|---|---|---|
| **Tactical** | 1 - 12 Months | 80% Focus |
| **Short Term** | 12 - 24 Months | 15% Focus |
| **Strategic** | 24 – 36 Months | 5% Focus |

*Table 41 - Tactical and Strategic Opportunities*

- **Your Pipeline should answer the following questions:**
  - Do you have enough opportunities to make Tactical and Short-Term revenue?
  - When will each opportunity close and how much will book?
  - How much is anticipated to book at the end of each quarter?

## The Pipeline is a Decision Support System (DSS)

- **A strong pipeline will provide 'laser-focus' for Sales and Management**
  - Cross-walk opportunities to your Market Sales Strategy
  - A solid list of opportunities which other internal business units can support
  - Synchronizes BD, Marketing, Recruiting, CFO, and other Management
  - Utilizes drop-down selection whenever possible (minimize errors)

- **Dashboard that consolidates the data and information**
  - Many commercial CRM solutions provide pipeline solutions (if you want a recommendation, look at Zoho, HubSpot, and SalesForce).

- Automatic generation of statistics to augment financial planning
- Anticipated revenue by quarter
- Snapshot of how your employees are progressing
- Value of opportunities based on the level of penetration into every organization
- Number of proposals in the next two, four, or six months
- Contracts won
- Identifies market and vertical (DoD, Federal, Commercial)
- Identifies contract type and set-asides

## Your Sales Dashboard

Let's take a moment to clarify what you see below in the example dashboard versus what you will see in a Customer Relationship Management (CRM) system. Many companies utilize systems like Zoho and HubSpot to manage their pipelines. They are excellent, cost effective (not expensive), and provide strong baselines for you to manage from.

However, more than half of our clients use a Microsoft Excel workbook that we developed at RSM Federal. I won't go into extensive detail on it, simply providing a graphical snapshot of what it looks like. If you currently use a third party CRM but like what you see in our Pipeline and Dashboard tool, feel free to download it and test it. Some companies simply aren't ready for an online CRM. Simply using Microsoft Excel makes them feel for comfortable.

That said, even though I developed the Pipeline and Dashboard tool, I always recommend that companies with multiple business developers strongly consider using a third-party online CRM.

# Example Sales Dashboard

Figure 75 - Sales Dashboard

# Your Pipeline

If you're set on using Microsoft Excel, then don't consider using any template other than RSM Federal's Pipeline and Dashboard. If you use our pipeline tool, here's a graphic of what the pipeline looks like.

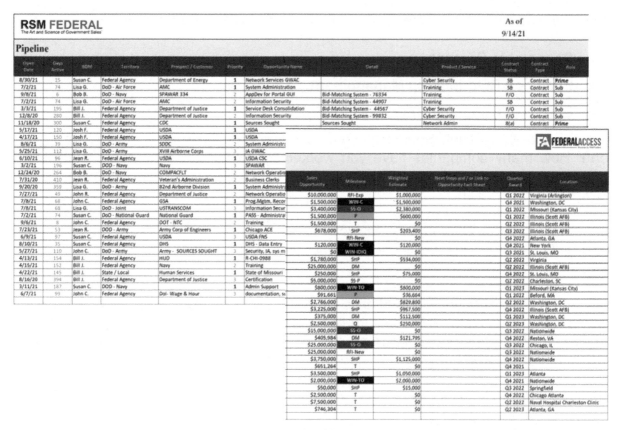

*Figure 76 - Pipeline*

# Pipeline Milestones

Every major pipeline tool, whether ours or third party CRMs, utilizes "Stages." Simply, just because you found an opportunity worth $1 million in SAM.gov doesn't mean it's worth a million in your pipeline! Have you spoken to a government decision maker about that opportunity? If yes, then it's worth 30% of $1,000,000 → $300,000. Are you in the Proposal phase? If yes, then it's worth 40% of $1,000,000 → $400,000. Are you optimistic about being awarded the contract? Then it's worth 70% of $1,000,000 → $700,000.

- **Repeatable Process**
- **Focus on Relationship Management**
- **Supports Company CFO Projections**

This is a bloody brilliant method of understanding exactly what your pipeline is *really* worth. How many companies have you worked for or current own where there are 60 opportunities on the pipeline worth $3.2 billion? This means absolutely nothing to you. It provide little to no value.

But, what if every opportunity in your pipeline was weighted, by phase, where opportunities without any intelligence, without any discussions with the government, have a weighted value of zero dollars?

Both RSM Federal's pipeline and third-party pipelines calculate your weighted values automatically. If you look at the picture of the dashboard earlier in the chapter, you'll see weighted percentages and dollar amounts on the left side. *This ensures you are truly realistic about the worth of your opportunities.*

Imagine going into a sales meeting and you are managing a sales team and you say:

> *"Okay, Sally, you have six opportunities in the 'Territory' phase. This means we don't have any intelligence yet, no discussions with potential teaming partners, and we have yet to reach out and talk to the government buyer. What are your next steps on each of these?"*

This facilitates responsibility and accountability. You're asking Sally to do one of the most important activities for a business developer → ***Walking opportunities through the pipeline so that you are more and more competitive.***

If you are interested in learning more about the concept of "Walking opportunities through your pipeline," read Chapter 10 in *An Insider's Guide To Winning Government Contracts* on Amazon. The entire chapter is dedicated to it.

To reiterate, RSM Federal is a GovCon Ecosystem of resources and industry best practices for government contractors. You've spent the money and time learning from this Manual, do not stop there! Buy the book above and join Federal Access. You will then have EVERY resource our company bares on the market.

| Weighted Pipeline Milestones | | |
|---|---|---|
| Pipeline Code | Phase | Weighted % |
| T | Territory | 0% |
| DNQ | Does Not Qualify | 0% |
| Q | Qualified | 10% |
| DM | Decision Maker / Champion | 30% |
| SHP | Shaping Requirements / Influencing the Acquisition | 30% |
| RFI-New | RFI or Sources Sought – Not Expected | 0% |
| RFI-Exp | RFI or Sources Sought – Expected Release | 10% |
| P | Proposal Phase | 40% |
| SS-O | Source Selection – Optimistic | 70% |
| SS-P | Source Selection – Pessimistic | 40% |
| WIN-C | Contract Win | 100% |
| WIN-IDIQ | IDIQ Contract Win | 100% |
| WIN-TO | Task Order Win | 100% |
| Lost | Lost Award to Competition | 0% |
| Cancel | Opportunity Cancelled | 0% |

*Table 42 - Weighted Pipeline Milestones*

- **If your objective is to increase revenue by $5 Million**
  - You must have at least ***$20 Million*** in ***Weighted Estimate*** (not pipeline value)
  - If we are in a recession and your commercial contracts are in jeopardy, you have to increase your pipeline even more to cover the potential loss of existing contracts.

- **Ease of Use**
  - Once implemented, easy to maintain and update
  - Requires tailoring to your specific market, products, and services
  - Training business developers on milestone definitions is critical to success

# Conferences and Trade Shows

Trade shows, symposiums, and conferences are very important to setting up your government sales strategy. You get to meet government buys, decision makers, influencers, champions, and future teaming partners. This 10th edition of the manual has come out during the COVID years. However, in-person events are coming back so make sure you take advantage of them.

## Common Misperceptions

- **If we don't exhibit, our competitors have a competitive advantage**

    - False. They may have a competitive advantage because it's only because they set-up several meetings in advance prior to the conference. . . and you did not

- **If we don't exhibit, customers will think we're not focused on them**

    - False - There are thousands of trade shows every year

    - You need to research and know which ones will provide best value

    - You should know which ones to exhibit at or to simply register as attendee

    - Exception - your customer or prospect asks you to exhibit

    - If you do not plan to exhibit, let your customers / prospects know and schedule meetings with them during the conference. Schedule these meetings several weeks or months before the show.

## Actionable and Measurable Objectives

- **Define your Objectives**

    - Develop sales leads

    - Qualify existing opportunities

    - Product demos

    - Enhance your brand and image

    - Talk to current customers (collect new requirements and new issues)

- **Manning the Booth**

    - Dress sharp - no black tennis shoes – You are "branding" yourself

    - Don't eat in your booth

    - Pay for the extra padding (sore feet & backs take precedence over prospects)

- **Booth Teaming**

    - Cost effective for small businesses

    - Other company must "Add Value" / "Be Complimentary" to your solutions

    - Solutions must truly be complimentary

# Event Coordination

- **Attending a trade show without a formal plan is a *waste of money***
  - Applies to being an exhibitor or an attendee
  - Attending without a formal plan is simply a company paid vacation

- **Activities before getting on the plane**
  - Coordination with prospects and customers
  - Identify attendees and speakers (get previous year's list from event planner)
  - Identify exhibitors (get previous year's list)
  - Are exhibit hours all day or just an hour or two in the morning and afternoon?
  - Which seminars will you attend?

- **Schedule meetings with prospects and current customers**
  - Breakfast meetings before the seminars begin
  - End of day happy hour
  - When possible - attend the VIP social gatherings
  - Always have something of value to discuss ("know your customer / prospect")

- **Getting a hotel suite for meetings**
  - Even small businesses can afford a small suite
  - Pay additional $60 a night for one employee to stay in a small suite
  - That $60 is worth having two or three prospects or customers meet with you
  - Suite must be in same hotel where conference takes place

- **Business Cards**
  - Capture what you discuss with each prospect on the back of every card
  - Capture socio-economic statuses, current customer base, products, and services
  - If they don't have a card, capture name, phone, email, address, and comments

- **If you are registering only as an attendee**
  - Must still schedule two or three meetings with prospects prior to conference

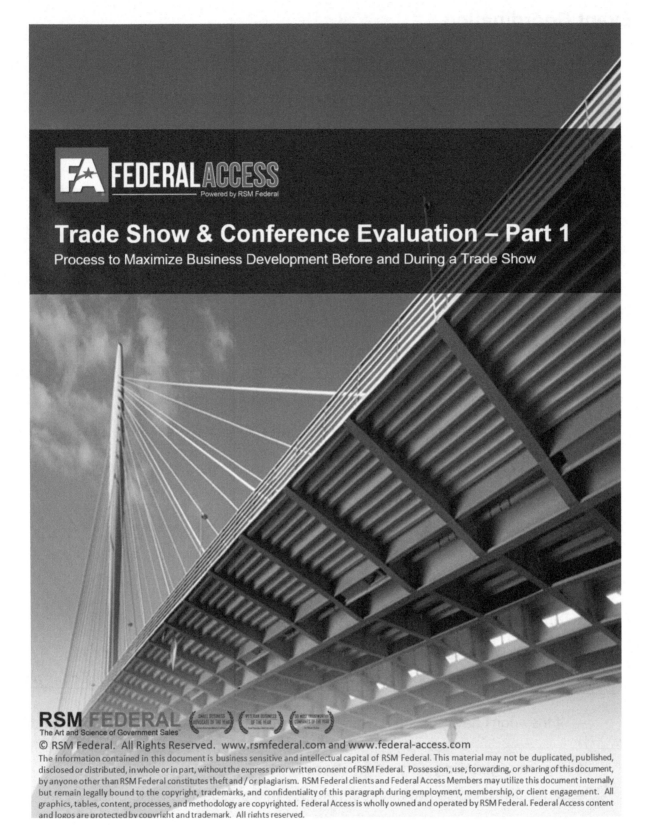

*Figure 77 - Trade Show and Conference Evaluation*

# Trade Show Evaluation

In general, trade shows, specifically setting up a booth, is a waste of time, money, and manpower if not properly evaluated and prepared for beforehand. Companies, large and small, that are successful and obtain multiple qualified prospects at a trade show, perform targeted planning and coordination with customers and prospects *prior to arriving at the event*.

## Common Misperceptions

- "Your competitors are exhibiting and if you don't exhibit they will have a competitive advantage." This is absolutely not true. If they have an advantage, it's because they set up meetings with two or three key prospects before they ever arrived at the conference.

- If you don't exhibit, your customers and prospects will think you're not interested. 99% of the time this is not true. There are thousands of local, regional, and national trade shows and conferences every year. You should know which conferences are important and which ones you should attend or exhibit.

- You have to attend the major shows to get new business. This is also incorrect. The only mandatory shows are ones which your current customers require or ask for your attendance. If you feel you have to attend a show it is because a customer, not a prospect, asked to see you there. In this case, you don't need to exhibit - just ensure your customer(s) see you in several of their seminars and / or you stop by to talk.

- Teaming with another company. Sharing a booth with another company can add value and decreases costs as well. But ensure that the other company is "complimentary" to your offerings and adds value. Do not simply team on a booth to save costs. It looks a bit odd if you sell construction services and your booth partner sells shampoo.

- Follow-up all meetings with an email within 12 hours after the event.

## Trade Show Planning Process

The first two steps are to identify your budget and objectives. When you define your objectives, at a minimum, they should support:

- Develop sales leads

- Qualify existing opportunities

- Provide product demonstrations

- Enhance your brand and image

- Talk to current customers (collect new requirements and new issues)

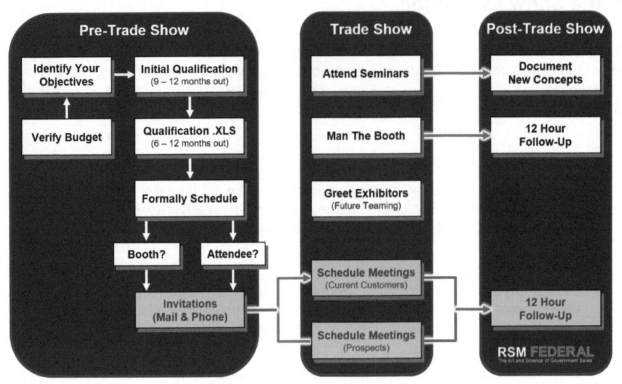

*Figure 78 - Trade Show Planning Process*

The next step is identifying which conference and trade shows you are interested in attending or exhibiting. But before you can make a final decision, you need to research each conference to validate whether or not there is value in attending.

## Ask the following questions:

- Who are the speakers and who are on the panels? This is normally a very good indicator of how many people will attend the conference. A low-level program manager for a government agency will not have the same turnout as the Director of Homeland Security. A Lieutenant General (three star) responsible for Army process improvement will not have the same turnout as a Brigadier General (one star) for IT transformation. The title and position are key for speakers and those on panels.

- Who attended last year? Rarely will you be able to get this list online but if you call the event planner you may be able to convince them to send you a list (just tell them you are interested in exhibiting - even if you don't end up exhibiting). If you don't

- see people for the organization's you are targeting then the organizations you are targeting may not even be sending the people you need to speak with.

- Which vendors are exhibiting this year? Which vendors exhibited last year? Are your competitors exhibiting? Is there a drastic reduction in exhibitors from last year? If the companies exhibiting change from year to year, then you can assume that

they went through the process identified in this document and felt the return on investment was not viable.

- How many vendors are exhibiting? Recommend you consider the *over-under-bump rule* for trade shows. Every show is different based on attendees, speakers, and panels, but knowing the number of exhibitors is key. For some shows, less than 30 or more than 200 exhibitors makes your job either more or less difficult in qualifying opportunities for future business. Based on attendees, speakers, and the type of show, if under 30 and over 200, then one option is to hang around similar companies and "bump" into prospects interested in your type of offering. This is very subjective but a potential solution and you save a lot of money not having to exhibit.

- What are the exhibit hall hours? If it's only 30 minutes in the morning, between sessions, 45 minutes during the lunch break and 30 minutes in the afternoon – don't waste money on a booth.

- Based on the above review, it may not make sense to setup a booth but the conference may have some excellent seminars and you know your targeted agencies will have employees or decision makers present. In this case, pay to be an attendee and attempt to find out which seminars / sessions your prospects are attending.

## The Number One Success Factor

*If you don't have a meeting setup before the conference – 9 times out of 10, you've wasted your money on the conference.* With the information you researched, you should call several of your prospects and ask them for a 15 minute meet and greet (you'll get 30 minutes if they agree to 15). You should have already researched the prospect's pain-points / challenges and what programs are currently in process. When you meet, provide a quick synopsis of your company, customers (past performance), what differentiates you, but do not tell them how you can support their requirements. **This is not the time for that.** You simply provide a 45 second pitch of the value your company provides. Do not give your company's capabilities like every other company. Your objective is to learn about their organization, their programs, needs, challenges, etc. or to validate what you believe you already know. Best case scenario, with or without a booth, is having two to three meetings setup before you ever arrive at the trade show.

## Manning Your Booth

- Video Screens and Capability Briefs. Most businesses setup a laptop under one of their tables and connect it to a screen sitting on the table or hanging from the booth structure. Many small businesses waste their time and put their standard Capabilities Presentation on the screen. Do you really think anyone is going to come to your booth and stand there for five minutes watching your PowerPoint slides? Of course not. Instead of your standard presentation - tailor it! Use organizational graphics of your prospects. If DoD, use graphics of military equipment.

  - At your next trade show walk around the exhibit hall and watch the videos from

other exhibitors. Focus less on the message and more on the format.

- – Many of the larger companies have in-house graphic and video specialists that create these videos. In today's economy, you can find graphic and video specialists who will take your information and develop a very nice video for less than a thousand dollars. Better yet, if you develop a short video that is more for the company and not the trade show, you can then reuse the video (reuse content) on your website as well! Better yet, there are now a ton of companies online that will create a marketing video, presentation, or infographic for less than a $100! (www.fiverr.com)

- – If you don't have a solid video that will catch the eye of your prospects, don't use a video.

- Dress sharp. Just because black tennis shoes are more comfortable does not mean you should wear them. You act like you look. Dress formal. As a small business you need to work very hard to change the perceptual maturity of your organization. You want prospects to see a viable solution to their challenges – not a small business with several capabilities.

- Don't eat in your booth.

- Pay extra for padding. A sore back and sore feet will *always* take precedence over prospects.

## Final Points

- The day after the trade show is always hectic, travelling home, putting your equipment away, and catching up on other requirements. Have your follow-up emails and follow-up plan already staged and ready to go.

- When someone walks-up to your booth, don't start with "Good morning, how are you?" Everyone understands it's a trade show and expects a pitch. Make yours clear and concise. "Good morning, what organization do you work for?" *Then follow their response with a leading question that focuses on whether or not they could become a qualified prospect.*

- Don't do all the talking. *It's not about you.* Even behind the booth, your job is NOT to talk about your company. You'll do that in 45 seconds. Your objective is to collect information and qualify the people that stop by.

- Have a good time! If you are bored - you will come across as bored. Seriously, have a good time. If you're a business developer and you're worried about proving to your boss that the conference "was worth the time and money," you're going to come across as an obnoxious sales person in your booth! When folks come to our booth, I normally start with something like, "Are we having fun yet!"

- Create an "Account Management Support CD/DVD/USB." If you have never seen one, you should consider creating one. When you get to a trade show, it is sometimes difficult to get a strong internet connection (whether or not you paid for it) so everything you need may be back at the office or on your laptop. Most companies send a laptop with the booth for the presentations you show. What happens if you forget to send the presentation? What happens if you don't have the current version of the video? What happens when a hot prospect says, "Here's my USB thumb drive. Can I get a copy of that?"

- Experienced sales managers and business developers use an Account Management Support CD/DVD/USB similar to what is shown below. The image below is the screen that executes as soon as the CD/DVD/USB is put into the drive. In this example, RSM Federal has all of its marketing material, pricing, teaming agreements, non-disclosure agreements, capability briefs, teaming documentation, various templates, and the most current version of the sales presentation or video.

- We recommend that someone in your organization create this CD/DVD/USB. In addition to having everything at your fingertips, senior management can be confident that their business developers have everything they need when they fly to California for a conference. One final note - this is an excellent tool to provide to new business developers and sales representatives.

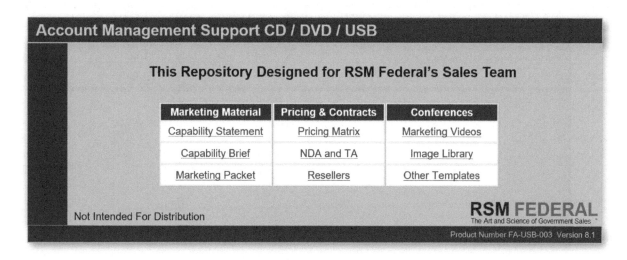

*Figure 79 - Trade Show Support CD*

## Summary

Some shows should be attended (not exhibited) in order to hear the positions of multiple decision or policy makers which will impact, strengthen, or realign your business development, positioning, and sales strategy. If only going as an attendee to learn about changes in the market, *you still want to setup meetings with prospects and / or prospective teaming partners prior to arrival*. If exhibiting, you should have those meetings with very few exceptions. Based on research and a prospect-rich environment, you make the decision to exhibit. The decision to attend as an attendee or as an exhibitor is based on your research and discussions with customers and prospects as well as internal company reviews.

# Trade Show Annual Cost and Decision Template

Remember: every activity in your Marketing-Mix must be mapped to revenue producing activities. How will attending or exhibiting at a specific tradeshow impact revenue and how will you measure success?

These and hundreds of other templates are available for download in the Federal Access Coaching and Training Platform.

**Annual Tradeshow and Conference Worksheet**
MSR Services

MSR SERVICES

| Date of Show | Tradeshow Name | Location | Attendees | Travel & Per Diem | Marketing Give-aways | Exhibit Cost | Registration Only | Total Cost | Notes |
|---|---|---|---|---|---|---|---|---|---|
| 10/29/21 - 11/1/21 | AFA Air Warfare | Orlando, FL | John, Sally | $1,720 | $100 | $2,000 | | $3,820 | |
| 12/20/21 - 12/21/21 | ATC Global | Chicago, IL | Bill, Mary | $1,720 | $100 | | $800 | $2,620 | |
| 1/12/22 - 1/14/22 | Space Symposium | Colorado Springs, CO | John, Sally | $1,720 | $100 | $1,500 | | $3,320 | Sharing Booth with Z3 Tech |
| 2/5/22 - 2/8/22 | Joint Warfighter Conference | Virginia Beach, VA | Sally | $860 | $100 | | $400 | $1,360 | |
| 2/28/22 | NGA Technology Day | Vienna, VA | Josh | $740 | $100 | | $250 | $1,090 | |
| 3/28/22 - 3/31/22 | LandWarNet | Fort Lauderdale, FL | Bill, John | $1,720 | $100 | $2,000 | | $3,820 | |
| 5/2/22 - 5/4/22 | DISA Partnership Conference | Orlando, FL | John, Sally, Mary, Bill | $3,440 | $500 | $3,500 | | $7,440 | |
| 6/6/22 | AFCEA West | San Diego, CA | Sally, Bill | $1,480 | $100 | | $600 | $2,180 | |
| 7/1/22 - 7/4/22 | Defense Logistics | Arlington, VA | Josh, Mary | $1,720 | $100 | | $700 | $2,520 | |
| 8/20/22 | USDA Industry Day | Kansas City, MO | John, Evette | $1,480 | $100 | $800 | | $2,380 | |
| 9/4/22 | DOL Small Business Day | Washington, DC | Bill | $740 | $100 | $800 | | $1,640 | |
| | | | | | | | | $32,190 | |

*Figure 80 - Trade Show Annual Cost Tracking*

# Chapter 11
# Develop a Market Sales Strategy (MSS)

**RSM FEDERAL**
The Art and Science of Government Sales™

Figure 81 - Market Sales Strategy Cover

# Basic Sales Strategy and Process Overview

Having a business development and sales refresher is good for any size business, small or large. Quite a few of our clients and Federal Access members, who are small businesses, requested a **Market Sales Strategy (MSS)** with step-by-step processes. This MSS is designed to support all businesses, all verticals, and all markets. It is not specific or unique to any industry and in many ways, is market agnostics. I want to reiterate, you can use these tactics and strategies for commercial opportunities as well. For example, instead of talking to the federal small business office, you'll be engaging the prospect / corporation's diversity or small business office.

For our Federal Access Members that are small business, this is probably one of the five most valuable resources across all Federal Access resources. Don't forget that there is also an example of a real-world company's MSS in Federal Access.

These strategies are based on proven tactics and strategies that our clients and members have used to close billions in government contracts.

---

*Applying What You Learn*
*"Tactics and strategies are the foundation for repeatable processes."*

---

While this prospecting and sales process will provide value to large companies (because sales is sales), this MSS example was developed for small business. That said, these strategies apply to both small business as well as larger companies with multiple capture management and business development teams. Again, the size of your company is not the point of focus - *it's understanding how to perform business development*. The learning curve may be greater for small business but the end result for acceleration of process and revenue remains the same. The end-result is a proven business development and market sales strategy that will accelerate the maturity of your business by three to five years.

Although you will be able to understand and implement this strategy as a baseline, you will not achieve the growth and accelerated revenue without understanding the tactics and strategies for Value-Mapping™ and Programmatic Teaming Strategies™ (PTS). Prospecting, business development, sales, marketing, teaming, relationship management and proposal development are highly incestuous and cross-walk with each other, with inputs and outputs between them. If you have the repeatable processes which employ the right tactics and strategies, you will understand how to maximize the impact and success of your sales strategy.

It should be noted that this MSS is a *template* which should be modified and tailored for your business. The products and services you sell, the prospects you target, the companies you team with, and the intellectual capital and capabilities of your employees are all unique. It only makes sense that companies should use the MSS as a baseline and modify as appropriate.

No matter how much content or information I pack into this Manual, I simply can't include everything. Don't forget that RSM Federal is more than just a Manual or an online coaching and training platform. Our ecosystem includes much more.

This manual is but one small part of that overall ecosystem. I also recommend that you look at these other resources.

For more information, visit
www.rsmfederal.com

We will start with a high-level overview of the Market Sales Strategy (MSS) and then discuss specific activities to achieve each objective.

Figure 82 - RSM Federal GovCon Ecosystem

# Parts of Your Sales Strategy

- **Step-by-Step Process for Prospect Engagement and Follow-Up**
  - Focus on education followed by selling
  - Focus on prospect and customer problems and challenges
- **Consolidation of Key Tactics and Strategies**
  - Value-Mapping™
  - Bulls-Eye Decision Support System (BDSS) in absence of a formal CRM tool
  - Tailored Opportunity Capabilities Brief
  - Bridging -Strategy™
  - Programmatic Teaming Strategy™ (PTS)
  - Introduction and Capability Statement™ (ICS)

# Overview - Market Sales Strategy Process

- **Step by Step Process for Prospect Engagement and Follow-Up**
  - Realignment Solution Methodology uses the Market Sales Strategy to focus and qualify opportunities
- **Sales Strategy Steps**
  1) Research your prospect
  2) Meet with Office of Small Business Programs (OSBP)
  3) Meet with one of the prospect's Program Managers
  4) Initiate Value-Mapping™
  5) Facilitate or update Programmatic Teaming Strategy (PTS) ™
  6) Educate and network with prospects twice a month
  7) Network up, down, laterally into other agency / military commands

*If you are new to the Government market, this is one of the
more valuable strategies in the manual*

# MSS High-Level Process Overview

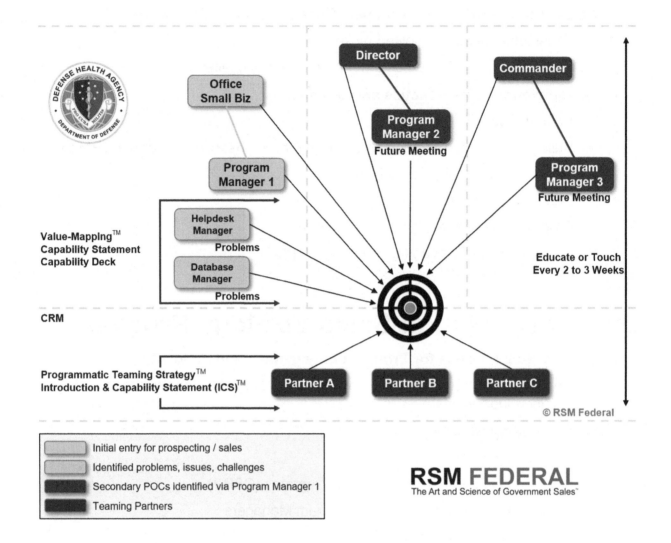

Figure 83 - Market Sales Strategy Graphical Overview

# Steps

1. **Research your prospect**
   - Utilize a Customer Relationship Management (CRM) tool to capture data
   - Initiate Bulls-Eye Decision Support System (BDSS) for each agency or service if you don't have an online CRM system

2. **Engage Office of Small Business Programs (OSBP / OSDBU)**
   - Post meeting activities
   - Update CRM
   - Update pipeline

3. **Meeting with a Program Manager**
   - Post meeting activities
   - Update CRM
   - Update pipeline

4. **Initiate Value-Mapping™**
   - Perform Value Mapping (see section of manual on value-mapping)
   - Develop tailored opportunity capabilities deck / brief
   - Call OSBP and PM after delivery of capabilities deck
   - Send a hardcopy, by mail, to both the Small Business Office and PM

5. **Facilitate or Update Programmatic Teaming Strategy™ (PTS)**
   - Initiate or continue "Sell-The-Prime" process (discussed later in the manual)
   - Develop Introduction and Capabilities Statement™ (ICS)
   - Call partners after delivery of ICS
   - Send a hardcopy, by mail, to your potential teaming partner
   - Update CRM and pipeline

6. **Educate and Network with Prospects twice a month**
   - Educate and provide value every two to three weeks
   - Call after every document is delivered
   - Update CRM
   - Update pipeline

7. **Network up, down, and laterally into other agency / command programs**

   – Utilize Bulls-Eye template to help focus and identify other programs and opportunities

   – Update pipeline

   – Identify and attend agency / military command events (conferences, discussion panels, social events)

# Sales Strategy - Scenario Based Example

## Phase 1 – Research Your Prospect

## Phase 2 – Meeting with the Office of Small Business Programs

### Prior to Meeting

Research agency's mission, vision, agency priorities, current and future programs, subordinate agencies

### Schedule the Meeting

Always try to schedule first thing in the morning. The small business advocate is less likely to be rushed.

### The Introduction

The small business representative has held these type of meetings for hundreds if not thousands of companies. ***You are not there to talk about your company or your solutions.*** You are there to build a relationship and collect information that will allow you to position the value and benefits of your company's solutions (not your features or capabilities). When you leave this meeting, you have several pre-determined activities which you will undertake. Therefore, you need to be very focused during your meeting and ask questions that will allow you to identify and start engaging prospects within that agency.

If you are asked what your company does, your response should be short in order to refocus on the agency and not your company. A good technique is to answer the question with value and benefit statements and finish with a transition question. Since the small business office is not a prospect who will buy your products or services, make sure that you focus on what services and support the small business office provides.

Let's stop for a moment. Have you completed your 45 Second Pitch? If you don't know what I'm referring to or you haven't completed it yet, make sure that you complete it before engaging prospects or teaming partners. The 45 second pitch requires that you communicate the value you provide, proof of that value, and how you differentiate. An example and template for the 45 Second Pitch is included in the Federal Access Coaching and Training Platform as well as outlined in various RSM Federal books on Amazon

The example below is a 45 second pitch for a company that only has commercial contracts and performs system and network engineering and database administration. (If you don't have any government contracts yet, don't worry because you are not there to talk extensively about your capabilities or past performance. You are there to collect information on the agency. Additionally, if you are not in the technology industry, simply follow the example and consider how you would communicate your value, proof, and

differentiation.

## 45 Second Pitch

① *"We are in the business of streamlining and consolidating information and data across multiple geographically dispersed networks to increase the visibility, accuracy, and speed of access across the enterprise. On average, we save our clients 30% in operational expenses and more than a 45% savings in data integrity and database cleansing costs.*

② *We have provided these benefits to Monsanto, Blue Cross - Blue Shield, and the Parkway School District.*

③ *Like most companies in our space, our website and marketing collateral list half a services (or products), but the two that provide the most value to our customers are network engineering and application development.*

④ *But before I go into more detail, can I ask several questions to better help me understand your organization?  Would that be okay?"*

*Figure 84 - 45 Second Pitch*

## Questions to ask during Meeting

It's okay to have this list with you and use it.
*The following are example questions for a technology firm. Modify for your industry.*

- **What is your approach to working with Small Businesses?**
  - Always the first question - people are proud to talk about what they do for their organization
  - You want to hear what kind of impact the advocate has on set-asides or sole-source opportunities
  - The answers will tell you if the small business advocate is strong, weak, and if they have influence
- **What are the agency's key initiatives?**
  - Not specifically technology - you want to get an idea of the agency's priorities
- **What are the key technology programs?  Which contract vehicles are used?  Which vehicles are preferred?**
- **What are the key challenges facing the agency today?**
- **What are the key issues that small businesses have in doing business with the agency or command?**

- Not specific to technology

- **How often do small businesses turnover their contracts? (get an idea of loyalty and vendor entrenchment)**

- **What are the agency's small business prime and subcontracting targets?**

- **Did the agency meet its small business goals last year?  Exactly, how much below, how much above?**

  - This is an important question because it will tell you if the agency has the "Propensity" to use small business

  - You should already know this… via the annual reports in SAM.gov's Data Bank

  - If they have the propensity, then you will be able to find out in mid Q3 how much money remains unused and still needs to be "set-aside" in Fiscal Q4 in order to meet statutory set-aside requirements.

- **Which organizations manage the technology programs?**

- **Who are the Program Managers for these programs? (don't be shy - ask for it)**

  - You want their name, position, phone, and email

  - If the small business advocate won't give a phone number – ask for an email (this is key as you'll see below)

- **Do the different programs use the same contracting office or are there multiple contracting offices?**

- **Who do you recommend I speak with to "start building a relationship" with the agency?**

- **What separates the successful small businesses from the weak ones?**

- **How often do you recommend I speak with you?**

- **How often should I update and send you a copy of our capability statement?**

- **Can you help facilitate a capability briefing with one of the program teams?**

## Post-Meeting Activities

- **Post Meeting Review**

  - Clean-up your notes, identify deliverables, problems and challenges, next steps

  - Enter key information into your CRM

- **Thank You Letter**

  - Send via email **same day**

  - Send a short hand written letter via postal service

# Phase 3 – Preparing to Meet with the Program Manager

## Prior to Meeting

Your objective is to build relationships while penetrating the organization. You may or may not get the names of program managers or decision makers from the small business office. If you don't, then the small business advocate *has little influence within the agency*. If they know but won't tell you because "that's their job," then you know they are either afraid or were told to stop giving out contact information and if that is the case, again, they don't have the necessary influence. Even though they may not know or want to give you the names, the advocate may still be very good at facilitating set-asides for the small business community. If the small business advocate simply doesn't know the answer, ask them to do you a favor and find out. Regardless, never burn a bridge. If you build rapport during your meeting with the small business office, 95% of advocates will give you the names and contact information and simply say, "Don't tell her where you got her contact information!"

Getting the names of Program Managers is not difficult. It simply requires a few well-placed questions. Have you asked companies you are building relationships with for help with contact information? Have you worked the room at an AFCEA Luncheon or S.A.M.E. event and walked up to a service member in uniform and asked where they work? (You will get a lot of good information from the younger service members who are not usually spoken to at these events.)

Regardless, once you have a name and a number, introduce yourself and if you are able to communicate your value via a 45 second pitch, you'll schedule a meeting.

## Schedule the Meeting

Remember, it may take six calls to get them on the phone. Expect them to say "no" several times. They get dozens of calls from companies that want to get their business so be aggressively persistent. Also remember that if you're unable to communicate your value, you'll just come across as begging and immature.

## Call When Prospects are Receptive:

- **Best Week To Call – After Month End**
    - First week of the month (after month-end reporting and close out activities)
    - Second best week is the last week of the month
- **Second Best Time – Last week of the month**
- **Best Day – Friday after 4PM**
    - Secretary and support staff are likely gone (no gatekeeper)
    - Is happy about pending weekend and is more personable

- Best calling period is between 4PM and 6PM on Friday

- **Second Best Day – Thursday early morning**

- **Third Best Day – Tuesday early morning**

  - Monday, all day, is the worst time to call

## Prior to the Call

Since you are already expecting to be told "I don't have time" to meet with you, you should already have prepared yourself for that response. But what if you could positively influence the Program Manager before you ever made the call? This is where some simple tactics comes into play. Based on the questions you asked during your meeting with the small business specialist and prior research, you have enough information to develop an introductory email *before* you call to setup a meeting. This is why getting the email address from the small business specialist or someone else is important.

An introductory email takes the "edge" off the initial cold-call and speaks to a level of maturity and professionalism. It is a very short and simple email:

**Alex Martin**                    Sent: January 14, 20xx    10:15am

To: rjones@scott.af.mil
Subject: Introduction

Mr. Jones, my name is Alex Martin and Ms. Johnson recommended I reach out. My company is in the business of streamlining and consolidating data and information across geographically dispersed networks for increased visibility, accuracy, and speed of access for the DoD enterprise. Based on our past performance, Ms. Johnson recommended I validate with you whether or not it makes sense to start priming and subcontracting on your requirements.

At a high level, I want to validate if it makes sense to spend time and money engaging Scott AFB. Just wanted to quickly introduce myself. I'll reach-out in the next couple of weeks to follow-up and introduce myself.

Until then, have a good week.

Thanks,
Alex Martin
ABC Technologies

*Figure 85 - Prospect Email Before Call*

When you read the email above, consider how it's written:

- **Don't give Ms. Johnson's title or office (OSBP, Small Business Advocate)**

  - When the Program Manager reads "SB specialist," the immediate response is

*"another small business to waste my time. . ."*

- **Don't give too much detail on your capabilities or features**

  - You really don't know his challenges or problems so giving him the kitchen sink on your capabilities only positions you to be *"like all the other small businesses"*

  - Every small business "lists their capabilities" so don't do it.

- **Set conditions for the future call**

  - Tell him when you will call

  - Although you indicate you want to "learn more about their programs, you KNOW they won't have the time which is the segway on your call to set-up a face to face meeting. (More on this below).

## Making The Initial Call

If you are like most people, you are uncomfortable cold-calling. But have confidence! You know that the Program Manager has already received your email introduction; that you were *referred* to him; and that your call is an introduction, not a sales pitch. When you think of it in these terms, you should feel more confident about your call. Now you understand the importance of sending a simple note before you call. It also *turns a cold-call into a follow-up.*

Your introductory call is planned and scripted. If you have learned one thing from RSM Federal and our other resources, it is that repeatable processes are what helps you understand what works and accelerates the maturity of your processes. Repeatable processes are a key driver to facilitate revenue growth. With that said, here are some tips when making the call:

- **Don't say, "I know your time is busy so this won't take long." This indicates his time is more important than your time.**

- **Don't use his / her first name until they tell you it is okay – you need to build trust first.**

- **Be ready with your 45 Second Pitch. Give some quasi-personal details.**

  - You are a "Senior Account Executive", a "Vice President", etc.

  - You are not a Senior Business Developer or Sales Representative

  - If the title on your business card says sales or business development manager, you need to talk to your management and have them authorize **external** titles. Internally, they can call you whatever they want. Externally, your title needs to convey more than a salesperson. Do not take this lightly. Your external title is important to how you are perceived by your prospects.

  - Personal details - moved to St. Louis with your wife two years ago – she works over at St. Johns Hospital as a recruiter for nurses.

- Where you came from before your current company

- **Ask him about his position and what he does for the agency**
  - Most people enjoy explaining what they are responsible or accountable for
  - Don't ask questions that are too personal – you need to build trust first.

- **You control the call. It's your call.** If he asks what your company does, give your 45 second pitch and then quickly move to asking questions and collecting intelligence to learn more about the agency or program. You don't know enough about his requirements or problems to give a tailored or detailed description of your capabilities.
  - If he still wants you to tell him your competencies, give a "Reality Pitch" -- "Although we market eight capabilities, realistically, we have three core competencies, A, B, and C. (You've already prepared for this based on your initial research (such as SAM.gov's Data Bank), discussions with other companies, and the small business office.) This makes the PM sit-back and think, "Okay, I have a company that understands they don't do everything."

- **Once he has given you some detail on his programs, which may only be a sentence or two, close the call with the following:**

---

*"Mr. Jones, our company is interested in supporting future requirements. In order to do that, I would like to ask a few questions and learn more about your mission. Can I get a half hour on your calendar in the next three to four weeks?"*

---

- **Everyone wants to talk to him next week but that makes it easy for him to say, "Nope, too busy. Thanks for calling."** Instead, asking in the next three or four weeks makes it much more difficult for him to say no.
  - Send him an email thanking him for speaking with you and reiterating you will follow-up in several weeks if you're not already on his calendar.
  - Send a hand-written note thanking him again
  - Be aggressively but softly persistent! You expected him to say no.

- **If he says yes, schedule and prepare for your meeting.**

# Phase 4 – Meeting With The Program Manager
## Prior to Meeting

When you first start to prospect, your objective is to identify the champions, decision makers, and influencers; avoid or mitigate / influence the competition (adversaries); and find the individuals who have a challenge or problem where your solutions will provide value and benefit. By following steps 1 and 2, you will already have some valuable information. (And you have already put it into your CRM or Bulls-Eye Decision Support System (BDSS).

*Figure 86 - Buy Authority Levels*

You should approach your meeting with the understanding that this Program Manager or buyer *may not be the right person* and you will know fairly quickly if he or she is going to be a champion. Remember, by definition, a champion is someone that has a problem or challenge and can see where your solutions will resolve those problems with clear value and benefit.

If this program manager is not a champion, he can always be an *influencer*, helping you connect to other key individuals within the agency. This is why your CRM or Bulls-Eye is so important. If you quickly look at the high-level graphical overview at the beginning of this document, you can see where Program Manager 1 provided other names and positions with other programs (Program Manager's 2 and 3). All of this information goes into your CRM or Bulls-Eye. It really doesn't matter where you put it... as long as you are tracking it! This helps you focus and identify penetration points that often go unnoticed or fail to receive follow-up. For the purpose of this example, we will assume that this program manager has the challenges and problems which your solutions will rectify.

Similar to the introductory call, your meeting is fairly scripted. Yes, you need to be flexible. If you come across as providing a scripted meeting, you're done. It is not a formal script but a set of objectives which you need to successfully meet in order to properly complete your Value–Mapping with follow-on education and marketing.

## Meeting Objectives

- **Identify challenges and problems facing his program**
  - You are there to learn about the prospect, not to sell your products or services (repeat this to yourself over and over again)

- **Understand the challenges and problems**
  - **Who** is affected by these problems? End users? The PM? Senior Leadership?
  - **How** do these problems affect them?
  - **Which** current contractors / vendors support these problems?
  - These are all awesome questions with very valuable answers!

- **Understand the impact if these problems and challenges** *are not resolved*
  - Requires the program manager to admit cause and effect.
  - What pain will he or the agency deal with if the problems are not resolved?
  - The answers to these questions can help you differentiate and provide win themes for your proposals

- **Continue mapping your Bulls-Eye (Again, if you're not familiar with the bulls-eye, go take a look at it in the Sales Module of Federal Access)**
  - If he tells you that a senior manager is impacted by a specific problem, get his or her name
  - If there are other managers in the agency that work on these issues, get their names
  - Identify problems, clarify the problems, who is affected

- **Build rapport with the Program Manager**
  - Building a relationship is more important that the solutions or services you sell
  - You build rapport throughout the conversation - don't force it
  - If the first thing you do is walk into his office and stare at a picture of his wife in order to build rapport, you're in trouble. This probably made you chuckle but it happens more often than you may think.
  - Are you originally from this area? Oh, is that your family?
  - Look at what is on his desk and hanging on his walls. Do you have any common interests?
  - If he has a miniature golf green on his desk, ask him if he's going to play at the AFCEA scramble in July
  - Building rapport is just as important as understanding their problems and challenges

- **Close the meeting strong**
  - It is very important that you, not the program manager or buyer, close the

meeting. If the PM starts looking at his watch or his body language tells you he is ready for the meeting to close, then you initiate the close at the earliest opportunity, **once you have met your objectives**. If you ask the right questions, he will appreciate your interest in his role and problems and this won't be an issue.

- Standup, shake his hand, and thank him for speaking with you and that once you've had an opportunity to review your discussion, you will follow-up.

| | Collecting Prospect Information During Meetings |
|---|---|
| 1 | Review / enter data in the "Bulls-Eye" decision support template |
| 2 | Identify prospect's key personnel and their roles |
| 3 | Identify prospect's program and key activities |
| 4 | Identify current vendors / contractors supporting these programs |
| 5 | What is the prospect's mission and requirements |
| 6 | What challenges or issues does the prospect have today |
| 7 | Who is impacted by these issues (internally and externally) |
| 8 | What opportunities are expected to be released as RFPs in the next 12 months |
| 9 | What is the prospect's agenda underlying a specific opportunity |
| 10 | What is the prospect's budget for the fiscal year (or remaining) |
| 11 | What are other major programs at the agency and who are the PMs |
| 12 | For questions relating to contracts, who are the contracting officers |
| 13 | What contract vehicle(s) does the prospect prefer |
| 14 | Does the prospect have a propensity to use small business |
| 15 | What are the prospect's priorities |

*Figure 87 - Prospect Meeting Questions*

The above table is a list of questions that can help keep you focused. You don't have to ask every question or get all the answers during your first meeting. Clearly this list is not all inclusive. Every company is different. How your discussion progresses will let you know how to proceed. Remember that any questions left unasked are excellent for follow-up and future discussion.

There is an outstanding on-demand webinar in Federal Access called *"How To Engage and Position During Government Prospect Meetings."* One part of the video is outlining the three core objectives when meeting with a prospect. None of them are to sell your products or services.

## Three Sales Meeting Objectives

1) **Collect Intelligence**

2) **Build Rapport**

3) **Position yourself as a Subject Matter Expert (SME)**

You know if this is a skill you have or need to develop. If you would like some help contact the RSM Federal Team.

The questions you ask and the follow-up you give them is based on the responses you receive. If you carefully review these objectives, you will recognize the value you should get from this meeting. The value comes from focusing on the prospect and not your capabilities or solutions. (Internally, you're thinking about all these things but not externally during your meeting)

The answers to these questions provide you with detailed information and intelligence to:

## Internal Activities

- Update your CRM and Bulls-Eye

- Provide one or more opportunities to your pipeline

- Perform Value-Mapping for differentiation and initial win-theme concepts

- Information which may provide a competitive advantage in a future proposal

## External Activities

- Provides the problems and challenges you need to tailor your strategy

- Provides the problems and challenges to develop educational whitepapers and case studies

- Competitive information which is used to "Sell-The-Prime" with potential teaming partners

- Develop an Introduction and Capability Statement (ICS) for potential teaming partners

A key part of your sales strategy is the *domino effect that comes from the use, reuse, and dissemination of information and intelligence*. A little bit of information impacts **every** activity within your sales strategy. The more information you have and how you shape and position that information with your prospects and teaming partners is how you develop the perception of being a mature business with a strong understanding of a specific prospect's programs, challenges and issues. This process may look complicated but it is simple because you're asking common-sense questions and follow-up questions to collect as much information and intelligence as you can.

## Post-Meeting Activities

### Post Meeting Review
- Clean-up your notes, identify deliverables, problems and challenges, next steps
- Enter key information into your CRM / Bulls-Eye

### Thank You Email
- Send same day

**Alex Martin**    Sent: January 27, 20xx    1:15am

To: rjones@scott.af.mil
Subject: Follow up

Mr. Jones, thank you for spending time with me this morning. It's good to know I'm not the only fair-weather golf fan in the area. If you attend the AFCEA golf-scramble in July, you want to play **behind** my team or my balls will keep hitting you.

Thanks for giving me the one-over on your program. I've met with several dozen PMs over the last couple months and it's pretty clear you've doing this for a while. Easy to understand your role, requirements, etc.

Once I get a chance to review our notes, I'll follow-up. Till then, have a week!

Best -
Alex Martin
ABC Technologies

FOLLOW-UP #1 IMMEDIATELY

*Figure 88 - Thank You Email*

When you look at the prior email, consider the language:

- Start the email with a personal item from when you were building rapport. You saw golf items on his desk; discussed how good he is; joked about how bad you are.

- Compliment them on their knowledge and / or management of their program

- Notify him that you will review your notes and then follow-up

## Thank You Letter

- Your next follow-up also occurs immediately. It is *very uncommon* for companies to send a hand written letter to their prospects, which is something that will differentiate you and your company.

- The letter is a very simple thank you with no focus on what was discussed or the value your company provides. It is as simple as shown below:

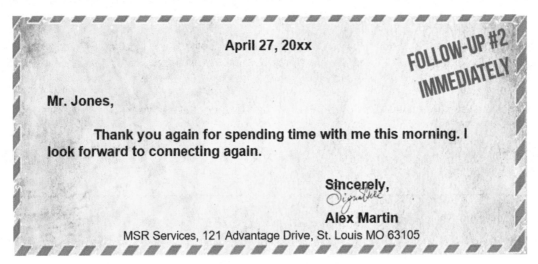

*Figure 89 - Thank You Letter*

### Tailored Email - Reiterate PM's Problems and Your Recommended Value
*Provide to the PM three business days after your meeting*

This is where you start to map your capabilities and value to the Program Manager's known problems and when you start to position for opportunities. This is where the business development and capture management techniques come into play.

Up until this point, you have emailed the PM twice, sent a personal letter, and met with him face to face. This will be your fifth contact with the PM in the last week. It does not matter what market or vertical you are in. You need to stay in front of your prospects.

You will notice that you are keeping your emails and communications short and to the point. *You're not stalking him!* You have designed them to be focused on building a relationship, not selling your services or solutions.

As a result, you have started to build credibility and trust. The program manager or buyer recognizes that you are not wasting his time, that your messages have been brief and easy to read, and that *you have asked for no action or decision on his part*.

Now that you have started to build a relationship, you need to start building your credibility:

- **Your company is very strong in supporting his type of requirements, even**

**subject matter experts**

- **Your company has proven they have resolved these type of problems with other customers**

- **You are personally credible and can be trusted**

- **You are extremely interested in supporting his agency**

You start building the above credibility by listing the problems he gave you and then following them up with potential ideas or concepts which may not have crossed his mind.

An example of this follow-up email follows.

---

**Alex Martin**          **Sent: January 30, 20xx    9:22am**

To: rjones@scott.af.mil
Subject: Re: Follow up

Mr. Jones, thanks again for walking me through your program. It was interesting to learn that a potential consolidation of the network operations center may take place near end of year. Regardless of the consolidation, I wanted to make sure I understood the various issues and nuances we discussed.

You indicated three challenges, if I captured them correctly:

First item – As part of the BRAC realignment, difficulties in database integration leaving users unable to access information, specifically between AMC and SDDC. Support to the Warfighter slightly degraded which causes extra hours for govies and vendors alike.

Second item – Network outages

Third item – The recently deployed Oracle database for the primary transportation systems where the CRON jobs and scripts from the legacy system aren't running correctly on the new system. This is impacting the real-time transfer of data. Impact is both to USTRANSCOM and other commands that use the data.

Six months ago, the Department of Energy had a similar issue with their data. They had also just migrated to the same Oracle version.

So with these similarities, I asked one of our PMs on a contract with the Department of Energy to document the best practices and strategies we utilized to resolve the issues. I'll have it in a couple weeks. I'll forward you a copy when I get it.

Anything specific I should ask our PM that isn't included above?

Thanks Ron –

Alex Martin
ABC Technologies

*FOLLOW-UP #3*
*3 DAYS LATER*

---

*Figure 90 - Prospect Meeting Detailed Follow-Up*

When you read the email above, recognize how it is designed:

- **Thank him again for meeting with you Reiterate any upcoming programs or acquisitions that may have been identified**
  - Potential consolidation of the Network Operation Centers

- **Make it clear that you are more interested in understanding his problems**
  - Restate the problem
  - Confirm who is impacted by these problems (users, management, warfighters, other agencies, etc.)

- **Map his problems to similar problems you have managed with other customers**
  - It's okay if you don't have exactly similar problems. Your objective with this email is to build credibility and create the perception, in the PM's mind, that you have managed the same or similar problems for other customers.
  - Don't lie or stretch the truth. This is where you use Value-Mapping to help you position.

- **Make a commitment to "Educate" him, at no cost, on how another federal entity or commercial companies dealt with similar issues.**

- **Close with a request for him to confirm that you properly captured his issues**
  - Notice that you're asking for the confirmation *after* you've made the commitment, at no cost, to educate him on the best practices, techniques, and processes that worked for another agency.

Now you are ready to tailor and position the value and benefits of your solutions, which is Step 5.

# Phase 5 – Value-Mapping™

This should look familiar from Chapter 5. Value-Mapping is a method that forces you to evaluate and map your capabilities and differentiate them based on a specific prospect, that prospect's unique problems or challenges, and when possible, a specific opportunity.

Bare in mind that Value-Mapping is a continuous process that takes place every time you get new information or learn of new opportunities. Initially, for the first opportunity with a prospect, it is a formal process. Afterwards, as you get new information, it is then updated since the results of mapping provide you with potential win-themes.

In the case of our ongoing example of working with Mr. Jones, the Program Manager, your next step is delivering a tailored "Opportunity Capabilities Brief."

Most businesses have a standard Capabilities Brief which is then thrown away by the prospect and never seen again. Generic capability briefs provide little value to your prospects or customers because they are not tailored to that prospect's issues or requirements. In effect, your presentation is no different than several dozen others that the Program Manager has on file.

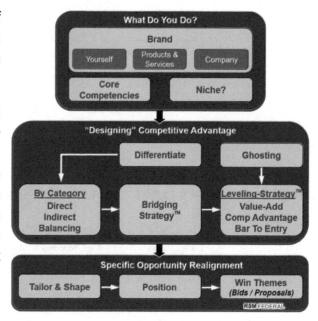

Figure 91 - Value Mapping Process

Value-Mapping is the foundation of your "Opportunity Capability Brief." It ensures that you are mapping the value and benefits of your solutions to specific problems or challenges of a specific opportunity within a specific agency. There may not be a specific opportunity which you will write a proposal for, but your efforts in creating your brief based on the problems identified during your initial meetings will help accelerate your position within the agency.

Once you have made your first pass at mapping your competencies to the three problems identified, you tailor your Capability Brief into an Opportunity Capabilities Brief.

When complete, you have multiple deliverables. The first goes to Mr. Jones, the program manager. This will be your fourth follow-up in one week. Your email will look similar to the following:

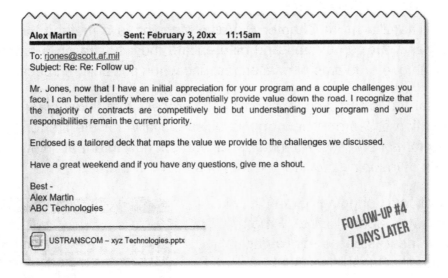

*Figure 92 - Prospect Meeting Tailored Cap Briefing*

Another copy goes to Mrs. Johnson, the Small Business Advocate you started with.

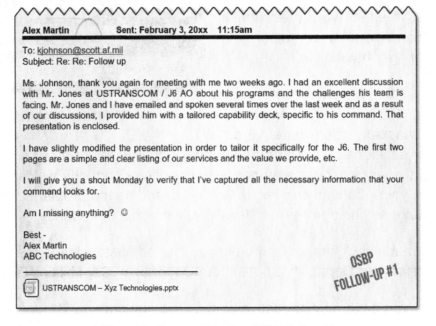

*Figure 93 - Prospect Meeting OSBP Follow-Up*

**A third copy** goes to one or more of your *partners* or *potential teaming partners*. But before we send this to another company, we first have to review how you manage your relationships with other companies.

Once you have emailed the Opportunity Capabilities Deck, send hardcopies, by regular mail, to your prospect and the small business advocate. Do this every time. Maximize the number of touches.

**Important Note.** You will recall that if the Program Manager chose not to meet with you, that we recommended you move immediately to Step 4, Value-Mapping. Just because the PM said no to your meeting doesn't mean you should remove this agency from your target list. *That is one of the key mistakes many companies make.* It also explains why most companies have a shotgun approach to business development and sales. If the program manager says no to your meeting, remember that "no means not now" and use the information you have from the small business office, from your partners, from Inspector General (IG) reports, or from any other reports and contacts to "educate" the program manager every month or two. Call the program manager after every marketing effort and after a month or two, he will most likely accept a meeting (or call) with you. Why wouldn't he? He has received multiple documents that have educated him on potential benefits - **all from a company that doesn't have a contract or legal obligation to do so.** Again, this is softly aggressive persistence.

# Phase 6 – Programmatic Teaming Strategy™ (PTS)

Now that you have provided your tailored deck to the Program Manager and SB Advocate at OSBP / OSDBU, you also have to review (or develop) your Programmatic Teaming Strategy (PTS). To learn more about Programmatic Teaming Strategies, review the Chapter on Teaming as well as the tactics and strategies in the Federal Access Coaching and Training Platform.

> *Programmatic Teaming Strategy*
> *A process and strategy designed to "build a relationship with another company in order to integrate your company's reputation, capabilities, and value into two or more of the other company's verticals, markets, or territories."*

It is about the best strategy to target multiple opportunities with limited resources, time, and money - a core focus for *any* business. The PTS utilizes a hybrid approach where your business development is both 'Direct' and 'Indirect' with the support of other partners. Let's evaluate your current relationships.

How many relationships do you have today? One, two, three, more? On average, most small businesses have strong interpersonal relationships with one and at most two large companies and many of these small businesses have never won work based on their current relationships. There is good reason for this and it is because small businesses fail to Sell-The-Prime. I've now mentioned the Sell-The-Prime concept several times throughout the Manual. We'll be getting to it shortly. Before we continue, pick the large business that you have the strongest relationship with and answer the following questions:

- **Does the large business have a relationship with Mr. Jones, the Program Manager?**

  - This will come out during your discussion with the PM or just ask the large business

- **If the large business supports Mr. Jones, is he pleased with the work they provide? There are several ways to identify the status of this relationship.**

  - Has the large business lost one or more re-competitions with the agency in the last 12 months?

  - Have you heard about problems via the "gossip-chain?"

  - Have you heard of any "cure notices" lately? (Government unhappy with contractor and documents it)

  - The PM will rarely tell you he's displeased but he will refer to that displeasure based on how he describes the challenges and problems he currently faces. (Read between the lines)

- **If not with the Program Manager, does the large business have other relationships with the agency?**

  - This one is easy. Ask the large business which programs they support at this agency

  - You should also check SAM.gov's Data Bank or USASpending.gov. You'll quickly be able to see all major contract actions between this agency / command and the large business. All you need is the large businesses DUNS number or SAM Unique Identifier.

- **Compared to other large businesses, what percentage of work does the large business have with the agency?**

  - Don't ask the large business

  - There are dozens of methods which include annual publications, contract management systems, SAM.gov Data Bank, USASpending.gov, etc. which can tell you the top contractors or vendors with any specific contracting office in any specific city and state.

**Special Note**. Even if the company you have built a relationship with has no work with either the program manager or this specific agency, do not immediately start shopping around for another partner. If you refer above to the definition of a Programmatic Teaming Strategy, it is not about a single opportunity or a single agency. It is about building a "Programmatic" relationship that gives you access to multiple capture managers in multiple territories. If you've done your research, you may find that this large business has strong relationships with two other agencies (e.g. Army and Department of Commerce) which are on your target list. One of the core activities to accelerate your sales and market penetration is the concept of quid-pro-quo. If you want to build a programmatic relationship and gain access to the other two agencies, then the information you've collected from your recent meeting with the Program Manager will be

highly desired by the large business. You can help them access intelligence for a new program.

The bottom line is that you do not want to provide your hard work and market intelligence to a large business (or any business) simply because they are the only one you have a relationship with. Think more than one step ahead – think strategically. In many respects, GovCon (Government Contracting) is like a chess board.

At some level, all large businesses within your industry have fairly similar capabilities. Their differentiation comes from the programs they manage and the infrastructure or

systems they support. As an example, all of the major defense contractors support USTRANSCOM (United States Transportation Command). But depending on the contract, they manage different systems. When an RFP or Task Order is released, regardless of the requirements, it's based on specific systems in that agency or command. As a result, the vendor / contractor who currently manages contracts for those specific systems will have a competitive advantage on subsequent RFPs. The question of which company to team with comes down to their reputation at each specific prospect location, the amount of work (past performance) they have with that customer, and the level of penetration and strength of relationships they have cultivated.

This document is not meant to replace the tactics and strategies presented in the Teaming Module of Federal Access. *This manual provides the process and methodology. The Federal Access Coaching and Training Platform provides the tactics, templates, and strategies.*

## Developing an Introduction and Capability Statement (ICS)

The Introduction and Capability Statement (ICS) takes your tailored capabilities deck to a new level. It is a five to seven page mini-proposal that maps the **value and benefits of your solutions** to a **specific prospect's program**, requirements, and challenges. Just as important, it maps these same criteria **to the other company's requirements**, gaps, and sales strategy.

Your objective is to build trust and credibility with all players within your sales strategy, which includes prospects and teaming partners.

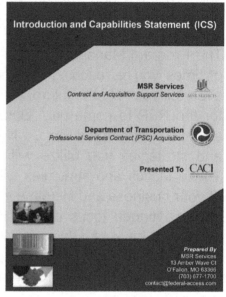

The ICS is your second follow-up with **one or more** selected potential teaming partners, small or large. However, it's used more often to convince larger primes. Remember that you will differentiate your company from the dozens or hundreds of other businesses by how you tailor, shape, and differentiate not only your solutions but in how you communicate your value. It is easy to use the same ICS for multiple partners but you must still modify what is inside the ICS to ensure it is tailored to each respective partner or company.

*Figure 94 - ICS Cover Sheet*

The ICS is a strategy under the process of Selling-The-Prime. Both are pieces of your Programmatic Teaming Strategy (PTS). Your PTS consists of all activities and data points *that make you valuable to another company.* Over the last ten years, we've tracked the use of the ICS with our clients and FA Members. **The success rate has been 98%.**

Almost every large business / Prime that received a tailored ICS sent a teaming agreement (TA) within 96 hours. If you understand how to Sell-The-Prime, the Introduction and Capability Statement (ICS) will become one of your primary tools.

---

*#1 Objective When You Want To Subcontract*
*Your primary objective is not convincing the potential teaming partner that you have outstanding products or services. Your one and only primary objective is convincing the other company that **you will make them more competitive!***

---

Once you have emailed the ICS, send hardcopies, by regular mail, to your potential partner. Do this every time. Maximize the number of touches.

# Phase 7 – Continue To Educate Your Prospects and Partners

At this point, you have communicated with Mr. Jones, your prospect, five (5) times in the last two weeks. The initial follow-ups were focused on building a relationship. The last several follow-ups were focused on improving the relationship as well as providing well-crafted documentation that makes it clear that you've carefully considered their challenges and problems and shaped your capabilities via values and benefits.

The Program Manager may get irritated with the number of times you're reaching out and touching him. He may even tell you - "In the future, just go to SAM.gov and wait for the RFP to come out." Don't listen to him. To make sure you understand, do. . . NOT. . . listen. The tactics and strategies you utilize will change their perception. These tactics and strategies will accelerate the maturity of your business and increase your revenue and win rate. Your continued focus on this PM and his program will eventually have him thinking, "***Wow, I have never been targeted like this.***" Keep in front of the PM and he will keep your name and company in front as well.

*Figure 95 - Prospect Education Timeline*

The remainder of your sales strategy is comprised of the following activities:

- **Keep your promises and follow-up when you are supposed to**

- **Continue to build a perception that you are a subject matter expert on this agency and its programs / their challenges and issues.**

  - Every time you talk to the prospect, you are getting information that makes you more competitive or that other companies need

  - A short email to one of your potential partners saying you just met with Mr. Jones and learned of a new acquisition being discussed - will have others perceive you as having the "pulse" of that agency or command and their opportunities. ***Companies will start bringing opportunities to you.***

- **Continue to focus on building rapport.**

  - Have drinks with them during social hour at a conference or trade show

  - Ask them to sit on a panel with you as a subject matter expert at a conference

  - Ask them questions about their hobbies and what they do on their days off (once you've built trust)

- **Continue to educate your prospect and help them at every opportunity. If your management will not allow you to spend time crafting whitepapers, case**

**studies, or other documentation that directly supports your prospect's challenges and problems, then ask for someone to help you. If your management team is unable to see the value, then there are operational challenges in addition to your business development requirements. There's a reason that a select few win large contracts.**

Consider every whitepaper, case study, or other document you prepare for your prospects as *mini-proposals*. Why do you write proposals in response to RFPs to win business? Of course you do. Why might you lose a bid? It may be the result of a poor proposal. Perhaps your pricing. But often enough, it's because you didn't have a relationship or the necessary intelligence.

"By educating their prospects. . . business developers are **100 times more efficient** and effective than their competition."

If you want to accelerate the maturity of your business by one to three years and accelerate the time it takes to sell to a federal agency or armed service, *make sure that your focus is on collecting information and intelligence and then educating the prospect – not selling to them*. Successful business developers know that by educating their prospects, they are laser-focused on the prospect's challenges, which makes them 100 times more efficient and effective than their competition.

## Follow-Up With Your Prospect Every Several Weeks

The most common question is what are you supposed to do every several weeks? First, make sure you understand The Standards of Ethical Conduct for Employees of the Executive Branch (5 C.F.R. 2635) which covers limitations on gifts to public officials. The key point is that government employees are not permitted to receive gifts in excess of $20 on any single occasion, e.g. a meal, and cannot receive gifts in aggregate of $50 in any calendar year. With the increase in protests and increased accountability and oversight being placed on government agencies, most government employees play it safe (with good reason) and refuse all gifts, even those under $20. A bit later we will identify how to use the $20 threshold as one part of your marketing strategy.

*Figure 96 - Case Study Cover Sheet*

In our current scenario, you've reached out and provided information to the Program Manager five times in the last two to four weeks. It is now mid-February and you know you need to follow-up again in a couple weeks. In the first week of March, you decide to "educate" your prospect, show them that your company is a subject

matter expert in some area or discipline that can help resolve their current problems or challenges. Furthermore, you will be able to use this in support of your Programmatic Teaming Strategy (PTS).

Remember when you told the Program Manager that you managed similar challenges with the Department of Energy? Since a key piece of your sales strategy is educating your prospect, the case study your project manager at DOE is helping you write will be your next contact in early March.

Every time you educate your customer, touch them again and mail a hardcopy. Do this every time. Maximize the number of touches.

## Other Follow-Up Techniques

The most powerful follow-ups are those that provide valuable information and compel the prospect to think about your company each time a specific type of problem is encountered. Educating your prospects with solutions of how your company resolved similar problems with other customers is a very simple yet powerful concept.

**Important point.** Do not think that these strategies are unique to your prospects. Your market sales strategy is for your entire business. You should be using it for

> "These techniques are not only for your prospects. They are also used to retain and grow your current contracts."

commercial prospects as well. Just as important, you should be using these strategies with your retention accounts - your *current* customers. Two years from now when one of your current contracts is up for renewal, whether it be commercial or government, imagine how much easier it will be to maintain the contract when you've been touching and educating your customers every month or two? This is not because you took them to lunch or called them every Tuesday for a project update. It will be because of the continued education you've provided them, above and beyond the work on their contract, that has them looking at you not only as a subject matter expert, but a subject matter expert for *their* organization. They trust you. You have credibility. **This is how you increase your revenue by 50% off of current customers and contracts.** When a new opportunity is identified, they will do everything they can to roll it under your current contract or put it out for competitive bid where you are "wired" to win the business.

The options you have are only limited by your imagination. How you educate your prospect is also based on the products you sell or the services you provide. Consider the following tactics and strategies:

## Multiple-Customer Best Practices and Whitepapers

Similar to the example above with the Department of Energy, if your prospect has a problem with how they manage helpdesk tickets, you can educate them – **even if you**

> "You are an expert at whatever you decide to be an expert at."

**don't have helpdesk contracts**. Go visit two or three of your current customers (commercial or government) and interview their helpdesk managers. You know what your prospect's challenges are so simply ask your current customers how they deal with those issues. By the time you have visited two or three customers, you will have a dozen pages of notes. Now, write a whitepaper or case study for your prospect. You don't have a helpdesk contract yet? Guess who Mr. Jones, your prospect, will think of tomorrow when his ulcer flares up because of helpdesk problems? Guess who Mr. Jones will recommend to his primary contractor when they have a problem with an incumbent small business? You should now understand the importance of going the extra mile and using education as part of your sales strategy.

## Marketing Give-Aways

Remember the Standards of Ethical Conduct for Employees of the Executive Branch (5 C.F.R. 2635) which we discussed earlier? This is how you build marketing into your strategy, keeping your dollar threshold under $50 annually - and ensuring your prospect *does not* consider what they receive as gifts.

An excellent strategy, best communicated by Chet Holmes in *The Ultimate Sales Machine*, is how to utilize small giveaways in parallel with education. When you send a document to your prospect, tie it to a small toy that relates to the concept of your document and something they will keep in or on their desk. It should have your company name or logo on it. Here are a few examples. They are all inexpensive and you can buy them online.

| Marketing Give-Aways | | |
|---|---|---|
| **Items** | | |
| Tape Measure | | "Measuring ROI for A/E/C contracts" <br> "Measuring ROI on infrastructure upgrades" |
| Carabiner | | "Protecting the lives of your employees" |
| Clip | | "We grasp the value you require" |
| Silly Putty | | "We are adaptable, flexible, and innovative" |
| Small Rubik's Cube | | "We can simplify the complex" |
| Coffee Mug | | "Some help on those Monday mornings!" |
| Calculator | | "We understand cost. We focus on value." |

*Table 43 - Marketing Give-Always*

*Make sure* that your gifts are not key chains, pens, or other common giveaways. You want something that they will chuckle at or really appreciate and then place on their desk. If you send silly-puddy to your prospect, chances are the next time you visit their office you will find silly-puddy in the shape of a tank, plane, or an impression from some other item in the office.

A business developer who worked for Chet Holmes called one of his prospects and the prospect said, "I've been meaning to talk to you! When I'm on the phone I'm always playing with one of these damn toys! Every time someone comes into my office to talk about something, they're rummaging around my desk for one of my toys!" The business developer definitely made an impression. *Just make sure that the documentation which accompanies the toy is providing clear value to the prospect*.

**This also works with your partners!** Remember, you need to have a similar level of effort for your desired teaming partners as you do for your prospects. If you think the program manager will smile at the silly-puddy, think about what your colleagues at other companies will do.

## Maintaining a Calendar of Events

To ensure that you maintain your follow-up schedule, annotate what documentation you are sending or planning to send to your prospects on your daily calendar. Everyone has their own method to managing their calendars.

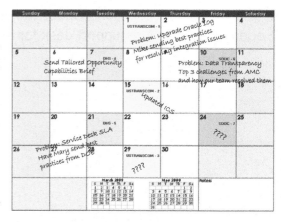

*Figure 97 - Calendar of Contact Events*

# Summary

As you network into an agency or command, your information and intelligence will become progressively more extensive and detailed. As you identify new contacts who may be champions for your products or services, you re-initiate your sales strategy at Step 3 and build the necessary relationships. You will find that by asking the right questions and educating each contact that your CRM / Bulls-Eye will expand exponentially. As you start to educate your prospect, you will find yourself *tailoring documentation you have already provided to other prospects* - even within the same agency or command. It becomes easier and easier to maintain your networking and follow-up schedule. You will have a robust library of educational reports, whitepapers, and case studies which you can modify for almost any opportunity.

Your sales strategy is about networking, building relationships, and building credibility. An interesting question is, "Should you *act like* a competent small business or simply a competent business?" In other words, should you approach your prospects with the arrogance and confidence of a business that is larger than you are or with the humbleness of a growing small business? The answer is both. You have to be confident without being arrogant. You have to be humble while proving subject matter expertise.

On the subject of set-asides, when you perform business development, *never discuss the socio-economic status of your company except as an afterthought*. If they ask you what status your company holds, answer the question with an immediate transition into the value or benefits that your company provides; not the features or capabilities of your solutions. Ironically, many small businesses believe this in theory but few practice it daily.

Ask the right questions and focus on your prospect. Don't focus on yourself or the sale. Do this and you will more strongly position your company for exponential growth. Educate your prospects and provide them with assistance at every turn and you will have stronger and more viable opportunities than your competition. This is how you build the strongest relationships; how you accelerate the maturity of your business; and how you double your annual revenue. *You must have the desire to learn*, the ability to accept rejection, and the aggressive yet soft persistence to become known as one of the strongest businesses (not small business) in your market and industry. These tactics, strategies, and processes can take your company to the next level.

If you have any questions about these tactics and strategies, either contact your RSM Federal coach or the support desk for Federal Access.

# Example – Step-by-Step Market Sales Strategy

This resource is Part 1. Now that you understand the baseline for Realignment Solution Methodology (RSM), Part 2 is a real-world example of a sales targeting strategy from an actual company. Part 2 combines daily business development and sales activities with historical contract data from USASpending.gov and SAM.gov's Data Bank.

Part 1, provides all the core requirements and activities necessary to engaging the government market. Part 2 provides a use-case of how these activities cross-walk to actual agency and DoD engagement. Part 2 is available to Federal Access Members in the Sales Module. Access at www.federal-access.com/manual.

# Your Contact and Call Plan

Every business developer operates differently. However, what if you don't understand the basics or you're the owner and you're curious about how often government contacts should be touched? These recommendations include both prospects and current customers.

| High Level Contact / Call Plan and Metrics | | | |
|---|---|---|---|
| **Sales Rep / BDM** | **Contact** | **Occurrence** | **Activities** |
| **Business Developers** (All Targeted Prospects) **Market Sales Strategy** | Senior Buyer / CO | Monthly | Contract Vehicles<br>Timing of Opportunities<br>Position for Set-Asides |
| | Program Manager | Twice Monthly | Current Problems and Challenges<br>Educate, Educate, & Educate<br>Identify Upcoming Opportunities<br>Identify Mission, Goals, Objectives |
| | Lead Technical | Once or Twice Monthly | Current Technical Problems<br>Educate, Educate, & Educate<br>Identify Upcoming Opportunities<br>Required Certifications |
| | Other Personnel | As Required | Competitor Information<br>Current Problems and Challenges |

# Chapter 12
# Teaming and Partners

**RSM FEDERAL**
The Art and Science of Government Sales™

# Teaming Methodology

- **Develop "True Partnerships"**
  - A partnership is not a company you teamed with 6 months ago on an RFP
  - Proactive and continuous communication and relationship building
  - Active versus passive communication
  - Forward opportunities within their competencies which are not yours
- **"Programmatic Teaming Strategy™" (PTS)**
  - "Building a relationship with another company in order to integrate your company's reputation, competencies, and products into two or more of the other company's verticals, markets, or territories."
  - It is not about the best partner. It's about the best strategy to target multiple opportunities with limited resources, time, and money
  - Increases qualified opportunities and increases number of contract vehicles
  - Level of trust and confidence which places you above other teammates

# Teaming Considerations

- **Teaming Agreements should be put in place BEFORE the RFP is released (whenever possible)**
- **First-Tier or Second-Tier Subcontractor?**
  - Multiple advantages to being a First-Tier Subcontractor
- **Teaming with a Large Companies**
  - Never pull out of proposal phase after it begins *(Quick way to destroy reputation)*
  - Be consistently aggressive

# Building an Unsolicited Tiger Team

- **Building a team of cross-functional capabilities and competencies,** supporting key products and services, to target select organizations for RFPs and unsolicited opportunities
- **An advanced teaming methodology**
  - Must be built into corporate sales strategy (Management rejects without vision)
  - Requires well planned Teaming Agreement (TA) strategy
- **Positioning**
  - Build joint marketing capabilities brief

– Joint press release

– Joint meeting with targeted agencies

# Teaming Agreements Between Large and Small Business

- **Common Problems**
  - Small Business gets on a winning team and receives minimal or no business
  - Small Business fails to "Sell The Prime" after contract award
- **Guarantee of Work?**
  - Standard for large Primes to mandate percentage from other large companies
  - Some large businesses are easier to work with and do not mandate a percentage
  - It is unusual for small business to leverage specific percentages with large companies
  - Common between small businesses
- **How To Position**
  - Instead of "Guaranteed Dollars" – Negotiate specific "Functional Areas"
- **Example Teaming Agreement, JV, CTA Templates & Checklists**
  - You can download multiple examples of teaming agreements, non-disclosure agreements, and other templates from the Federal Access Coaching and Training Platform.

# Case Study – First vs Second-Tier Sub-Contracting

- **The Second-Tier Domino Effect**
  - 5% average loss in bill rate

| Prime | $70.00 | First Tier / Discounted Rate |
|---|---|---|
| ↓ | $66.50 | Mandated Second Tier Rate |
| 1st Tier Sub | 1920 | Annual Billable Hours |

| First Tier Sub | $70.00 x 1920 = $134,400 |
|---|---|
| Second Tier Sub | $66.50 x 1920 = $127,680 |

*Figure 98 - 1st versus 2nd Tier Subcontracting*

- **Much more than Money!**
  - Only 5%?  The above example is $6,720 annually!
  - Impacts salary decisions
  - Can't communicate with customer without notifying Prime or first-tier sub
  - Difference between a 9 to 5 employee and one that calls you with opportunities!
  - Impacts Future Business

# Know Your Partners (and know your competition)

- **Your Network – By Customer, Contract, Competency, Market**
  - You qualify an opportunity but don't have the past performance for 2 Task Areas
  - Which company gives you the best win probability?
  - You do not build overnight - is an ongoing effort

# Develop a Stable of Companies

We teach every client to create a "Teaming Stable." You should have one to two of every socio-economic status, small and large. With strong proactive relationships, no matter what opportunity you find, you or one of your partners can pursue it. This and all other Teaming templates are in the Federal Access Coaching and Training Platform.

To crystalize the value of creating a "Teaming Stable," imagine the following scenario. You are a small woman-owned small business. You find an opportunity that is set-aside for service-disabled with the US Army and it's due in 10 days. You have almost no time to start your teaming process. BUT, your teaming stable has an SDVOSB, with DoD past performance, specifically for financial services. You quickly call your partner and you've just saved seven days of trying to convince some other company to put you on their team or they on yours to fill your gaps. It's not enough to have teaming partners. You need to document your stable of preferred partners so you can quickly and easily look at an opportunity and then evaluate which companies in your stable have worked with that agency, have the necessary competencies, their statuses, and contract vehicles. You think you can do this in your head. As you start engaging more and more opportunities and partners, this tracking mechanism becomes irreplaceable.

| Teaming Stable | | | | | |
|---|---|---|---|---|---|
| **Company** | **Status** | **Clients** | **Vehicles** | **Competencies** | **POC** |
| Krater Inc. | Small VOSB | Intelligence | ESITA Emerald | Software Development | Mary Smith (703) 665-8874 |
| Value Unite LLC | Small WOSB | HHS / CMS Defense Health USDA Homeland Security CDC | CIO-SP4 NITAAC | Systems Architecture IT solutions Workforce Development Financial Systems Management | Craig Jones (202) 551-7785 |
| Battle Casing Inc. | Large | Homeland Security Defense | EAGLE CASES TASER | Remote Portals | Dean Lannister (202) 663-2231 |
| ASERT Tech | Small WOSB 8a | DoTR GSA Gallery of Art SEC | GSA Schedule eFAST | Strategy Technology Operations Financial Management Org Management | Phillip Smith (618) 555-7777 |
| Blue Council LLC | Large | GSA Commerce Defense | None | Financial Services Federal Government Healthcare Life Sciences | Mary Jones (314) 651-7759 |
| Brighten Partners | Small SDVOSB | Intelligence Defense | SeaPort-E | System Engineering Financial Management IT Infrastructure Engineering Risk Management | Lisa Slater (703) 662-1145 |

*Table 44 - Your Teaming Stable*

# Working with Large Companies

- **Most Common Complaints:**
  - They won't call me back
  - We're on a winning team but we never get any work
  - The big boys take care of themselves
  - We are just as good as the other small businesses who received work or sales

> The number one reason that companies won't call you back or respond to your emails is because you have not communicated *enough value*

# How Large Companies Evaluate Small Business

There are five functional areas. They won't say these outloud or tell you that they are looking at these, but if you're a small business, you need to recognize this is how you are being evaluated for any given teaming opportunity.

- **Market Acumen**
  - You Know the Customer
  - Geographical Location

- **Back-Office Maturity**
  - Business Developers – Strong Interpersonal Skills
  - Investment Potential (Time?) (They will ask around)
  - Teaming Maturity
  - Proactive versus Reactive
  - Follow-Up What is Promised
  - Program Management
  - NAICS Codes – Back them up
  - Beneficial Agreements
  - Company Reputation
  - Competitive Pricing

> "You may have superior capability, great products and past performance, but a strong back-office is equally important to a teaming decision."

- **Competencies**
  - Complimentary Capabilities

- – Niche Capability?

- – Capabilities Brief is "Reality"

- – Past Performance (Mix Commercial & Government)

- **Quid-Pro-Quo**

  - – Common Interests

  - – Bring Them Business First

- **Acquisition Differentiators**

  - – Socio Economic Status

  - – Size Standard (How many years left?)

  - – NAICS Code Coverage

  - – Notice that acquisition differentiators. . . is last

# Meeting with a Large Company For Teaming

## Example #1

- **Your number one objective is convincing them that you will make them more competitive**

- **Your focus is mapping your capabilities and past performance, whether commercial or government, to complementary capabilities provided by the other company**

- **They are looking to see how mature you are as an organization**

- **The first meeting should be YOU bringing an opportunity to THEM**

  - – Should be a small business opportunity, one which they can not prime themselves → common practice and expected by larger companies. There is no stronger way to build a relationship with a large company

  - – Sometimes team even if you can do 100% of the work on your own

- **Example: you have identified an opportunity on Whiteman AFB and have:**

  - – Performed an initial qualification

  - – Confirmed that you have past performance on 65% - 95% of the requirements

  - – You need another company to fill the gaps

  - – You've been trying to build a relationship with a larger company…

  - – Provide an Introduction and Capability Statement (ICS) which we'll discuss later in this chapter

## Example 2

- **You are meeting with a large company to get on *their* team:**

  - Shape your core competencies to map to the RFP requirements

  - A large IDC / IDIQ Contract for the Air Force is heavy on Database Administration

  - Have a copy of your tailored Introduction and Capability Statement (ICS)

IDC – Indefinite Delivery Contract
IDIQ – Indefinite Delivery Indefinite Quantity Contract

---

"We are in the business of streamlining and consolidating data and information across multiple and geographically dispersed networks in order to increase the visibility, accuracy, and speed of access for the Enterprise.

We have increased the visibility and accuracy of data for Monsanto, Ralston Purina, and the Department of Defense, specifically at Offutt Air Force Base.

But before I go into too much detail, can I ask you some questions to help me better understand the services and type of teammates you are looking for? Would that be okay?"

---

*Figure 99 - Introduction for Joining a Team*

# Teaming with Large Companies

- **Don't Make Common Mistakes**

  - No begging or looking for handouts (You bring them the first opportunity)

  - Do not steal the work after an agreement is reached

  - Do not fish and pitch

- **Have "Quiet Confidence"**

  - Be confident without being cocky

  - Do not act bigger than you are (a common problem for small businesses)

  - They know you're small – so be small but mature and competent

- **One Primary Contact is critical**

  - But they must see there is a back-office supporting you

# Without CUF – Someone Is Going To Jail

- **Commercially Useful Function (CUF)**

  - Common issue / challenge for small business suppliers

  - Especially an issue for 8(a) / DBE minority suppliers

  - As Prime, you must perform four (4) functions to be classified a CUF:

    - ➤ You must be the one to negotiate price

    - ➤ You must determine quality and quantity

    - ➤ You must order the materials

    - ➤ You must pay for the material itself

## Commercially Useful Function (CUF)

| Small Business / DBE Responsible For |
| --- |
| • Negotiating price |
| • Determining quality and quantity |
| • Ordering the supplies |
| • Storing the supplies |
| • Paying for the supplies (key challenge for smaller DBEs) |
| • Receiving the supplies |
| • Delivering the supplies |
| • Supervision and management |
| • Customer service |

*Table 45 - CUF Responsibilities*

| Small Business / DBE Has The Following |
| --- |
| • Warehouse / storefront (or owns / operates distribution equipment for products) |
| • Inventory stored at warehouse or storefront |
| • Delivery vehicles |
| • Loading equipment |
| • Employees |
| • Website |
| • Industry standard insurance policies |

*Table 46 - CUF Has The Following*

## CUF Red Flags for Suppliers

- Does not normally buy, ship, support, or invoice the products
- Materials for the DBE are ordered or paid for by the prime or other team member.
- Prime discusses price or negotiates pricing for the DBE with another subcontractor
- Does not supply similar supplies for non-DBE projects
- Company other than DBE schedules delivery of supplies credited towards DBE participation.
- Obtains supplies for the contract from another supplier that is also on the contract.
- Owner / senior management provides little or no supervision of the work.
- DBE manager no a regular employee of the DBE firm.
- Key personnel / staff not under control of DBE.
- Inquiries of DBE activities answered by the Prime.
- DBE employees found on payroll records of two companies. . . on the same team.
- DBE owner has never visited the job site.
- Two-party or joint checks sent to manufacture for payment . . . versus from the DBE.
- Materials delivered to jobsite by company other the DBE.
- Prime contractor deducts payment for materials from payment for work performed.

# A Winning Team and No Work

- **Common statements made by Small Business:**

    - Not Fair

    - Unprofessional

    - Unethical

    - We just can't figure out how to convince the Prime to give us work!

- **The reason you don't have work is because you failed to:**

### *"Sell The Prime"*

*As a member of a team, you must position **your value** with the Prime before the RFP is released, during proposal phase, **during source selection**, after award, and if an IDIQ contract, for every task order*

# Sell The Prime™

- **Methodology:**

  - Under Multiple Award Contracts (MAC) and other type of contracts, is a post-award process to realign and shape your capabilities against a specific task order's requirements; to differentiate from the other companies on the team; to influence decisions on what work the Prime will give your company upon task order award.

- **Result:**

  - The overall team has the capability but your company positioned with the strongest differentiation and relationship with the Prime to provide value; and a competitive advantage so that the Prime selects your company for that specific Task Order or Functional Area when awarded.

- **Essential Tactic:**

  - You're fellow teammates are treated as the competition when it comes to market intelligence. Never share the information and intelligence you collect from potential agencies and military commands with any teammate until AFTER you've passed-on your intelligence to the Prime. When it comes to Indefinite Delivery Contracts (IDCs) (e.g. MAC, IDIQ, MATOC, GWAC, etc.) the subcontractor who identifies competitive intelligence is the company that the company that is awarded the work if the team wins the task order. Don't share market intelligence with your friends or fellow teammates until after you've notified the Prime.

# How Important Is Website To Teaming?

- **Large companies will evaluate more than a 100 small businesses for teaming on major contracts**

  - They immediately weed out companies with unprofessional websites

  - A broken link or two?  You've already been cut.

  - Are your core competencies listed and easy to find?

  - Does your website list every competency known to mankind? (not good)

  - Do your core competencies *match* what you have told them previously?

  - Are your NAICS codes prominently listed?

  - What is the breadth and depth of your company?

# "Balance of Strategies" In Teaming

- **"How to utilize your strengths"** and *"why you will help them win."*

- **Vision and Strategy**
  - Large companies develop strategy **months** or **years** before RFP is released

- **Reviewing their small business size standards**
  - How many of their current small businesses are at $10M, at $15M, at $20M?
  - Small businesses close to threshold rotated off *(Especially on 10 Year contracts)*
  - This may open the door for your company to join the team *(rare)*

- **How will the government apply small business credit?**
  - First Tier or Second Tier Sub?
  - Some agencies don't receive socio-economic credit for 2nd Tier Sub-Contractors

- **The Incumbent's Transition Plan**
  - Will review Small Business Goals and positioning prior to RFP release
  - Will bring-on new teammates and integrate *into existing work* to position the Proposal response *before* contract is awarded. This is a strategic plan.

# On Two Teams & Conflict of Interest (COI)

**Common Situation:** Large Multiple Award Schedule (IDIQ) with Small Business complement contract. In other words, you can both prime the small business contract and sub to a large company as a member of their team.

**Scenario:** You are on two teams and one team wins the award. The other team believes that you used information from their win-themes, ghosted their weaknesses, or utilized their key proposal concepts.

**Result:** Potential lawsuit, damage to reputation, burned bridge

**Solution:**
- "Run a Screen" to mitigate Conflicts of Interest (COI) (2 x Proposal Writers)
- Treat the RFP as two distinct opportunities
- Notify both teams of Screening during proposal process

# Introduction and Capability Statement (ICS)

The ICS is one of the most valuable tools you have for larger opportunities where you want to get onto the team of a large Prime. Simply, an ICS is a five to seven page mini-proposal that is used to convince larger (and smaller) Primes to put you on their team. Since its inception in 2008, this simple yet complex marketing / teaming tool has been successful 95% of the time! This means small businesses have successfully achieved a teaming agreement (TA), with a large business, 9 out of every 10 times.

*Figure 100 - Introduction and Capability Statement*

# Introduction and Capability Statement™ (ICS)

- **Detailed mapping of**
  - Prospect's Program
  - Prospect's Requirements
  - Prospect's Problems / Challenges
  - System Integrator's Small Business Requirements
  - System Integrator's Gaps and Penetration Strategy
- **Characteristics**
  - 5 to 7 page mini-proposal
  - Helps a company look more competent and mature to larger companies
  - Level of differentiation that validates you will provide value and be strong partner
- **Proven Success**
  - Specifically designed for teaming

# Sections

- Introduction and Summary
- Company Overview
- High-Level Benefits to Teaming
- Prime and Subcontracting Strategy
- Opportunity or Agency Requirements or Task Areas
- Corporate Competencies and Capabilities
- Past Performance Mapped to Government Opportunity
- Past Performance Mapped to Teammate
- Competency Crosswalk
- Standard Company Data (NAICS Codes, Cage Code, etc.
- List of Contracts / Past Performance

# Example ICS

### Before You Read

This hypothetical procurement has two acquisitions, one for large business and one for small businesses. We call these complimentary acquisitions. The large companies will compete against each other and the small businesses will compete against other smalls. In this example, MSR Services plans to Prime the small business track but wants to get on CACI's team for the full and open track.

### Introduction and Capabilities Statement (ICS)

**October 20, 2021**

Janet, *(Name of CACI capture manager, business developer, etc.)*

This document was designed to facilitate and augment our process of positioning MSR Services for the Department of Transportation's Professional Services Contract for the small business compliment acquisition. As we are already partners on the DISA Defense Transportation Services (DTS) effort, where we team with CACI, we also wanted to communicate our strengths for DOT's upcoming acquisition. We have past performance in several task area groups (TAGs) and we have a competent management team and back office to facilitate and support proposal development, resource delivery, and contract execution.

Even though this document is part of our overall strategy to build a strong team for the small business compliment contract, we also want to help map our capabilities to CACI's strategy and requirements as part of an early programmatic teaming strategy (PTS). I have not spoken with you or your capture management team since the acquisition strategy was modified by the government. As a result of the government's modifications to the acquisition, including scope and timeline, we are proactively positioning our capabilities and value to support CACI's bid decision and subsequent proposal.

Our intent is to position MSR Services *as a **primary first-tier subcontractor on Task Area Group 3*** to CACI. MSR Services wants to strengthen the relationship we have with CACI, developing a more programmatic relationship to increase and accelerate revenue for both companies.

We have provided a detailed background of our company, our capabilities, how and where those capabilities map to our existing customer base; how these capabilities map or potentially map to CACI's capture management activities; and increase CACI's competitive position. Our teaming and business development strategies have been modified for this effort.

Just as important, our methodology for supporting opportunities includes: identification and qualification of the themes and then mapping our capabilities, specifically those that allow us to shape and influence requirements, in order to communicate competitive advantage and differentiation to the CACI capture manager.

MSR is a growing small business, $4M revenue, and has an excellent reputation in the federal space as well as with the Department of Transportation (DOT). I look forward to continuing our discussions and joining the CACI Team.

Best regards,

*Michael Bauer*

**Michael Bauer**
Senior Account Executive
Government Technology Group
MSR Services
Mobile (703) 677-1700
mbauer@MSRServices.com

*Proprietary Notice*

*This document includes data that shall not be disclosed outside the receiving organization and shall not be duplicated, used, or disclosed—in whole or in part—for any purpose other than to evaluate MSR Services' role. If, however, a contract is awarded or in connection with the submission of this data the receiving organization has the right to duplicate, use, or disclose the data to the extent provided in the resulting contract. This restriction does not apply where information was known to the recipient prior to receipt of such information from MSR Services, or becomes publicly known through no fault of the recipient, or is received without obligation of confidentiality from a third party owing no obligation of confidentiality to MSR Services. The format of this document is business sensitive.*

## OVERVIEW

**Purpose:**

The purpose of this document is to communicate MSR Services' position in regards to DOT's Professional Services Contract; communicate our competencies that map to the anticipated / expected requirements; and where we will provide competitive differentiation. It is anticipated that MSR Services will develop a team to prime the DOT Professional Services Contract, NAICS Code 561110, where the government anticipates two to three (2-3) IDIQ contracts.

**MSR Services Corporate Profile:**
- Founded in 20xx *(10 Years)*
- 45 Employees
- SDB 8(a)
- Small Business *(SB)*
- WOSB
- Awarded KS Top 50 Companies
- *Differentiator*
- *Differentiator*
- *Differentiator*

**Why MSR Services? How do we Differentiate the Team?**
- Strong back-office focus on collaboration and teamwork

- We currently prime 7 DoD and 4 Commercial Contracts

- Secret Facility Clearance *(Headquarters in Kansas)*

- Strong Information Assurance (IA), Information Security (IS), and Cyber Security Services

- Key Certifications across lines of business *(i.e. CISSP, PMP, MBCP, MCP, etc.)*

- Utilization of Earned Value Management System *(EVMS)*

- Performance-based contracts with NAVSEA, GSA, and HUD

- ISO Certifications

  *[Note: Differentiators should map to both the opportunity and to CACI's requirements and gaps, where applicable.]*

## TEAMING WITH MSR SERVICES

### Why MSR Services?
MSR has excellent past performance, certifications, and back-office management to successfully manage government contracts and their respective proposals. You will find that our back-office operations are advantageous with strong process and cultural focus. We are a successful business as a result of our relationship, teaming, and channel methodologies.

## PRIME AND SUB-CONTRACTING STRATEGY

### Department of Transportation (DOT) Professional Services Contract (PSC):
The major changes between PSC and PSC 2 is a heightened focus on small business acquisition and training as a result of challenges faced during the first five years of the original contract. *From our discussions with the DOT Program Manager and Contracting Officer*, we have identified five key themes which the source selection committee will be looking for in the proposal response *[Note: do not provide the themes until a **teaming agreement is signed**. You can discuss your findings with them at a high level but do not lose your competitive position or leverage until a teaming agreement is signed]*. MSR Services is in final discussions with several small businesses to finalize our team as part of our capture management strategy. Our desire is to join the CACI team as a primary first-tier subcontractor and given the responsibility for Task Area Group (TAG) 3 for Professional Administrative Services, as part of the Full and Open acquisition. As a primary first-tier subcontractor, we would like to be responsible for managing the team's efforts on TAG 3, which is a core competency with solid past performance and CPARS ratings.

| Acquisition Strategy | | | | |
|---|---|---|---|---|
| **Service** | **Acquisition** | **Awards** | **Prime** | **NAICS** |
| Professional Services | SB | 2-3 | MSR Services | 561110 |
| Professional Services | Full / Open | 2-3 | CACI | 561110 |
| IT A&AS | Full / Open | 2 | CACI | 541512 |

*Table 47 - ICS Acquisition Strategy*

### MSR plans to Prime:
- DOT Professional Services (Small Business) – Team build pending final TAs.
- *Teaming Agreement with CACI in process*

### MSR plans to be a Primary First-Tier Subcontractor to CACI on TAG 3
- DOT Professional Services (Full and Open) – Discussion with CACI in process.

## MSR Services – COMPETENCIES / CORE CAPABILITIES

### Competencies and Capabilities

MSR's Core Services are listed below in Figure 1. Like other businesses, we provide Help Desk and Resource Delivery. However, MSR more strongly supports a team's differentiation through our data management and training services.

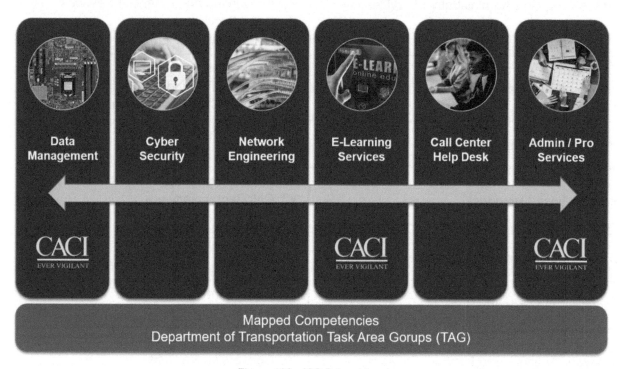

*Figure 102 - ICS Prime Mapping*

| MSR Solutions | |
|---|---|
| **Competencies** | **Detail** |
| Professional and Administrative Services | ✓ Project Management<br>✓ Personnel Administration<br>✓ Accounting and Financial Services<br>✓ Legal Services<br>✓ Staffing and Placement |
| Training and E-Learning | ✓ Management Training<br>✓ Systems Training<br>✓ LMS & LCMS Development |
| HIPPA and Information Security | ✓ Medical Records<br>✓ Medical System Analysis |
| Service Desk / Helpdesk | ✓ Telecommunication Coordination<br>✓ Call Center Software<br>✓ Tier 1-3 Support Levels |
| Data and Documentation Management | ✓ Data Entry<br>✓ Documentation Management |
| Logistics and Property Book | ✓ Equipment Management<br>✓ Parts Management |
| Software Analysis and Network Services | ✓ Network Administration<br>✓ Conversion Analysis<br>✓ AppDev and Code Reviews |

*Table 48 - ICS Competencies*

## Specific Past Performance Mapped To Capability

### MSR Services HIPPA and Information Assurance:

  MSR Services supports contracts with the Department of Defense, federal civilian agencies, as well as state and local governments. We provide Information Assurance (IA) services to the the Department of the Interior as well as the Department of Transportation. MSR Services has been awarded three contracts in support of Information Assurance. As a result of our contracts, we have mitigated more than 500 attacks on government networks and have become the 8(a) vendor of choice for the Department of Transportation. Our niche in HIPPA compliance, risk mitigation, and security oversight provides competent and recognized differentiation in the combination of HIPPA and Information Assurance.

> **HIPPA and IA Competencies**
> ✓ Program Management
> ✓ HIPPA Compliance
> ✓ Vulnerability Assessment, Penetration Testing, Risk Assessment
> ✓ Incident Response
> ✓ IT Security Training

## Enterprise Level Training / E-Learning

| DoD Training | Services |
|---|---|
| ✓ Program Management | |
| ✓ HIPPA Compliance | |
| ✓ Vulnerability Assessment, Penetration Testing, Risk Assessment | and |
| ✓ Incident Response | |
| ✓ IT Security Training | |

MSR Services provides comprehensive tailored training services are part of the deployment of an agency's enterprise technology deployment. MSR Services provides cradle to grave training services as part of DISA's Defense Transportation System (DTS), supporting the Army National Guard for the States of Alaska, Illinois, and Rhode Island. Our relationships with both the Commanders and the contracting officers has helped position MSR Services to accelerate the success of our Market Penetration Strategy (MPS). Our efforts with the Alaska National Guard provided training for 15 Army contract specialists in support of more than 23,000 soldiers. We trained 5 contract specialists at the Rhode Island National Guard in support of another 15,500 soldiers. Our contract with the Illinois ARNG supports more than 32,000 soldiers. Our training and E-Learning services, for both DTS and other DoD information technology systems has helped build our reputation as the "go-to" for IT and system training.

## Other Competencies…

| DoD Training |
|---|
| ✓ … |
| ✓ … |
| ✓ … |

## MSR Services Competency Crosswalk

The following table maps MSR's core competencies to current contracts within the Department of Defense, US Federal Agencies, State and Local, and the Private Sector.

| MSR Services | |
|---|---|
| **MSR Services SOW Crosswalk** | **Past Performance** |
| **Professional and Administrative Services**<br>• Project Management<br>• Personnel Administration<br>• Family Support Programs<br>• Accounting Services<br>• FOIA Services<br>• Legal Review<br>• Underwriting | ✓ State of Indiana<br>✓ Nestle Purina<br>✓ Illinois Army National Guard<br>✓ Rhode Island Army National Guard<br>✓ US Transportation Command<br>✓ Department of Labor<br>✓ General Services Administration<br>✓ US Navy<br>✓ Railroad Retirement |
| **Training and E-Learning**<br>• Defense Travel System (DTS) | ✓ Alaska Army National Guard<br>✓ Illinois Army National Guard |
| **HIPPA and Information Security (IS)**<br>• Medical Records<br>• Medical System Analysis | ✓ State of Illinois<br>✓ Illinois Army National Guard<br>✓ Rhode Island Army National Guard<br>✓ Indian Health Services |
| **Service Desk / Helpdesk** | ✓ US Army Reserve<br>✓ US Department of Agriculture |
| **Data and Documentation Management**<br>(Includes Database Administration)<br>• Data Entry<br>• Documentation Management | ✓ Nestle Purina<br>✓ Illinois Army National Guard<br>✓ US Transportation Command<br>✓ Indian Health Services<br>✓ Department of Labor<br>✓ US Department of Agriculture<br>✓ US Navy<br>✓ Railroad Retirement |
| **Logistics and Property Management**<br>• Equipment Management<br>• Property Management | ✓ Illinois Army National Guard<br>✓ US Department of Agriculture<br>✓ General Services Administration |
| **Software and Network Services**<br>• Network Administration<br>• Conversion Analysis<br>• Code Review | ✓ Nestle Purina<br>✓ State of Illinois<br>✓ US Transportation Command<br>✓ Indian Health Services<br>✓ Department of Labor<br>✓ US Navy |

*Table 49 - ICS Past Performance Crosswalk*

## OTHER COMPANY INFORMATION AND RESOURCES

### Company Data

| | | | |
|---|---|---|---|
| # Employees | 45 | Annual Sales | $4M |
| Status | 8(a), SB, WOSB | Cage Code | 4GJS4 |
| DUNS | 665334755 | GSA IT-70 | GS-35F-4423K |
| GSA 8(a) STARS | GS-44F-5589Z | | |

### NAICS Codes

| | |
|---|---|
| 541519 (7379) | Other Computer Related Services |
| 541611 (8742) | Admin Mgt & General Management Consulting Services |
| 541710 (8731) | R&D in the Physical, Engineering, & Life Sciences |
| 611420 (8243) | Computer Training |
| 811212 (7378) | Computer & Office Machine Repair & Maintenance |

| Contract Vehicle | Number |
|---|---|
| GSA Schedule | GS-35F-4423K |
| GSA GWAC 8(a) STARS | GS-44F-5589Z |
| GSA Polaris GWAC | GSA-667-44TH7 |
| CIO-SP4 | Sub to SRA<br>DISA Mentor / Protégé with NGC |
| DISA / DITCO BOA | HC1002-08-G-5669 |
| USTRANSCOM A&AS | HTC 711-07-D-0006<br>Full and Open – Teaming with CACI<br>Small Business - Teaming with S4 |
| VETS (Teaming with VETS-Inc.) | GS-03F-0433Z |
| Seaport-Enhanced | N55578-02-D-4431 |
| DoD BPA for DTS Training | ARNG-334-44776 |

*Table 50 - ICS Corporate Data*

# Chapter 13
# The Bid – No Bid Process

**RSM FEDERAL**
The Art and Science of Government Sales™

# Bid – No Bid Process Overview

This is a fairly short chapter but important nonetheless. The bid - no bid process starts during business development and ends when you complete the proposal. Some companies, which you don't want to be like, get 80% complete writing the proposal and then realize there are gaps they can't fill, that they are not competitive and decide not to submit a bid or proposal.

Can you imagine how much time and money they just wasted? This happens much more regularly with smaller businesses. How do you prevent this from happening? By ensuring you *understand every requirement in the solicitation*. You use a **Compliance Matrix** which we cover in the next chapter.

- In the Federal Market, the *timing* of when you "engage" an opportunity is the key criteria in your decision to bid

- Bidding on government RFPs takes time, money, and resources

- A bid decision is like being pregnant:
  - You are either fully committed or you are not
  - Resource intensive

- Lack of focus = you are wasting time, money, and manpower

- Doing the bid process in your head? You are probably not winning.

# Poor Bid Decisions?

- Business Developers have trouble meeting quotas so they bid everything "that looks good"

- Too many agencies or organizations targeted – can not properly focus

- The only time you don't bid an opportunity is when your resources are at maximum capacity

- *You must have a formal Bid – No Bid Process (repeatable process)*

## Poor Bid Decisions Cost Money

- **Potentially spend weeks or months on a proposal and find out half-way through that you do not have the necessary capabilities**

  - Too late to find teaming partners

  - If you find teaming partners – they are the wrong ones (better ones are taken)

  - You don't have the competencies and past performance to win

- **What is the cost to No-Bid after you've starting writing the proposal?**

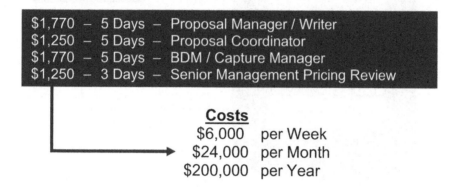

$1,770 – 5 Days – Proposal Manager / Writer
$1,250 – 5 Days – Proposal Coordinator
$1,770 – 5 Days – BDM / Capture Manager
$1,250 – 3 Days – Senior Management Pricing Review

**Costs**
$6,000    per Week
$24,000   per Month
$200,000 per Year

# The Bid – No Bid Process

- **Step 1 – Initial Qualification**

  - Was it already released as an RFP or RFQ when you learned of it?

  - Do you know the prospect?

  - Is there an incumbent and is this a recompetition?

  - Have you spoken to this prospect or customer about this opportunity?

  - Bottom Line: Was this RFP on your radar?

- **Step 2 – The Bid - No Bid Qualification Worksheet**

  - Do you understand the scope and requirements of the RFP / PWS?

  - Do you understand the customer's vision and objectives?

  - Do you have the core competencies? Did you shape? Can you differentiate?

  - Is the contract wired for another company?

  - Is there acceptable risk?

  - Can you develop a winning staffing strategy, if applicable?

- **Step 3 – Bid Decision**

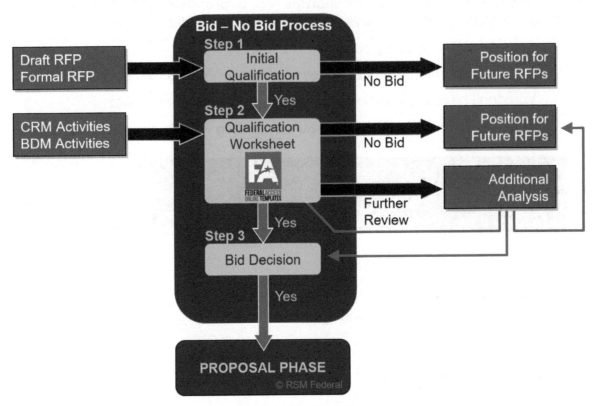

*Figure 103 - Bid - No Bid Process*

# How Do You Make a Bid Decision with Vague Requirements?

- **Vague requirements are *common* in Government RFPs**
  - Prospect may be unsure of what they are looking for
  - Scope may be poorly defined due to lack of experience or knowledge
  - Prospect may have an incumbent in mind and does not make an effort to clarify
  - Sometimes it is a combination of factors
  - Normally, when the government refused to answer your questions, it's because they feel you should know the answer or they purposely want companies to not have the answers so that you explain why you are using a specific number of FTEs, etc.

- **Clarify requirements**
  - Develop comprehensive list of questions and submit during Q&A phase
  - Attend pre-proposal conference / Industry Day to ask questions in person

- **Contracting Officer still refuses to answer your questions**
  - Unfortunately, this happens
  - When answers are not provided, you *build assumptions into proposal*

- **Companies may change their bid decision after the Q&A phase**

# Bid – No Bid Qualification Worksheet

If you look at the figure on the preceding page for the bid – no bid process, Step 2 is using a qualification worksheet to make sure you should or not be writing a proposal. Like every other strategy and work product outlined in this Manual, this qualification worksheet can be downloaded from the Federal Access Coaching and Training Platform. The template allows you to tailor the worksheet to your company and your specific products or services.

As the business developer, the Director of Sales, or the owner, you can tailor the worksheet so your know your team is only writing proposals where it is clear that your business development activities have made you competitive.

**Bid - No Bid Qualification Worksheet**
MSR Services

MSR SERVICES

| RFP Title | USDA IT Services and Helpdesk |
| Capture Manager | Michael McBride |
| Date/Time Receipt | October 1, 20xx |

| | | KEY | Evaluation | |
| --- | --- | --- | --- | --- |
| | | | Yes / No / Blank | F = FAV  U = UNFAV |

**Section 1 - RFP / SOW / PWS Review**

| # | | KEY | Yes/No/Blank | F/U |
| --- | --- | --- | --- | --- |
| 1 | Do we have the identified NAICS code? | ► | Yes | F |
| 2 | Did we have prior knowledge of this opportunity prior the RFP being released? | | Yes | F |
| 4 | Do we know the Independent Government Cost Estimate (IGCE) (their budget)? | | No | U |

**Section 2 - Customer Vision and Objectives**

| 5 | Do we understand the customer's current challenges and "hot buttons" (regardless of the RFP)? | ► | Yes | F |
| 6 | Are we able to qualify and quantify the value / return on investment in responding to the requirements? | | Yes | F |

**Section 3 - Core Competencies Positioning, Differentiation**

| 7 | Have we positioned requirements / ghosted requirements to give us a competitive advantage? | | No | U |
| 8 | Do we have all of the core competencies required by this opportunity? | | Yes | F |
| 9 | Do we have direct and relevant technical past performance with this customer? | | Yes | F |
| 10 | Do we have direct and relevant technical past performance with other government customers? | | Yes | F |
| 11 | Do we have direct and relevant technical past performance with other commercial customers? | | Yes | F |
| 12 | Can we differentiate our products / services in our response to faciliate a perception of stronger value? | ► | Yes | F |
| 13 | Can we successfully deliver without using teammates? | | Yes | F |
| 14 | If we don't have all the core competencies, do our team mates have the missing competencies? | | Yes | F |
| 15 | Do our teammates have direct and relevant technical past performance with this customer | | Yes | F |
| 16 | Do teammates have direct and relevant technical past performance with other government customers? | | Yes | F |

**Section 4 - Is This Contract Wired**

| 17 | Is this a new opportunity? (No indicates an incumbent performing the work today) | | Yes | F |
| 18 | Is this opportunity for work-continuation?  2nd Phase of a current contract? | ► | No | F |
| 19 | If there is an incumbent, is the customer satisfied with their work? (If you don't know - answer Yes) | ► | No | F |
| 20 | If there is an incumbent, are they eligible to re-bid? | | No | F |
| 21 | Is Past Performance selection criteria weighted low? (<=30%) | | Yes | U |
| 22 | Do you have at least 10 business days to respond? | | Yes | F |
| 23 | Are the requirements clear and well defined to understand scope and pricing? | | No | U |
| 24 | Do we have competitive intelligence on other companies planning to bid? | | No | U |

**Section 5 - Risk**

| 25 | Is the contract Firm Fixed Price (FFP)? | | Yes | F |
| 26 | Do we have a current relationship or had prior discussions with this customer? | | Yes | F |
| 27 | Do we have a current contract with this customer for other services? | | No | U |
| 28 | Is this customer specifically identified in our annual business development target list? | | Yes | F |
| 29 | Have we met with the customer's decision makers / program managers? (not contracting officers) | | Yes | F |
| 30 | If we are building a team, do any of our team members have a relationship with this customer? | | No | U |

**Section 6 - Multi-Disciplined Staffing Approach (MDSA)**

| 31 | Do we have a resume database with at least 50% of required personnel and all Key Personnel? | | Yes | F |
| 32 | Have we staffed at this location before (within the last three years) | | No | U |
| 33 | Are the requirements clear and well defined to accurately identify labor categories and number of FTEs? | | Yes | F |
| 34 | If the RFP requires security clearances, do we have the ability to locate the necessary personnel? | | Yes | F |

| | |
| --- | --- |
| Total Favorable | 25 |
| Total Unfavorable | 8 |
| % Favorable | 75.76% |
| Bid Decision  > 75% Fav = Bid Decision  <50% Fav = No Bid Decision  >50% or <75% = Move to Next phase | **Bid** |

Approval Authority _____  Date _____

*Figure 104 - Bid - No Bid Qualification Worksheet – 'Bid'*

| | Bid - No Bid Qualification Worksheet | | | |
|---|---|---|---|---|
| MSR SERVICES | | | MSR Services | |

| | | | KEY | Evaluation | |
|---|---|---|---|---|---|
| **RFP Title** | USDA IT Services and Helpdesk | | | Yes / No / Blank | F = FAV |
| **Capture Manager** | Michael McBride | | | | U = UNFAV |
| **Date/Time Receipt** | October 1, 20xx | | | | |

| | Section 1 - RFP / SOW / PWS Review | | | |
|---|---|---|---|---|
| 1 | Do we have the identified NAICS code? | ► | Yes | F |
| 2 | Did we have prior knowledge of this opportunity prior the RFP being released? | | Yes | F |
| 4 | Do we know the Independent Government Cost Estimate (IGCE) (their budget)? | | Yes | F |
| | Section 2 - Customer Vision and Objectives | | | |
| 5 | Do we understand the customer's current challenges and "hot buttons" (regardless of the RFP)? | ► | Yes | F |
| 6 | Are we able to qualify and quantify the value / return on investment in responding to the requirements? | | Yes | F |
| | Section 3 - Core Competencies, Positioning, Ghosting | | | |
| 7 | Have we positioned requirements / ghosted requirements to give us a competitive advantage? | | Yes | F |
| 8 | Do we have all of the core competencies required by this opportunity? | | Yes | F |
| 9 | Do we have direct and relevant technical past performance with this customer? | | Yes | F |
| 10 | Do we have direct and relevant technical past performance with other government customers? | | Yes | F |
| 11 | Do we have direct and relevant technical past performance with other commercial customers? | | Yes | F |
| 12 | Can we differentiate our products / services in our response to faciliate a perception of stronger value? | ► | No | U |
| 13 | Can we successfully deliver without using teammates? | | Yes | F |
| 14 | If we don't have all the core competencies, do our team mates have the missing competencies? | | Yes | F |
| 15 | Do our teammates have direct and relevant technical past performance with this customer | | Yes | F |
| 16 | Do teammates have direct and relevant technical past performance with other government customers? | | Yes | F |
| | Section 4 - Is This Contract Valued | | | |
| 17 | Is this a new opportunity? (No indicates an incumbent performing the work today) | | Yes | F |
| 18 | Is this opportunity for work-continuation? 2nd Phase of a current contract? | ► | No | F |
| 19 | If there is an incumbent, is the customer satisfied with their work? (If you don't know - answer Yes) | ► | No | F |
| 20 | If there is an incumbent, are they eligible to re-bid? | | No | F |
| 21 | Is Past Performance selection criteria weighted low? (<=30%) | | No | F |
| 22 | Do you have at least 10 business days to respond? | | Yes | F |
| 23 | Are the requirements clear and well defined to understand scope and pricing? | | Yes | F |
| 24 | Do we have competitive intelligence on other companies planning to bid? | | Yes | F |
| | Section 5 - Risk | | | |
| 25 | Is the contract Firm Fixed Price (FFP)? | | Yes | F |
| 26 | Do we have a current relationship or had prior discussions with this customer? | | Yes | F |
| 27 | Do we have a current contract with this customer for other services? | | Yes | F |
| 28 | Is this customer specifically identified in our annual business development target list? | | Yes | F |
| 29 | Have we met with the customer's decision makers / program managers? (not contracting officers) | | Yes | F |
| 30 | If we are building a team, do any of our team members have a relationship with this customer? | | Yes | F |
| | Section 6 - Multi-Disciplined Staffing Approach (MDSA) | | | |
| 31 | Do we have a resume database with at least 50% of required personnel and all Key Personnel? | | Yes | F |
| 32 | Have we staffed at this location before (within the last three years) | | Yes | F |
| 33 | Are the requirements clear and well defined to accurately identify labor categories and number of FTEs? | | Yes | F |
| 34 | If the RFP requires security clearances, do we have the ability to locate the necessary personnel? | | Yes | F |

Do not mark in this section

| | | |
|---|---|---|
| | **Total Favorable** | 32 |
| **AUTOMATIC NO BID** | **Total Unfavorable** | 1 |
| **REQUIRES SENIOR MANAGEMENT TO CHANGE DECISION** | **% Favorable** | 96.97% |
| | **Bid Decision** > 75% Fav = Bid Decision <50% Fav = No Bid Decision >50% or <75% = Move to Next phase | **STOP** |

Approval Authority _____   Date _____

*Figure 105 - Bid - No Bid Qualification Worksheet - 'Stop'*

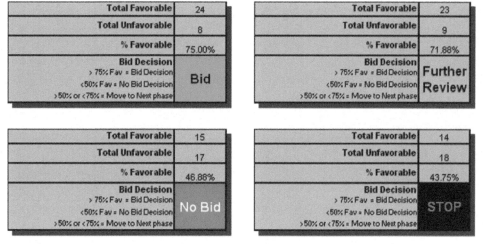

*Figure 106 - The 4 Bid Decisions*

---

# Chapter 14
# Proposal Tactics and Strategies

# Chapter Objectives

- **Provide key concepts, tactics, and strategies**
- **Introduction to the Multi-Disciplined Staffing Approach (MDSA)**
  - Impacts all sections of the RFP
  - Provides competitive advantage
- **This chapter is not designed to teach end-to-end proposal development**
  - There are many books and training courses. However, all the books and training courses can not replace experience.
  - Anyone can teach you how to format a proposal, but proposals win because of the strategy.
  - All of the tools and templates outlined in this chapter can be downloaded from the Federal Access Coaching and Training Platform.

    www.federal-access.com/manual
- **The objective of this chapter** is to provide you with tactics and strategies that cross-walk your Market Sales Strategy (MSS) into the acquisition and proposal phase.
- The tactics and strategies in this module should be integrated into any proposal you work on as either a Prime or Sub.

# A Winning Proposal

- **Comes from a well executed Market Sales Strategy (MSS)**
  - Proposal development and storyboards (when applicable) become much easier
- **A strong Market Sales Strategy 'enables' a stronger proposal response**

## Business Intelligence *Drives* Successful Proposals

- **Performed during sales activities and prior to any specific acquisition**
- **Sources Sought and Requests For Information (RFI)**
  - Best time to shape and *ghost* requirements
  - Initiate Teaming Agreements (TA) in pre-acquisition, before the RFP or RFQ is released! *(Your competition will wait for the RFP)*
- **Industry Comments on Draft RFP**
  - Another opportunity to shape and ghost requirements
  - Contracting Office may be looking for feedback to decide on acquisition strategy and other requirements

---

- **Pre-Proposal Conference / Industry Day**
  - You talk to the customer, perform site survey, hear questions from competition
  - Obtain Information that will NOT be in the RFP (competitive advantage)
  - You will better understand the status of the incumbent *(indirectly)*
  - If one is scheduled - you or a teammate *should* attend
  - If you are the Prime - you *must* attend (if you want to be competitive)
- **Post RFP Q&As**
  - Questions to clarify RFP intent and language
  - Remember that the agency will share your questions and answers with other bidders

# Insights on Government Proposals

- **Public Sector Proposals are highly detailed and "integrated"**
- **"Early Engagement" (Market Sales Strategy)**
  - Spend time upfront → not simply responding to RFPs
  - Practice "Early Engagement" before RFP is released
  - Qualify, shape, and position opportunities before RFP is released
- **Responding to RFPs without knowing the prospect is "Activity"**
  - Don't be a proposal sweatshop
  - You will lose 99% of your proposals without knowing the prospect
- **40% - 60% of RFPs – Procurement decision is already made**
  - You must be involved with the prospect before the RFP is released
  - By being involved and as part of your sales strategy, you can "shape" the RFP
  - Shaping requirements is a Pipeline Milestone
- **Arrogant to believe you can unseat an incumbent without relationships** and the prospect having a perception of proven differentiation
- **Stability *Often* Overlooked**
  - Lowest price does not provide customer with sense of stability
  - If attempting to unseat incumbent, speak to "transitional stability"
  - Taking stability into account builds prospect / customer confidence
- **Don't use RFP response to "Show what we can do"**
  - The Source Selection Committee may not be the right audience
  - Better to build relationships via Market Sales Strategy

- Exception: Providing additional capability not requested = Value-Add
- **Always cite value / benefits before features** – tie to requirements
- **It's about the Prospect – Not about you**
  - If you find it difficult to write the majority of your proposal about the prospect's challenges, systems, and processes, then you probably do not understand the prospect well enough to win the contract
- **Use Active vs Passive voice**
- **Always write from the prospect's perspective – not your perspective**
- **Use different font color to emphasize differentiation and value**
- **Format and respond to the proposal *as requested in the RFP***
  - Often used to quickly eliminate unknown or undesired bidders
- **For alignment, do not justify text. Leave left-justified.**
  - Easy for reader to skip a line
- **Utilize Call-Out boxes to draw attention to key value and benefits**
- **IBM coined a phrase called Unsubstantiated Bold Allegations (UBAs)**
  - Do not use UBAs. If it can not be validated, use another verb or statement to describe
- **Do not assume the Prospect:**
  - Understands the benefits of your solutions
  - Understands the "best value" of your solutions
- **Respond to EVERY requirement listed in the RFP**
  - Even the small / minor / less important requirements
  - Failing to respond to a requirement makes you "non-responsive"
  - Non-responsive will eliminate you from competition
- **It is not enough to meet or exceed the requirements**
  - Must exceed the competition's solutions to be recognized as "best value" and the RFP or RFQ clearly states that the procurement is Low Price Technically Acceptable (LPTA).
- **Your company's writers and reviewers are NEVER the same people**
  - Even in small companies
  - You can not see the errors in your own writing (the Prospect will)
- **Establish and ENFORCE schedules and timelines**

## Proposal Writing – Common Challenges

- **Don't measure success via Red Team (Final Proposal Review)**
  - Measure success by constantly asking "How competitive are we?"
  - How well do we communicate our "value" and "win themes"?

- **Don't focus on spelling and grammar in your draft**
  - You won't lose because of spelling and grammar
  - Spelling and grammar are resolved in future iterations
  - Focus on whether or not your draft communicates best value and win themes are clear and consistent.

- **Don't focus on style – Focus on Content**
  - You never have enough time so writers should focus on content, not style
  - Provide a style sheet during the Kickoff Meeting

- **"We always use this graphic"**
  - Don't use a graphic unless it adds *significant value*

- **Don't format until the final review**
  - Why not format as you go? The proposal manager can't focus on the important items if they are focused on making it pretty

## The "Loss-Leader"

A Loss-Leader is when you write a proposal, which you expect to lose (or win with little profit), in order to collect business intelligence and to create a competitive advantage for follow-on procurements. Your proposal is designed to collect information and intelligence for a **_known_** and future solicitation that is on your **_pipeline_**.

- **Rarely a Good Idea**
  - Not a viable or productive activity
  - Might be an option if the agency is in the top 3 of your annual target list
  - Expensive! Two week proposal effort averages $12,000 (time / resources)

- **Most companies will call a proposal a loss leader →**
  - As an excuse after loss of award
  - In the middle of the proposal effort when they realize they aren't competitive

- **Strong adherence to Bid – No Bid Qualification Worksheet**
  - A strong bid process ensures you're not wasting money and resources

- **Except under very rare circumstances, don't "fall-into" loss-leaders**
  - Spend your time building a strong relationship with the prospect

- It is arrogant to think you can unseat an incumbent without a relationship

- **If you decide to do a loss-leader, first consider:**

  - Historically, does the contracting officer provide sufficient feedback?

  - Is a known future opportunity worth the effort of performing a loss-leader?

  - Have you assessed your own risk? (Time, money, labor, resources)

- **A loss leader is almost never a smart choice**

  - Review the RFP and utilize the Q&A process to collect what you need for future opportunities. You can do all of this without writing a proposal!

# Understanding and Mitigating Risk

When writing a proposal, you need to consider the perceived level of risk during source selection.

- **Federal customers are risk adverse!**

- **Any new company is perceived as a risk by the government**

  - Educate your prospects and become subject matter experts (SME)

  - Become a respected source for your core competencies

- **Remember FFP contracts have more risk than T&M contracts**

  - Review all SLAs and Metrics

  - For FFP, the longer the timeline for development / implementation the more risk

  - Consider, account for, and possibly speak to risk in various proposal sections

  - Measure the risk through your prospect's eyes (understand your prospect)

  - You can not do this without strong Market Sales Strategy activities

- **Three Key Questions**

  - How does the customer assess risk?

  - Who is responsible for assessing risk?

  - Who is responsible for mitigating risk?

- **If proposal requires risk mitigation – touch on risk in executive summary**

  - Depends on RFP and identified risk and level of mitigation

- **Risk Management Strategy**

  - Emphasize strengths

  - Mitigate weaknesses

  - Neutralize competitor strengths

  - Ghost competitor weaknesses

## Risk Management Matrix

Not to be confused wih a Requirement Traceability Matrix (RTM), the Risk Management Matrix is included in your proposal, if necessary, to show the government you have mitigated any actual or perceived risk. If you need a copy of a risk management matrix / template, log into the Federal Access Coaching and Training Platform. You may add one into a proposal where the RFP requests one or you feel it's warranted.

| # | Risk Management Matrix | | | | |
|---|---|---|---|---|---|
| # | Risk Area | Risk Level | Mitigated Level | Summary of Approach | Proposal Section |
| 1 | Unanticipated surge | Medium | Low | Using a Multi-Disciplined Staffing Approach (MDSA) | 3.4.2 |
| 2 | Ability to meet transition schedule | High | Low | Pre-Award activities and offsite preparation | 4.1 |
| 3 | Key Personnel not available | Medium | Low | MDSA Approach and Alternate's identified | 2.5 & 3.4.2 |
| 4 | *Another Risk* | *Medium* | *Low* | *Summary* | *2.5.1 & 4.1.1* |

*Table 51 - Risk Management Matrix*

# Win Themes

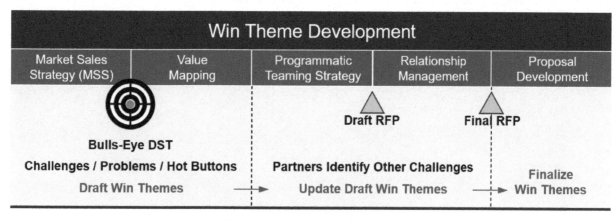

*Figure 107 - Win Theme Development*

- **Win theme development:**
  - Identify win themes during relationship management
  - Recorded within your CRM or on the Bulls-Eye DSS
  - Whenever possible - draft win themes are developed before RFP release
  - Themes are based on the challenges and problems you identify during Market Sales Strategy activities

- **Finalizing win themes after RFP is released will have low win percentage**
- **Win themes are how you communicate Best Value**
- **A win theme takes your core competencies and:**
  - Clearly depicts unquestioned ability to meet requirements
  - Clearly depicts unquestioned ability to manage the contract
  - Captures known challenges, problems and hot-buttons
  - Differentiates and shapes the value and benefit of your capabilities
  - Your solution is a better-value than the competition
- **A win theme takes your competitor's win themes into account**
- **Clear statement of how your solution benefits the prospect**
  - Fulfills prospect needs
  - Resolves specific issues
- **From Value-Mapping:**
  - Ability to communicate competitive advantage (if possible)
  - Ghosts the weaknesses of your competition
- **Focus on Value – not Features**
  - Imagine you are the prospect and what is most important to you
- **Start developing Win Themes before RFP or Draft RFP is released**
  - You should have draft themes before acquisition phase

CRM – Customer Relationship Management System
DSS – Decision Support System

## Win Theme Components

The Win-Theme Worksheet is comprised of four primary fields

- Prospect's Objectives
- Your Approach
- Your Value and Benefit
- Proof (Past Performance)

| # | Prospect Objective | Approach | Value & Benefit | Proof |
|---|---|---|---|---|
| | **Win Theme Worksheet** | | | |
| 1 | Provide experienced contractors to minimize change orders for surge or unanticipated events | Multi-Disciplined Staffing Approach (MDSA) | ✓ Cross-Functional Capabilities<br>✓ Alternates and Backup<br>✓ Save overtime $$$ | AFMC<br>USACOE<br>St. Louis Orthopedic |
| 2 | Consolidate network operations from five to one site for centralized operations and management under a Performance-Based Contract | Communicate National versus Regional using two performance-based contracts with DISA in California and St. Louis | ✓ Experience managing centralized network operations<br>✓ Successfully manage multiple sites across the country today<br>✓ Already perform work at 4 of 5 geographical locations | AFMC<br>AMC<br>DOT |
| 3 | Close interaction with the OCIO's office for current and future IT planning requirements | Have two government and two commercial contracts where we work with and provide value to the CIO | ✓ Strong competency in helping CIOs manage IT direction | Department of Labor<br>HUD<br>St. Louis Orthopedic<br>Lumber Associates |
| 5 | | | | |

*Table 52 - Win Theme Worksheet*

# Storyboards

- **Hearing the word "Storyboard" makes most people cringe**
- **Storyboards are not for common or simple procurements**
- **When should you utilize Storyboards?**
  - Complex acquisitions
  - New opportunities which are different from previous proposal efforts
  - Due to time management issues, small businesses often don't have the time to complete storyboards
  - Rarely applicable or viable for Task Orders with a 2 week timeline
- **Value of Storyboards**
  - Plan, develop, and review key requirements before writing
  - Reduce time and preparation costs
  - Help you quickly identify requirements, strategy, and graphics

# Storyboards for Small Business

- **Storyboards provide:**
  - Graphical breakdown of the RFP
  - Short descriptions how to respond to each task, paragraph, and functional area
  - Visually tells the story of how you will respond
- **Storyboards do not have to be an exercise of PhD proportion!**
- **Multiple formats but most common:**
  - Column 1: Proposal Preparation Instructions
  - Column 2: Evaluation Criteria
  - Column 3: Statement of Work
- **Many small businesses believe that large company storyboard activities are too complicated and time consuming**
  - *They are right* – as long as the RFP is not a complex acquisition
  - Some version of the storyboard MUST be performed for complex acquisitions
  - If you have properly executed a Market Sales Strategy – it is a simpler process

# Collecting Market and Opportunity Intelligence

## Questions to Ask the Government Pre-Acquisition

To level-set, these are the questions, or similar ones, you look to ask the government when they release an RFI, a sources sought, or a draft solicitation. When the RFP is released, it has moved from pre-acquisition to acquisition stage. When it hits acquisition stage (contractors are now writing proposals), the government is unlikely to talk to you or answer questions (other than responding as part of the formal Q&A period. Remember, every question you ask during the RFP's formal Q&A period will be shared with your competition along with the government's response.

This is why it's best to ask questions and ghost requirements in pre-acquisition. The government is allowed to speak with you, one on one, before the RFP is released!

The table below includes several example questions you can use:

| Questions When You're In Pre-Acquisition |
| --- |
| What are the agency's key initiatives? |
| What are the key solutions or programs? |
| What are the key challenges or problems? |
| Who is affected by these challenges or problems? |
| How are they affected by these problems? |
| Who manages these requirements today? |
| Which vendors do the majority of business with this prospect? |
| Does the prospect like the incumbent today? |
| What is the contact number for the PM of this project? |
| If not a set-aside, is there a possibility it will change? |
| Does the small business office know about this requirement? |
| Is this contract a part of a larger effort not identified? |

*Table 53 - Questions When You're In Pre-Acquisition*

# Questions to Ask the Government After the RFP is Released

In order to maintain communications with the Agency, Prospect, or Contracting Officer:

| Questions Post RFP |
|---|
| Is there anything else we need to provide? |
| Do we need to extend the pricing expiration? |
| Will a decision be made in the next 45 days? |
| Have any vendors been eliminated yet? |
| Is the decision close or pending? |
| Are we still in the running? |
| Will you let me know as soon as a decision has been made? |
| Has the source selection team started their review? |
| When would be a good time to follow-up with you? |
| Are there any issues we should look at? |
| Did anyone internally recommend us?  OSBP? |

*Table 54 - Questions Post RFP*

# Collecting Intelligence after RFP Release

- The Contracting Officer and Program Manager are free to answer questions during the RFI / Sources Sought and Pre-RFP phases.

- Once the formal RFP or RFQ is released, the government is not "supposed" to answer your questions except by formal Q&A identified by date in the RFP. However, sometimes they will answer your questions even after the RFP is released.

- Caution. Once the RFP is released, any questions you ask and the responses you receive from the contracting officer (CO) will be shared with ALL interested bidders. This is important because you don't want to ask questions that involve strategy or win themes.

- There is no crystal ball for which questions to ask.

- If you have a strong market sales strategy, you will know the answers before RFP release. Step-by-step sales strategies are located in the the Federal Access Coaching and Training Platform.

## ⚠ Important Note on Intelligence After RFP Release

Remember that all of the questions you ask during the formal Question and Answer (Q&A) and the answers you receive will be recorded and provided to all vendors. Whenever possible, ask questions of the PM versus the CO. Once the RFP is released, attempt to ask the questions verbally in an attempt to keep the answers from being provided to all vendors.

# Freedom of Information Act (FOIA)

The Freedom of Information Act (FOIA) generally provides that any person has a right, enforceable in court, to access of federal agency records, except to the extent that such records (or portions thereof) are protected from disclosure by one of nine exemptions or by one of three special law enforcement record exclusions.

- **As a general rule, legislative or judicial branches do not apply**

- **Documents that contain proprietary information are exempt from being released - however, sometimes agencies will release them**

- **Timeline:**
    - Government will verify receipt of request within 20 business days
    - Response with documentation within 60 – 120 days

As a result, it may take 3 to 5 months to get what you're asking for. FOIA's are performed during pre-acquisition because by the time you see an RFP, the proposal will likely be due before you receive the FOIA response.

To be clear, if the RFP has already been released, it is too late to submit a FOIA request.

## Why FOIA?

- **The following are the most common FOIA requests:**
    - Past contracts
    - Prior RFPs and solicitations
    - Copies of prior task, delivery, and purchase orders

- **Recommend a 3rd party request -** *agency doesn't know it is you*

    - Whenever possible, request FOIA's through a 3rd party
    - RSM Federal can submits FOIA requests on your behalf
    - You don't want the agency to know you're the one... *causing them work*

- **The following is protected from FOIA release:**
    - Source Selection Documents and Performance Reports
    - Bid Abstract

- Proposals (unless incorporated into the contract. A small percentage of contracts incorporate sections from the competition's winning proposal because it's easier for the contracting officer to copy and paste sections from the proposal into the contract.

- Any Subcontracting Information

- List of companies that submitted bids or proposals

| FOIA Exemptions and Exclusions ||
|---|---|
| Exemption (b) (1) | National Security Information |
| Exemption (b) (2) | Agency internal personnel rules and practices |
| Exemption (b) (3) | Specifically prohibited by statute |
| Exemption (b) (4) | Trade Secrets and Financial Information |
| Exemption (b) (5) | Inter-agency or Intra-agency memorandums |
| Exemption (b) (6) | Personnel Files / Medical Files |
| Exemption (b) (7) (a) | Law Enforcement – Interfere with proceedings |
| Exemption (b) (7) (b) | Law Enforcement – Impact fair trial |
| Exemption (b) (7) (c) | Law Enforcement – Records and invasion of privacy |
| Exemption (b) (7) (d) | Law Enforcement – Identify of confidential source |
| Exemption (b) (7) (e) | Law Enforcement – Techniques and procedures |
| Exemption (b) (7) (f) | Law Enforcement – Jeopardize physical safety |
| Exemption (b) (8) | Regulation and Supervision of Financial Institutions |
| Exemption (b) (9) | Geological and Geophysical information |
| The (c) (1) Exclusion | Federal law shielding entire programs |
| The (c) (2) Exclusion | Federal Informant Information |
| The (c) (3) Exclusion | Specific files held at the FBI |

*Table 55 - FOIA Exemptions and Exclusions*

# Past Performance

In government language, past performance is simply your current and past work, experience, and contracts. If you don't have government past performance, no problem! Commercial past performance is just as valuable and viable. If your company doesn't have any contracts yet, then you will use your individual past performance and that of any employees you have.

- **Past Performance is always mapped to RFP / RFQ requirements**
    - Not what you do – but how it relates to each respective RFP task area
    - Cross-walk your past performance to your capture win-themes and differentiators
- **Does your past performance communicate quantifiable improvements in process?**
- **Integrate into each section of your Proposal**
    - Identifying past performance only in the Past Performance section *is not enough to communicate a best-value proposal*
    - Refer to past performance throughout the proposal to communicate ability to meet requirements based on solid past performance
- **If you don't have the past performance**
    - Team with another company
    - Utilize commercial past performance
    - Utilize past performance from similar tasks on similar contracts

# Establish and Maintain a Past Performance Database

You and everyone in your company who responses to Sources Sought, writes proposals, and facilitates relationships with teaming partners, needs to be able to quickly identify the scope, value, and metrics for your current and past contracts. Imagine bringing in a new proposal writer…don't you want to say, "Here's everything you need on our contracts and if you go here, you'll find past proposals, a library of graphics and images, past performance writeups that you can tailor, etc.?"

Your database may be a folder on the network, SharePoint, or other system.

You will use this information over and over again. Just remember, everything gets tailored for each specific opportunity. If all you do is copy and paste, the government will clearly see that you copied and pasted without tailoring it to their specific requirements in the RFP.

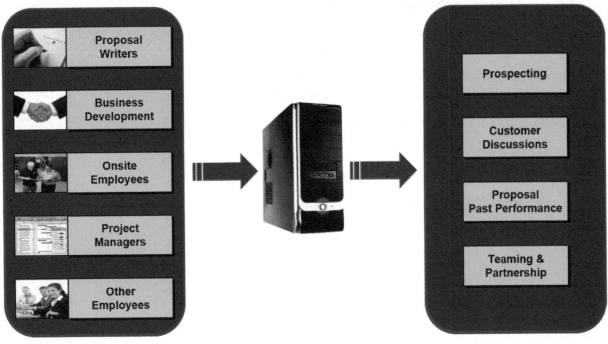

*Figure 108 - Past Performance Database*

# Past Performance Proposal Template

If you're not very familiar with government proposals and responses, this template is a very powerful tool. Even if you don't download the template from the Federal Access Coaching and Training Platform, pay attention to the highlighted numbers in the figure below. The five blocks are the core requirements / scope in the RFP. We call these Task Area Groups (TAGs). When you write your past performance section, you map / cross-walk the TAGs against your past performance. This helps eliminate any assumptions that your past performance does not correlate to the contracts objectives and requirements.

| Department of Transportation (DOT) Network Engineering Services | |
|---|---|
| Company: RSM Capital Group LLC, 13 Amber Wave Ct., O'Fallon, MO 63366 | |
| DUNS / SAM-UEID: 829431191 / DBA1AF1MVKD8 | CAGE Code: 5G2B0 |
| Contracting Agency / Business: DOT-COR, 2300 14ᵗʰ Street, Washington, DC 20005 | |
| Contract Number: DOT-HS-6-667-12 | Place of Performance (PoP): Washington, DC |
| Contract Name: DOT Network Engineering Services | |
| Contract Type: FFP | Contract Role: PRIME |
| Total Dollar Value Awarded Including Options: $2,534,000 | |
| Contract Value for the Last Complete Government Fiscal Year: $858,887 | |
| Date of Contract Award: 2/14/20xx | Contract Completion Date: CURRENT Contract |
| COR / Procurement Official:<br>Name: Mary Caruso<br>Email: mcaruso@dot.gov<br>Telephone: (202) 332-2356<br>Address: DOT-COR, 2300 14ᵗʰ St. Wash DC 20005 | Program Management<br>Program Manager: John Smith<br>Email: jsmith@dot.gov<br>Telephone: (202) 332-4559<br>Address: DOT-COR, 1456 21ˢᵗ St. Wash DC 20005 |

Description of services as relates to Section C, Statement of Work and Section M, Evaluation Criteria

Relevant Tasks and Activities

| Program Management (RFP – **C1.12**) | Network Management (RFP - **C.2.1**) | Network Engineering (RFP – **C2.4**) | Tier 2 and 3 Helpdesk (RFP – **C4.1**) | Information Assurance (RFP – **C5.0**) |
|---|---|---|---|---|

RSM provides 24 x 7 x 365 network engineering services for the Research and Innovative Technology Administration (RITA). RSM has supported RITA on several contracts since 2004. Initially, this contract only supported Tier 2 Helpdesk services. However, as a result of our multi-disciplined staffing approach (MDSA™); the quality of our employee... contract only supported Tier 2 Helpdesk services. H...over key network protocol management and... ed staffing approach (MDSA™), the quality of our e...mendment to the contract. RSM provides T... Manager (C1.12), RITA turned-over key network pro... oversight and maintenance to ensure 99... requirements within four months, with an amendm... subject matter expertise (SME) for RITA... 2, and 3 engineering services (C4.1) as well as 24... 's manages the Department of Transporta... re 99% uptime (C2.1) for 3,000 end users. Our em... m (DOT-EnMDS) (C2.1) which is integrated with IB... tise (SME) for RITA's enterprise architecture and in... are responsible for tickets related to integrati...3 network issues (C4.1). ...s manages the Department of Transportation's Ent... RSM synchronizes RITA a... ashboard System (DOT-EnMDS) (C2.1) which is int... infrastructure to manage the life cycle of id...Identify Manager. RSM's engineers are responsibl... applications and information. Similar to the...n, Tivoli and EnMDS as well as associated Tier 2 an... currently support RITA's 7200 and 7300 Cisco routers (C3.8), a Cisco IP/MPLS Edge 7600 Series, Nexus 7000 switches (C3.9), and provides network management via the Unified Operations Manager and the Unified Service Monitor (C3.11). RSM also manages three Network Appliance network file servers (C3.3). In support of DOT's Information…

*Figure 109 - Past Performance Template*

# Past Performance Questionnaires

Many RFPs and RFQs will ask that you have your current and past clients complete a survey / evaluation so that the government source selection committee can get direct feedback on your company's performance.

Once the surveys are complete, your clients are required to mail them directly back to the government. This protects against you tampering with the comments. What is important to remember is that you need to proactively manage this process. Are you sure that your clients received the survey? Are you sure that they completed them and actually sent them back to the government?

- **Format is similar but may be tailored by the govenrment for that specific RFP**
    - You'll be provided the format / template as part of RFP
- **Important that you have strong relationships with your clients**
    - If you only talk to your current customers when you invoice, that's poor customer relationship management
    - Many RFPs have a two or four week turnaround so you need *expedited* support
- **Build into your proposal timeline**
    - 75 / 25 Rule:  Completed questionnaires delivered 25% into proposal cycle
    - Initiate early in proposal timeline
- **Proactive**
    - Call customers filling out questionnaires to verify receipt
    - Call customers to verify they have delivered the questionnaire
    - Call the agency or command to verify they received the questionnaires

# Building A Team

Many companies that Prime choose companies to be subcontractors for the wrong reasons. Perhaps they are close friends. They might be current teammates on other contracts. You met them at a conference and they seem awesome.

Building a team is based on requirements. Every member of a team has capability and / or past performance that makes the overall team *more competitive*.

There's more to teaming, both in the Chapter on Teaming and in *An Insider's Guide to Winning Government Contracts* (Amazon). When building your team, you don't simply look at another company's website or take their word at face value - no matter how great or competitive they appear.

You have to evaluate, validate, and ensure that they will make your team more competitive. You do this when performing business development. You research their DUNS number / SAM Unique Identifier in SAM.gov's Data Bank. Then when you have found a strong opportunity and you've decided to Prime it, you use a Teaming Capability Matrix to ensure EVERY requirement is fulfilled by a you or a potential teaming partner.

## The Teaming Capability Matrix For Selecting Partners

- **Matrix / Spreadsheet for Teaming**
    - Spreadsheet designed to identify strongest vendors for competitive advantage
    - Ensures you have strong past performance in EVERY requirement or task area

- **Format is not important**
    - Based on your Win Themes, "know" which capabilities you need
    - Do not team with another company simply because they are friends

- **If YOU are asked to fill out a Capability Matrix:**
    - Never provide all your information to the Prime or other teammates
    - Today they are partners – tomorrow they are competition
    - It is rarely a good idea to provide contact and contract information for all of your contracts, even under NDA or TA
    - Of course, if you are the prime having other companies fill out your matrix, get as much information as you can!

# Example Teaming Capability Matrix

Both example and template for this matrix is available in Federal Access. Provides instructions that you provide to other companies when filling out the matrix.

MSR SERVICES

**Teaming Capability Matrix**
Department of Commerce
RFP for IT Services

| | Lead Task Area? (Y/N) | Like to Participate? (Y/N) | Overall Rating (1-10) | Relevant Past Performance | | | | | | | |
|---|---|---|---|---|---|---|---|---|---|---|---|
| | | | | Dept of State | US Treasury | USACE | USTRANSCOM | DISA – Texas | DISA – Columbus | DISA – Wash DC | Air Mobility CMD |
| **System Administration (Task Area 1)** | Y | Y | 9 | | | | | | | | |
| NOC System Administration | Y | Y | 10 | 10 | 9 | 8 | 4 | 7 | | 8 | |
| SYSADMIN – Linux and Solaris | Y | Y | 9 | 10 | | 6 | 8 | | 6 | | |
| SYSADMIN – Storage Area Networks (SANS) | Y | Y | 10 | | | | | 10 | | | |
| Documentation Management | N | N | | | 4 | 7 | | | | | 9 |
| Data Migrations | N | N | | | 9 | | 9 | 9 | | 7 | |
| **Service Desk (Task Area 2)** | N | Y | 8 | | | | | | | | |
| Desktop Training | N | N | | | 4 | | 9 | | | 5 | |
| Implementation Support | N | Y | 10 | 10 | 9 | 10 | 9 | | 8 | | |
| Remedy Helpdesk System | N | Y | 10 | | | | | 10 | | 9 | 9 |
| Develop SLA (Industry Best Practice) | N | Y | 8 | | 5 | 8 | 8 | 8 | | | |
| Provide 1st and 2nd Tier Support | N | N | | 9 | | | | 9 | | 7 | |
| Maintain Accountability of Spare Equipment | N | N | | | | | | | | | |

*Figure 110 - Teaming Capability Matrix*

# Multi-Disciplined Staffing Approach™ (MDSA)

- **The MDSA validates, differentiates, and communicates value**

  - Validates that you understand the scope of each task

  - Maps each task area to specific labor categories

  - Primary and backup resources within each task area and *across tasks areas*

  - Strengthens the capabilities of the overall team

  - Minimizes actual or perceived overall risk

  - Communicated (directly or indirectly) within each proposal section

  - When properly integrated, communicates strength, benefit, and value

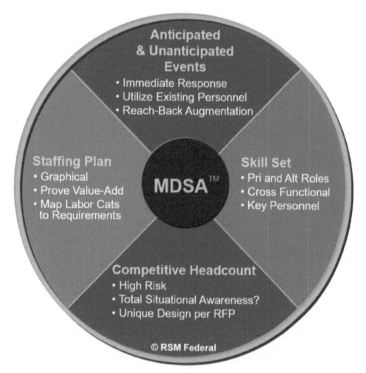

*Figure 111 - Multi-Disciplined Staffing Approach (MDSA)*

- ***Every* employee you hire** should have primary and alternate skills to provide backup and redundancy on the team

- **You don't hire the right person for a specific position.** You hire the right person who is cross-functional and provides "added-value" to the customer on multiple requirements

## Positioning For Unanticipated Events and Surges

- **Surge Requirements**
  - A process designed to facilitate *immediate* response to an unanticipated event
  - Initial response utilizes *existing* personnel and resources
  - Gives your PM or customer time to coordinate additional resources if necessary

- **Corporate Reach-Back Capability**
  - MDSA takes into account Subject Matter Experts (SME) at your corporate office or other client sites
  - If reach-back is a billable event, you must communicate this in the proposal
  - When combined, MDSA Surge and Reach-Back are key differentiators

- **Holidays and Medical**
  - Provides redundancy when team members go on vacation or get sick
  - Maintain operations during holidays

## Underbid Competition - Minimizing Head Count

- **MDSA provides the *ability* to decrease existing headcount on recompetes when you are not the incumbent**
  - Position your staffing plan with less Full Time Employees (FTE) than the competition

- **Advanced Startegy with *potentially high risk***
  - In general, customers are adverse to decreasing head-count once established
  - Your cross-disciplined approach must be clear
  - Must communicate mitigation of prospect's anticipated risks and perceptions

- **Not recommended unless you have *Total Situational Awareness***
  - You've had discussions with the prospect or customer
  - RFP *clearly* indicates that innovative approaches are desired
  - Most customers expect or dictate a specific number of FTEs

- **This approach must be *uniquely designed* for each opportunity**

# Key Personnel

- **Key Personnel**
  - If required by RFP, the labor categories (LCATS) will be outlined in the RFP
  - LCATS for leadership, management, and other key positions (e.g. project manager, senior engineer, foreman, etc.

- **Sources:**
  - Internal resume database (if you don't have one – start building one)
  - Monster, Careerbuilder, and other online job sites
  - Customer referrals
  - Incumbent contractors

- **Typically, key personnel are required to be present at Orals**
  - Not all RFPs require oral presentations

# Proposal Integration Points

- **Initiate your MDSA plan early**
  - Start reviewing during the bid - no bid process
  - Discuss during proposal kickoff meeting
  - Outline MDSA strategy for all writers in *Proposal Team Plan*
  - Key Personnel identified in RFP should not change
  - Resumes have annotations supporting the MDSA plan

| Multi-Disciplined Staffing Approach |
| --- |
| Executive Summary |
| Technical Approach |
| Past Performance |
| Management Approach |
| Staffing Plan |
| Quality Assurance / Quality Control Plan |
| Risk Management Plan |

*Table 56 - MDSA Integration Points*

# Resumes

- **Outline which RFP tasks are covered by each resume**
  - Annotate Section and Paragraph number within the resume
  - Cross-walk with what is communicated and graphically displayed in the Proposal Staffing Plan

- **Resume Guidelines**
  - Use Call-Out box to bring reader's attention to key position status and highlights
  - Annotate where resume experience matches or exceeds RFP requirements
  - Use the name of the customer in the first paragraph of the resume
  - Ensure that all resumes properly cross-walk to all RFP requirements

- **Time to Prepare**
  - Don't wait until the night before submission
  - You will often find that one or more resumes are NOT a good fit for the proposal or don't have enough experience to prove that you understand the requirements
  - Recruiters should have the necessary information at the same time you initiate proposal development!

- **Follow these guidelines:**
  - When possible, use the names of individuals in your technical response
  - Tailor each resume based on proposal requirements
  - Have resumes drafted before major writing effort
  - Utilize abbreviated resume summaries in the technical sections
  - Resumes should be no more than two pages – *preferably one*
  - Always include a "Proposal Staffing Plan"
  - Do not use photos in your resumes
  - Annotate key requirements in each resume, especially for key personnel
  - Use call-out boxes, tailored to RFP requirements:
    - ➢ Labor Category / Key Position
    - ➢ Key Experience & Security Clearance (if applicable)
    - ➢ Capabilities, Certifications, and Education

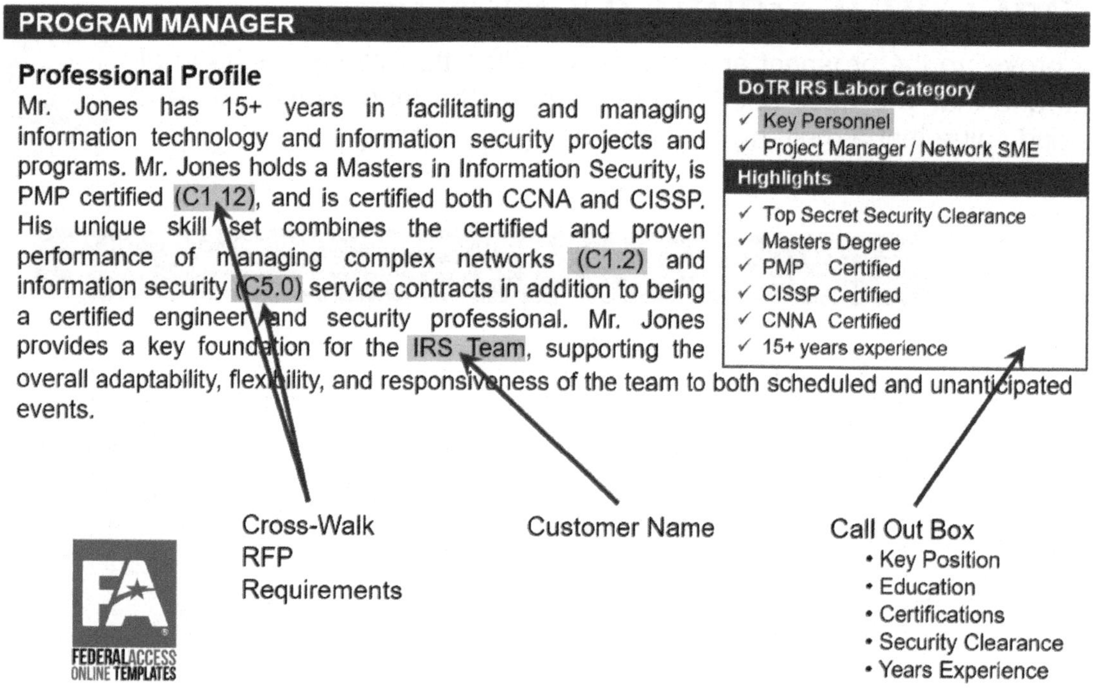

## PROGRAM MANAGER

### Professional Profile

Mr. Jones has 15+ years in facilitating and managing information technology and information security projects and programs. Mr. Jones holds a Masters in Information Security, is PMP certified (C1.12), and is certified both CCNA and CISSP. His unique skill set combines the certified and proven performance of managing complex networks (C1.2) and information security (C5.0) service contracts in addition to being a certified engineer and security professional. Mr. Jones provides a key foundation for the IRS Team, supporting the overall adaptability, flexibility, and responsiveness of the team to both scheduled and unanticipated events.

**DoTR IRS Labor Category**
- ✓ Key Personnel
- ✓ Project Manager / Network SME

**Highlights**
- ✓ Top Secret Security Clearance
- ✓ Masters Degree
- ✓ PMP    Certified
- ✓ CISSP Certified
- ✓ CNNA Certified
- ✓ 15+ years experience

**FA** FEDERALACCESS ONLINE TEMPLATES

Cross-Walk
RFP
Requirements

Customer Name

Call Out Box
- • Key Position
- • Education
- • Certifications
- • Security Clearance
- • Years Experience

*Figure 112 – Proposal Resume Header*

## PROGRAM MANAGER

### Professional Profile

Mr. Jones has 15+ years in facilitating and managing information technology and information security projects and programs. Mr. Jones holds a Masters in Information Security, is PMP certified (C1.12), and is certified both CCNA and CISSP. His unique skill set combines the certified and proven performance of managing complex networks (C1.2) and information security (C5.0) service contracts in addition to being a certified engineer and security professional. Mr. Jones provides a key foundation for the IRS Team, supporting the overall adaptability, flexibility, and responsiveness of the team to both scheduled and unanticipated events.

**DoTR IRS Labor Category**
- ✓ Key Personnel
- ✓ Project Manager / Network SME

**Highlights**
- ✓ Top Secret Security Clearance
- ✓ Masters Degree
- ✓ PMP    Certified
- ✓ CISSP Certified
- ✓ CNNA Certified
- ✓ 15+ years experience

| | | | | | | | | | | | | | | | | | | | |
|---|---|---|---|---|---|---|---|---|---|---|---|---|---|---|---|---|---|---|---|
| Senior Engineer (SW) **(Team Leader)** | 1920 | • | • | • | • | | • | • | • | • | | | | | | • | • | • | • | • |
| Senior Engineer (HW) | 1920 | • | • | • | | | | • | | • | | | | | • | • | • | • | |
| System Engineer | 3840 | | | | • | | | | • | | | | | • | | | | | |
| Database Administrator | 3840 | | | | | • | | | | | • | • | • | • | | | | | |
| Web Developer | 3840 | | | | • | • | • | • | | • | | | | • | | | | | |
| Graphics Designer | 1920 | | | | • | | | | | | | | | | | | | | |
| Senior System Administrator | 1920 | • | • | • | | | • | | • | • | | | • | • | • | • | • | | |
| System Administrator | 5760 | | | | | | • | • | | • | | | • | • | | | | | |
| Helpdesk Technician | 3840 | | | | | | • | | | | | • | | • | | | | | |

*Figure 113 - Resume Mapped to Staffing Plan*

# Proposal Labor Category Matrix

Graphically "prove" to the prospect and source-selection that you understand all requirements and that you have successfully mapped the labor categories and the benefits and value that a multi-disciplined staffing approach provides.

| Labor Categories | Hours | All Tasks Management | | | Task 1.4.1 Web Design Work | | | | | Task 1.4.2 Troubleshooting and Repair / Task 1.4.3 Hardware and Software Resolution / Task 1.4.4 Data Backup | | | | | | | | | Task 1.4.5 Modernization 5 Year Plan | | |
|---|---|---|---|---|---|---|---|---|---|---|---|---|---|---|---|---|---|---|---|---|---|
| | | Supervision (Key Personnel) | Liaison with COTR and Program Manager | Quality Control (QC) Plan | Graphics, content, HTML Coding & Scripting | Search Engines | Database Solutions | Statistical Traffic Reporting | Rebuild Site Navigation | Help Desk Tier 1 & 2 | Sustain Information Network Software (SW) | Sustain Information Network Hardware (HW) | Server Support | Data Base Administration & Data Service Assistance | Data Backup and Retrieval | Storage Area Network (SAN) | AntiVirus and Patches | Training | Website Architecture Analysis Review 5 Year Plan | 5 Year Website HW/ SW Plan (Bi-Annual Report / Quarterly Updates) | Technology Refresh (1/3 Annual) |
| Senior Engineer (SW) (Team Leader) | 1920 | • | • | • | • | | | • | • | • | • | | | | | | • | • | • | • | • |
| Senior Engineer (HW) | 1920 | • | • | • | | | | | | • | | • | | | | | | • | • | • | • |
| System Engineer | 3840 | | | | • | | | | | | | • | | | | | • | | | | |
| Database Administrator | 3840 | | | | | | • | | | | | | | • | • | • | • | | | | |
| Web Developer | 3840 | | | | • | • | | • | • | | • | | | | | | • | | | | |
| Graphics Designer | 1920 | | | | • | | | | | | | | | | | | | | | | |
| Senior System Administrator | 1920 | • | • | • | | | | • | | • | | | • | • | | | • | • | • | • | • |
| System Administrator | 5760 | | | | | | | | | • | • | | • | | | • | • | | | | |
| Helpdesk Technician | 3840 | | | | | | | | | • | | | | | | • | • | | | | |
| **28,800** | | | | | | | | | | | | | | | | | | | | | |

*Table 57 - Labor Category Matrix*

# Pricing Strategy

- **Small Businesses need a formal strategy to ensure competitiveness**
- **Do your recommended solutions really add value?**
  - Provide some capability that costs little but perceived by prospect as high value
  - Eliminate capabilities that are expensive which prospect perceives as low value
- **During sales activities, identify which contract vehicle is preferred**
  - Helps identify risk tolerance
- **Before you can price, you must understand:**
  - The prospect's price-capability trade-off
  - The market
  - Assumptions which the prospect used to develop their budget
  - Your pricing model and margins
  - Your competitors pricing model and margins
- **When pricing and technical proposal sections are managed separately, you get a technically strong but *high cost solution***
- **Critical that you record lesson's learned from prior efforts**
  - Information not written down is lost
  - What happens if a sales or capture manager leaves the company?
- **A pricing strategy evolves over time**
  - Through capture management and relationship management
  - Via Market Sales Strategy activities
  - Via Freedom of Information Act (FOIA) requests
  - Lesson's learned from previous competitions and bids won and lost
- **If you understand the prospect's budget and desired capability, you can identify one of three strategies in order to emphasize:**
  - Low Price
  - Best Capability
  - Best Value
- **If not identified in RFP, you must ascertain which is more important; low price, best capability, or best value**
- **Top-Down Costing**
  - Start with Prospect's budget
  - Comparison to similar projects managed by this prospect

- Tasks broken-down by price

- **Bottom-Up Costing**
  - Identifying your labor bill rates with associated overhead
  - Often used to underbid competition
  - Tends to incorporate higher margins to increase revenue
  - Results in higher and non-competitive estimates (relationships are important!)

- **If intelligence indicates a need to lower the price:**
  - Focus on efficiencies
  - Management positions responsible for more areas  (tie to MDSA)
  - Reducing senior positions = lower labor rates
  - Sub-contract tasks to teammates who have lower labor rates

- **Include cost summary in the proposal's Executive Summary**
  - Unless prohibited by proposal instructions (which is common)
  - Most companies are afraid their price will be too high and will not want to discuss it until the Pricing Volume.

- **Present cost data graphically to clearly identify cost points**
  - Standard deviation for high risk cost elements
  - Major costs' table, pie, or bar chart

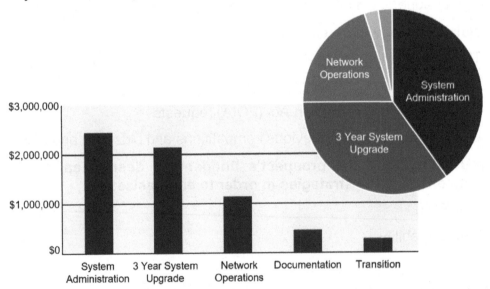

*Figure 114 - Proposal Pricing Bar / Pie Chart*

# "Best Price" or "Best Value"

- **Best Value**
  - Highly subjective
  - Source selection committee has discretion to decide
  - Must fully understand customer's requirements (from your sales strategy)
  - Proposal must respond to each requirement (be responsive)
  - Proposal does not respond to challenges not identified in the RFP
- *Best Value is communicated in your proposal via "Win Themes"*
- **If you know the prospect and have a strong sales strategy:**
  - You will have cost strategies before the opportunity hits acquisition phase
  - You sell the value of your solutions throughout the sales process
  - You validate the value of your solutions during acquisition phase
  - You have ghosted requirements into the RFP that are your strengths and your competition's weaknesses.

# Cost Volume Sections

- **Copy of Executive Summary (from Technical Proposal)**
  - Unless you have a specific page limit and can not include it
- **Summary for Cost Volume**
- **Your Approach**
  - Win Themes
  - Ghost competition's approaches and weaknesses
- **Discuss total cost of proposal (text and graphics)**
- **Emphasize fairness in cost**
- **'Estimating' approach**
- **How you manage and track costs**
- **Your cost system has been audited by the appropriate organization(s)**
- **No more than 15 pages** (but based on RFP guidance)

# The Proposal

## Proposal Alignment

- The Sales Strategy provides you with 90% of the key data and Win Themes

- Just as information is tailored and redistributed among the players in your sales strategy, proposal development is similar

- Proposal sections are not verticals. Each section has inputs and outputs to and from other sections to more clearly communicate the value of your products or solutions

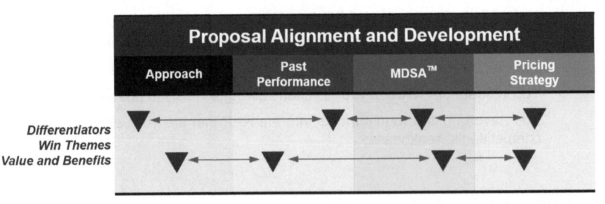

Figure 115 - Proposal Alignment

## Proposal Templates

- **Critical for Small and Large Companies**
    - Provides a repeatable process
    - Create your own digital library
- **Includes key graphics**
    - Organization, process, methodology, staffing plan, quality control, etc.
- **Irreplaceable on short-turnaround proposals**
    - Spend your time on writing - not formatting
- **Agencies often use the same format for their RFPs**
    - Go to SAM.gov and download an agency's current or previous RFPs
    - Modify your existing proposal template

Have a template ready before the RFP is released *(whenever possible)*

# Common Components of an RFP

| | Components - Request For Proposal (RFP) |
|---|---|
| A | General Information – Solicitation or Contract Form |
| B | Product / Services and Pricing |
| C | Statement of Work |
| D | Packages and Marking<br>Terms and Conditions (Reports, 508 Compliance, Invoice Format. . .) |
| E | Inspection and Acceptance |
| F | Deliveries or Performance |
| G | Contract Administrative Data |
| H | Special Contract Requirements |
| I | Contract Clauses / General Provisions |
| J | Attachments and Exhibits |
| K | Reps and Certs - Statements of Offerors |
| L | Proposal Preparation Instructions |
| M | Evaluation Criteria |

*Table 58 - Components of an RFP*

# Common Proposal Sections

| Common Proposal Sections |
|---|
| Executive Summary |
| Technical Capability & Approach |
| Management Approach |
| Quality Control Plan |
| Risk Management Plan |
| Past Performance |
| Proposed Staffing and Resumes |
| Pricing |

*Table 59 - Common Proposal Sections*

## Proposal Process – Type 1

### Release of Draft RFP

The data flow diagram below outlines the basic process for proposal development. In this example, there is a draft RFP in pre-acquisition. As a result, you have much more time to prepare your proposal.

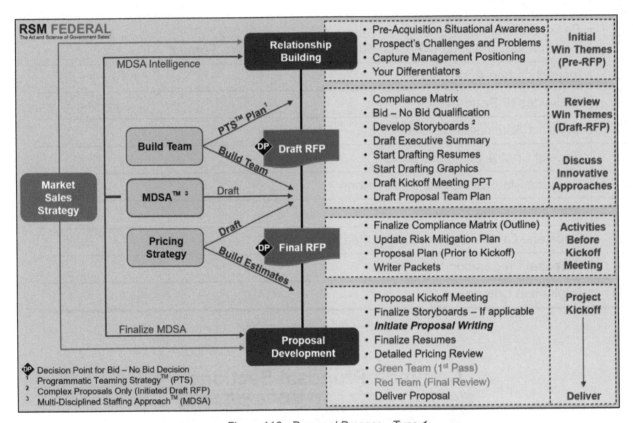

*Figure 116 - Proposal Process - Type 1*

# Proposal Process – Type 2
## Release of RFP without a Draft or Pre-Solicitation
In this example, the government doesn't release any drafts. You obtain the final RFP and have a set number of days to submit a proposal.

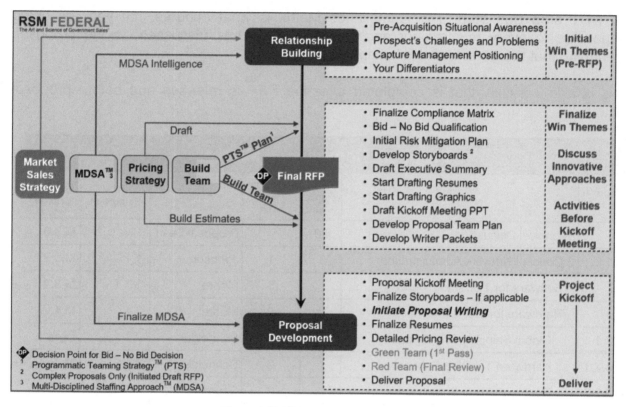

*Figure 117 - Proposal Process - Type 2*

# Compliance Matrix

This is one of the most important steps in responding to a proposal. Every large company creates a compliance matrix for each proposal effort. Most small businesses don't formally create a compliance matrix. Instead, they informally complete the process by highlighting and underlining key requirements in the RFP.

**Do NOT skip this step**. The Compliance Matrix is what ensures that you are being responsive to every requirement and that your team has discussed, in the proposal, everything that the government is looking for.

This is a key activity that is completed *after the RFP is released* and before proposal kickoff.

| Proposal Compliance Matrix | | | | | | |
|---|---|---|---|---|---|---|
| Proposal Section | Section Title | Total Page Limit | Section Page Limit | Author | SOW Paragraph | Eval Criteria |
| 2 | Technical Discussion | 20 | | Proposal Lead | 1 | M.3.0 |
| 2.1 | Concept Network Administration | | 1 | Johnson | 1.1 | M.3.2 |
| 2.2 | Software for Tier 2 and Tier 3 | | 5 | Moore | 1.1.1 | M.3.2 |
| 2.3 | Hardware for Tier 2 and Tier 3 | | 5 | Moore | 2.1 | M.4 |
| 2.3.1 | Global Shipping Grid System | | 2 | Schneider | 2.1.1 | M.4a |
| 2.3.2.1 | Hardware Tracking Subsystem | | 2 | Schneider | 2.1.2 | M.4b |
| 2.3.2.2 | Router and Hub Subsystem | | 2 | Schneider | 2.1.3 | M.4b |
| 2.4 | Quarterly / Annual Recommendations | | 3 | Johnson | 3.1 | M.5 |

*Table 60 - Proposal Compliance Matrix*

# Requirement Traceability Matrix (RTM)

On the previous page, we use the Compliance Matrix to ensure that we are responsive to all requirements in our proposal. However, we don't include the Compliance Matrix in our proposal. In the proposal, we submit a table that is called the Requirement Traceability Matrix (RTM).

Not every proposal will have an RTM. Sometimes, even when we want to use one, the page count limitation keeps us from using it. When space exists, including an RTM helps the government source selection committee to quickly and easily figure out *where* you have responded to *every* core requirement.

- **Submitted with Proposal**

    - Shortened version of the Compliance Matrix

    - Helps selection committee quickly locate responses to specific requirements

    - Proves to prospect that you covered all requirements

| Requirement Traceability Matrix (RTM) | | |
|---|---|---|
| RFP Requirements | | Proposal Section |
| SOW | Section Title | |
| 2 | Technical Discussion | 2 |
| 2.1 | Concept Network Administration | 2.1 |
| 2.2 | Software for Tier 2 and Tier 3 | 2.2 |
| 2.3 | Hardware for Tier 2 and Tier 3 | 2.3 |
| 2.3.1 | Global Shipping Grid System | 2.3.1 |
| 2.3.2.1 | Hardware Tracking Subsystem | 2.3.2.1 |
| 2.3.2.2 | Router and Hub Subsystem | 2.3.2.2 |
| 2.4 | Quarterly / Annual Recommendations | 2.4 |

*Table 61 - Proposal Requirement Traceability Matrix (RTM)*

# The Proposal Kickoff Meeting – When You Are The Prime

- **Two Types**
  - No Team Members
  - Team Members
- **No Team Members**
  - 100% internal to support your company's efforts
  - Still have to develop a Proposal Team Plan
- **Have Team Members**
  - You should have *two* kickoff meetings
  - First is internal to ensure you are ready to engage the team
  - Easier to make decisions and resolve initial issues with a smaller group
  - The second is for teammates to *receive clear guidance and assignments*
- **Do not hold a kickoff meeting as soon as you receive the RFP**
  - Upfront planning is critical
  - Holding a meeting without a plan will increase your writing time

## Running The Kickoff Meeting

- **Make sure all key people are present**
- **Set ground rules**
- **Whenever possible, meeting should be face to face**
  - Require teammates to fly to your corporate office if necessary; or
  - Facilitate via teleconference if COVID or other natural situation exists
  - Confirms intent and desire to fully participate
- **Provide a clear agenda before meeting**
  - The Proposal Team Plan is a baseline for the agenda
- **Provide kickoff package before meeting**
  - PowerPoint packet
  - Proposal Management Plan

## Kickoff Meeting Objectives

- Introduce all team members
- Outline the opportunity
- Deliver writing assignments

- Provide Proposal Team Plan
- Deliver via Kickoff Presentation
- Provide timeline and deliverables
- Make it clear your company is ready and has senior management support
- Is not a planning meeting – Educate and assign responsibilities
- *It is run by the Proposal Manager*
  - An introduction by senior management is an excellent starting point
  - Make sure the Proposal Manager and not the Executive runs the meeting or it will damage the Proposal Manager's credibility
  - *The Capture Manager / Business Developer supports the Proposal Manager*

## Proposal Team Plan

There's more on this in the Federal Access Coaching and Training Platform. However, here are the basic sections for running a kickoff for proposal development and the artifacts / documents you should provide to all writers.

- **Plan Sections:**
  - Project Summary
  - Proposal Team
  - Customer Profile
  - Scope
  - Competitive Analysis
  - Proposal Strategies and Themes
  - Assignments
  - Administrative
  - RFP
- **Attachments**
  - Proposal Schedule (Excel or Gant)
  - Compliance Matrix
  - Writer Instructions
  - Proposal Strategy
  - Draft Executive Summary

## Proposal Schedule

After completing the compliance matrix, many companies create a proposal schedule. Some are simple. Others are complex. They are more commonly used for larger acquisitions with multiple writers and / or multiple teaming partners.

| Example Proposal Schedule | | | |
|---|---|---|---|
| Requirement | Due Date | Time | Who |
| Initial Bid – No Bid Decision | 4/15/xx | | Capture Manager |
| **Blue Team** | 5/15/xx | | ABC Technologies |
| Teaming Agreements Complete | 5/30/xx | | Capture Manager |
| **Black Team** – Initial | 5/30/xx | | Capture Manager |
| Draft Kickoff Presentation | 6/16/xx | | Capture Manager |
| RFP Released | 7/3/xx | | Government |
| Complete Compliance Matrix | 7/4/xx | 1300 | Proposal Manager |
| Final Bid – No Bid Decision | 7/4/xx | 1700 | Capture & Proposal Manager |
| Build Proposal Team Plan | 7/6/xx | 1700 | Capture and Proposal Manager |
| Draft Executive Summary | | | Capture Manager |
| Resumes Drafted / Graphics Initiated | | | Recruiters / Graphic Design |
| Proposal Kickoff Meeting | 7/7/xx | 1400 | Capture Manager |
| Detailed Pricing Review | 7/9/xx | 1530 | Capture Manager and Mgt |
| Validate Strategy | 7/9/xx | | CM and Entire Team |
| Write Proposal First Draft | 7/15/xx | 1700 | Entire Team |
| Final Graphics | 7/15/xx | 1700 | Graphics Design |
| **Green Team** | 7/17/xx | 0900 | Entire Team |
| Gold Team | 7/20/xx | 1700 | ABC Technologies |
| Finalize Executive Summary | 7/20/xx | 1700 | Capture and Proposal Manager |
| **Red Team** | 7/23/xx | 1700 | Entire Team |
| Proposal Delivery | 7/30/xx | | Capture Manager |

*Table 62 - Example Proposal Schedule*

# Color Teams – The Review Process

We all learn through practice and experience. When you first enter the world of government sales, you will hear other companies and teaming partners talk about color teams. Like everything else in this Manual, you simply have to learn it the first time.

> *"It is amazing how much time, resources, and money is put into writing a proposal without any formal or detailed review process."*

The color teams listed below is an example. There are some variations. As an example, because 'green' is the color of money, some companies use the Green Team for pricing reviews. There's no right or wrong. What's important is that you understand the purpose of color teams and that you consider using them as part of your proposal process to validate concepts, validate win-themes, and ensure you are being responsive to all requirements.

The review process is just as important as writing the proposal. Color teams are one of the most cost effective activities to improve a proposal. You don't have to use all of them, but *Blue and Red are a minimum.*

| Color Teams | |
|---|---|
| Team | Purpose |
| **Blue Team** | Review Capture Plan and Validate Win Strategy |
| Black Team | Competition's Strategy |
| Pink Team | Validate Deployment Strategy (Story-Boards) |
| Green Team | First draft external review |
| **Red Team** | Evaluate For Customer Value and Benefit |
| Gold Team | Validate Profit and Risk (Pricing Strategy) |

*Table 63 - Proposal Color Teams*

# Colors and Graphics

- **Color**
  - Use color to grab the reader's attention
  - The proposal itself should be primarily black for text
  - The proposal cover-page can be a differentiator (Strong image with color)

- **Diagrams and Graphics**
  - Complex graphics can take too long to understand
  - A graphic has one primary message (easily identifiable when looked at)
  - Must be simple - if it requires an explanation under the graphic, it is too complicated
  - If you have to explain the graphic's purpose to a colleague - it is too complex

- **Graphics**
  - Every graphic has an action caption (lead with benefits and value, not features)
  - Cross-walk graphic to requirement

- **Master Graphics**
  - Common for large and complicated acquisitions
  - Often utilized by large System Integrators (SI)
  - *Rarely* makes the desired impact
  - Unless a complex graphic originates from the prospect – consider not using them
  - If they take too long to explain in person, why would you put it in a proposal?

- **Graphics go on the same page or facing page**
  - Do not make the decision maker flip to another page or appendix

- **Use specific colors that highlight differences or create associations**

- **Complimentary Colors**
  - Opposites on the color wheel
  - Used to bring attention and highlight differences

- **Harmonious Colors**
  - – Adjacent colors on the wheel
  - – Associations and harmony

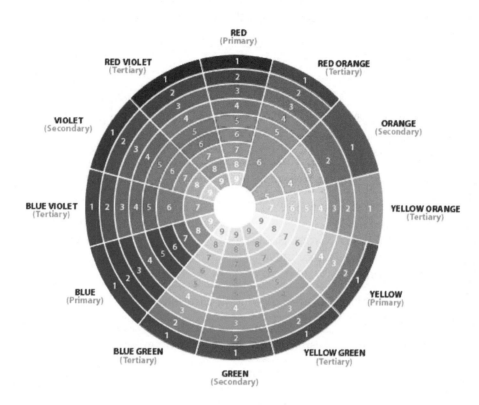

Figure 118 - Color Wheel

| Color Considerations for Proposal Development [8] | | |
|---|---|---|
| **Color** | **Meaning** | **Usage** |
| Black | Power, Strength, Authority, Boldness, **Stability** <br> Too much is ominous | Standard font color |
| Grey | Conservative, Traditional, High-Tech, Authority, Practicality, Creativity | Graphics |
| White | Soothing, Wisdom | Text on dark backgrounds |
| Brown | Solid, Credible, Mature, Reliable, calming | Text <br> Graphics |
| Gold | Wealth, Classy | Excellent for Tables |
| Purple | Luxury, Wealth, Sophistication | Use sparingly |
| Blue | Favorite for most businesses <br> Fiscal Responsibility <br> Inspires Confidence, Trust, Security <br> Darker shades are Authoritative <br> Pale blues can imply weakness | Common background <br> Graphics <br> Call-Out Boxes |
| Red | Sense of Urgency, Power, Excitement, Energy, Strength, **Risk**, Danger, Aggressiveness | Never use for text <br> Use sparingly |
| Green | Creativity, Tranquility, Status, Wealth, a calming color | Highlights |
| Yellow | Used to highlight or draw attention <br> Not often used alone | Bullets and Headings on dark backgrounds |
| Orange | Perception expensive solutions are more affordable | Pricing and Value Statements |

*Table 64 - Color Considerations for Proposal Development*

[8] http://www.color-wheel-pro.com/color-meaning.html

# Proposal Photographs

- **Photographs**

  - "A picture is worth a thousand words"
  - "Most-often" overlooked differentiator

- **Can be difficult to obtain permission for use in the Federal space**

  - Customer Locations
  - Collect photos from articles
  - Website
  - Public Relations
  - Conference / Trade Show Presentations

ABC Technologies has managed the systems in our command center for more than three years. They have consistently managed all issues in a collaborative and timely fashion. They are one of the strongest small businesses we have ever had the privilege to work with.

Air National Guard
Headquarters

*Figure 119 - Proposal Photo*

[9] Photo Source: Michael Vail, National Guard Center, Columbus Ohio

Page 349

# The Challenge of Communicating Innovation

- **Before you Innovate –** *You must fully understand:*
  - Existing processes and systems and how long they have had them
  - Are they planning, in the middle of, or just completed deployment of a new system or requirement?
  - *Are they truly open to change at this time?*
  - Are they *actually "looking" for a new innovative approach* or solution?

- **When is the government open to change or looking for innovation?**
  - Often mentioned in the Sources Sought, RFI, Pre-RFP, etc.
  - However, full understanding comes from one-on-one discussions as part of your prospecting and sales activities

- **If you decide to provide a new innovative approach:**
  - Based on industry best practices
  - Communicate an easy, confident and seamless plan
  - *Evidence of efficiencies* which will *alleviate risk of change*

- **Balance new processes / best practices with historic staffing levels**
  - If the RFP doesn't tell you historic staffing levels, you **must** find out

---

*How and when you communicate an "Innovative Approach"*
*(methodology and process) is* <u>*situation dependent*</u>

---

- **A new opportunity with no incumbent**
  - No current process or methodology
  - An innovative approach poses *less risk* to your proposal

- **A recompetition with incumbent**
  - Existing process and methodology have been designed and implemented
  - Prospect is likely tied to this process
  - *An innovative approach poses major risk to your proposal unless you've discussed with the prospect*

- **Proposal size is a major decision factor**
  - For recompetes with a 10 page limit, it is difficult to clearly communicate

innovation, as a competitive differentiator, while successfully mitigating the perceived risk of change

- **Recommendations for recompetes:**
  - Difficult to eliminate perception of risk
  - Sometimes difficult to respond to requirements when providing an "innovative approach."
  - *Answer the requirements first*

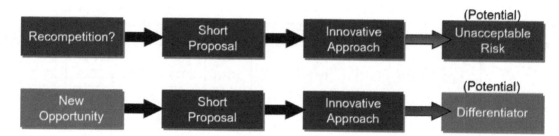

*Figure 120 - The Risk of Innovation*

# Protest Statistics

How and when to protest is outside the scope of this Manual. Every decision to protest is unique to every company, the products and services you sell, each specific acquisition, and the activities of yourself and the government's acquisition team. If you're a member of the Federal Access Coaching and Training Platform, send us a note and we'll help you make the right decisions.

In general, you should recognize that protests are rarely sustained. They are rarely found in your favor.

| Bid Protest Statistics for Fiscal Years 2010 - 2020 | | | | | | | | | | | |
|---|---|---|---|---|---|---|---|---|---|---|---|
| | FY 2020 | FY 2019 | FY 2018 | FY 2017 | FY 2016 | FY 2015 | FY 2014 | FY 2013 | FY 2012 | FY 2011 | FY 2010 |
| Cases Filed | ↓2,149 down 2% | ↓2,198 down 16% | ↑2,607 up <1% | ↓2,596 down 7% | ↑2,789 up 6% | ↑2,639 up 3% | ↑2,561 up 5% | ↓2,429 down 2% | ↑2,475 up 5% | ↑2,353 up 2% | ↑2,299 up 16% |
| Cases Closed | 2,137 | 2,200 | 2,642 | 2,672 | 2,647 | 2,647 | 2,458 | 2,538 | 2,495 | 2,292 | 2,226 |
| Merit (Sustain/Deny) | 545 | 587 | 622 | 581 | 616 | 587 | 556 | 509 | 570 | 417 | 441 |
| Sustains | 84 | 77 | 92 | 99 | 139 | 68 | 72 | 87 | 106 | 67 | 82 |
| Sustain % | 3.9% | 3.5% | 3.5% | 3.8% | 5% | 2.6% | 2.8% | 3.6% | 4.3% | 2.8% | 3.6% |

*Table 65 - Bid Protest Statistics 2010-2020*

In FY 2020, only 3.9% of protests files were sustained in favor of the protestor. Since 2010, there have been 27,095 protests with 973 cases sustained (3.6%).

# Your Final Mission...
# Should You Choose to Accept It

Thank you for reading this Manual! **PLEASE** leave a review on Amazon! Getting reviews is like pulling teeth!

Since its initial launch in 2007, the Manual has been purchased by thousands of companies, government contractors, and business professionals. The feedback has been inspiring!

If you gained value from this Manual, I would be *grateful* if you would do two things:

1. **Post a 5 star review on Amazon.** Even if you did not buy this book on Amazon, you can still leave a review! I hope you'll leave five stars!

2. **Take a picture of yourself holding this Manual and post the picture to LinkedIn** *and* say what value you gained. Please make sure to tag me – Joshua Frank in your post!

Publishing and marketing a book is not an easy task! My ability to share your picture with my network is 100 times more powerful than me saying, "Hey look, this is a good Manual."

Your support really does make a difference and I read all the reviews personally so I can gain feedback and improve this book.

Thanks again for your support!

Joshua Frank

# RSM Federal Ecosystem
# Training Resources

## RSM Federal

Our coaching and training ecosystem has so many resources that I recommend you visit our corporate website. Our GovCon Coaching and Training Ecosystem has supported more than 10,000 companies.
https://rsmfederal.com

## Federal Access (FA) Coaching and Training Platform

The flagship solution of RSM Federal. An award winning and nationally-recognized coaching and training platform, with hundreds of templates and step-by-step strategies that you need to win government contracts.
https://federal-access.com/manual

## Podcast Game Changers for Government Contractors

Available on iTunes and everywhere you listen to podcasts. Game Changers is one of the most listened-to podcasts in the nation for small business government contractors. Every month, two or more industry subject matter experts provide game-changing strategies for tips, tricks, and strategies in the government market.
https://GovConPodcasts.com

## Connect with Joshua Frank on LinkedIn

https://www.linkedin.com/in/joshuapfrank/

## Books on Amazon

If you enjoyed this Manual, you will gain even more value from the Amazon #1 bestseller *An Insider's Guide to Winning Government Contracts*. Whether you are new to the government market or been selling for 10 years, it is one of the most comprehensive resources for GovCon tactics on the market. To learn more about the Insider's Guide and other books, visit
https://Amazon.com

## Author's Website

https://AuthorJoshFrank.com

Made in the USA
Las Vegas, NV
16 March 2023